MW00763151

The Unknown
Connection: Spirituality, the
Paranormal and You

The Unknown Connection:

Spirituality, the paranormal and you

by

Phyllis E. Sloan, Ph.D.

Alpha Run Press
Washington, D.C.

Copyright © 2006 by Phyllis E. Sloan. Printed in the United States of
America.

All rights reserved. No part of this book may be reproduced or transmitted
in any form or by any means, electronic or mechanical, including photo-
copying, recording, or by any information storage and retrieval system
without written permission from the publisher, except for the inclusion of
brief quotations in a review.

Alpha Run Press, LLC
Washington, D.C.
www.alpharunpress.com
To place orders please visit the above web site
or call 1-800-BOOKLOG, 1-800-247-6553 or visit
www.AtlasBooks.com

This is a work of non-fiction. Some persons have chosen not to reveal their
real identities for reasons of privacy. Only in these instances, names have
been changed to protect the innocent. Any resemblance to actual events,
locales, or persons, living or dead is entirely coincidental.

Library of Congress Cataloging-in-Publication Data

Sloan, Phyllis E.
    The unknown connection : spirituality, the paranormal,
and you/by Phyllis E. Sloan.
p. cm.
    Includes bibliographical references and index.
    ISBN-13: 978-1-933289-07-6 (pbk. :alk. paper)
    ISBN-10: 1-933289-07-4 (pbk. :alk. paper)
1. Parapsychology–Case studies. 2. Supernatural–Case
studies. I. Title.

BF1031.S57 2005
133.8–dc22

                    2005028550

Contents

"God has placed a torch in your hearts that glows with knowledge and beauty; it is a sin to extinguish that torch and bury it in the ashes."

___ Kahlil Gibran

Acknowledgements

Writing this book has truly been a labor of love and I thank, first and foremost, The Creator, for aiding me and making her presence felt throughout every step of this process. I also thank my mother for her helping hands throughout my doctoral program and afterward. Without her help, my progress would have been delayed. I also thank my sisters for their moral support and encouragement. Many thanks to my father for instilling in me the courage to stand tall in the face of adversity and persevere. Also, I thank my daughter for fixing and bringing me food and drink to our computer room when I was literally living there, trying to meet critical deadlines.

This book is a revision of my doctoral dissertation; I thank the members of my doctoral committee: Rachel, Diana, Phyllis, "Bud", Herman and Bonnie for their contributions to this endeavor. I especially, thank Rose who is both a mentor and a sister-friend who has proven to be a strong warrior. Thanks, also to Dr. D. Klein for his guidance. Thank you, Jon, for your caring and helpful comments.

To my special friends at work, Bob, James and Dorothy, thanks for the encouragement, critiques and moral support.

Lastly, I want to thank the shamans who willingly and kindly gave of their time and who courageously shared their spiritual experiences with me. Without them, this book would not have been possible. In this age of agnosticism, atheism, skepticism and other spiritually negative "isms", sharing their lives took a special brand of courage because many of their experiences contradict orthodox religious beliefs. I, especially, thank Chief Joe Rain Crow whose knowledge of essiac tea that he shared with me helped improve my chronic fatigue syndrome and cured a foot problem. Many thanks go to the ordinary people who shared their spiritual experiences with me.

Thanks also to the many people who participated in the research part of this book, especially Frances and Mr. McKay for their statistical analyses of the data.

Preface

This book is about "psi" phenomena. Psi events or experiences are those that we call paranormal, psychic or supernatural. Psi events include, but are not limited to: precognitions or prophecies, sightings of unexplained events, visions, psychokinesis (movement of objects for no apparent reason), intuition, clairvoyance, clairaudience, telepathy, dreams, spirit communications, out-of-body experiences, sightings of apparitions, levitation, and psychic readings. A more recent "psi" category is that of the "missing time" phenomenon which people who claim to have been abducted by extraterrestrials experience.

It is a common belief among researchers in this field, who are called psychical researchers or parapsychologists, that all of the aforementioned terms refer to the same general process which is called ESP (extrasensory perception) manifesting itself in different ways. The terms psi, paranormal and supernatural will be used interchangeably in this book when referring to various phenomena.

This book consists of three main sections: (1) the psi experiences of extraordinary spiritual leaders or shamans, (2) the psi experiences of ordinary people and (3) a survey of the paranormal experiences of ordinary people.

I interviewed six shamans, and retold the story of one, Brother Andre, long deceased, but whose healings are widely known and documented. Most modern dictionaries of the English language define a "shaman" as: 1) a medicine man; or 2) one, acting as both priest or holy man and doctor, who works with the supernatural. The persons whom I call shamans all fit this definition. I have included two female shamans because they fit the definition of shaman, except for gender. Each of the shamans has a special spiritual gift or several gifts which they use to heal or help others. Five of the shamans are presented here using their actual names. Two of them, however, Reverend Clarence and Reverend Chloe, chose to tell their stories but remain anonymous because of the general non-acceptance of their spiritual gifts and shamanism by the Western World and because they have dual occupations.

This book is a revision of my doctoral dissertation, which, originally, related the experiences of three shamans and fewer ordinary people. The Interviews with the shamans spanned the years 1993 through 2003.

What led me to write this book? I have been turned off by the dicta and dogma of most orthodox religions for a very long time. I was raised as a Baptist in Gary, Indiana. Most of what I learned in church and Sunday school would have stood the test of time had I not been a curious soul. I wondered about other religions and about what they believed and why we all seemed to believe something different, all over the globe. Everyone is taught that their religion is superior to all others and people who believe differently are going to burn in hell or suffer some alternatively horrible fate.

Another religious issue that bothered me was the belief that God has so-called "chosen" people. Aren't we all "chosen", since God created us all?   Do we really believe that God plays favorite child? I don't think so. God even loves her wayward children, unconditionally. Then, there's that other thing about acknowledging the founders of some of the more well known religions and going through them or be damned to eternal Hell. Suppose you never heard of Jesus or Buddha or Mohammed or Zoroaster or anyone who founded a religion. Suppose you lived in a remote area in the jungles of Wherever and no missionary dared set foot upon your land. Would you be damned to Hell by God just because of where you lived or would God accept you into Heaven even if you never heard of some of these prophets and founders of religions? Also, what about pre-history? Man existed before churches were established. What about all those millions of souls? Most of the founders of our major religions had not yet been born? Did God make them wait for the advent of those men? Would God's word have been revealed if they had not been born?

Neither religions nor science had all of the answers for me. Religions put locks upon my mind because they dictate beliefs that you should not question, lest you burn in Hell. But, I did have questions and I didn't think that God gave me a brain just to let someone else pour their beliefs into it and have me " eat the whole thing raw". I embarked upon a lifelong quest for knowledge about God, life and its purpose, and more personally, who I am and what I am supposed to be doing here.

Science, on the other hand, believes it can find the answer to most questions, which life poses. The scientific method has its place and is well suited for researching and finding out truths about the material world, but ill-suited when it comes to explaining spiritual phenomena. So, what ňdoes science do when it comes to matters of the soul, mind-body phenomena, God and the unseen? I think many scientists are angry because they cannot explain spiritual matters. These matters fall outside the safe, narrow confines of the scientific method and they, therefore, debunk any notion of the supernatural as being "unscientific" as if being "scientific" is the requisite template for *all* knowledge.

My search for truth led me in many directions. I attended various churches, studied various philosophies and religions. I even studied how to give and receive spiritual messages in a spiritual science church. One of the chapters on ordinary people describes a one-day workshop, which I held on learning how to receive and give spiritual messages or *channel,* as it is called.

More compelling evidence that God exists and that life is everlasting was given to me through an experience many years ago which most people would call eerie or just plain scary. At the time that it happened to me, I really did not know what to make of it, so I told no one at the time because I did not know how it would be received.

I was twenty-something at the time and I was living in Chicago. It was very cold and snowy on this particular day. The thermometer read seventeen degrees below zero. I had just moved into my apartment over the weekend and this was my first day of work at a new job. I had very little furniture and utensils. To be exact, I had a sewing machine table, a sewing machine, a radio, a few dishes, a couple of glasses, two sets of eating utensils, a skillet and one medium sized pot. That was all. I had my clothes and some bath needs, sheets and toiletries. Where did I sleep? Even though it was a one-bedroom apartment, I slept in the living room because there was an old-fashioned bed-in-the-wall that came with the apartment. At night, I opened the closet doors and let down the bed for the night. The bed also served as a seat for eating meals because I used to pull the sewing machine table over to the bed and eat off it. If I had a guest for dinner, he or she would sit on the sewing machine case on the other side of the table.

On this cold and snowy day, I was exhausted after coming home from work. I pulled the bed down from the wall and decided to take a nap before I went out to dinner with a friend. The apartment was very cold because the heat had been turned down all day. I decided to heat up the apartment quickly, so I turned on all of the jets on the stove and I lit the oven and let it stay in the open position to maximize the heat distribution. I got into bed and closed my eyes. I don't really know how much time had elapsed before I heard my telephone ringing and I decided to answer it even though I didn't feel like talking. I opened my eyes and I was not in my bed. I was floating in a perfectly blue, cloudless sky! I was outside of my body! I could still hear my telephone ringing and I began to panic. Suddenly, I felt myself going back into my body at a point between the back of my head and the top of my neck! It felt like water flowing back into a vessel. Several times I tried to move my body, but I could not; I panicked even more. I must have tried to move several times, but my body felt too heavy to move. I couldn't budge it. My body felt like a herd of elephants was standing on it; that's how heavy it felt in comparison to the lightness of being outside my physical body. I must have fully connected with my body several moments after I tried to move it because suddenly I was able to move it. I rolled off the bed onto the floor. I smelled gas! I crawled over to the window and threw it open. The phone was still ringing, so I answered it. It was my boyfriend. He sounded very upset. He said," What's wrong? I let the phone ring about forty times. Are you alright?" I really did not know how to tell him what had just happened, so I just said, that I was fine and that I had been asleep. I didn't want him to worry about me. I knew that I had not been asleep. That was no dream. I felt everything and saw everything with a clear mind, both inside and outside my body.

People were not talking about out-of-body experiences then; but I came to realize, years later, that was what I had experienced. I know that God took me out of my body for a reason. Yes, I almost died, but I am convinced that God was showing me that there is more to life than our material world and that God let me return to Earth to complete my karmic goals. It was both a lesson and a warning. There were things, which I needed to change in my life.

Other experiences ensued after that out-of-body episode which involved a dream, which led to financial gains, a heightening of my intuitive sense, various unusual visual abilities among other phenomena. I started a day care center once and I had a dream, which led me to a place where I could get free equipment and supplies. I followed through on the information that God had given me through a dream and sure enough, I received about four thousand dollars worth of free equipment: desks, lockers, chairs and tables. The only supplies and equipment that I had to buy were the sleeping cots and a commercial stove. It was a tremendous help and the money that I saved helped me to keep the center afloat for the first several months.

Since then, I have had several spiritual experiences, some of which fall into the category of premonitions. I have had friends and relatives tell me about their experiences which I describe as 'psi' experiences. They include smelling scents which were not actually present, having dreams come true, and other types of paranormal experiences.

In many cultures it is not unusual to see someone who has died, to receive a communication from the other side via dreams or actual episodes of altered reality states or to just have strong feelings or hunches about people or impending events. But, in the Western World, we tend to look askance at those who have these feelings or experiences. Fear of ridicule or worse leads us to suppress our reporting of these very common experiences. The third section of this book, which includes a survey of paranormal experiences among ordinary people shows that many people have these experiences. They are just told to ignore them, doubt their veracity or just chalk it up to a "hallucination".

I hope that the testimonies of the shamans, the ordinary people and the survey results will help to dispel the shroud of mystery and taboo which surrounds psi phenomena. We all have an intuitive intellect which a part of our hard-wired equipment at birth. Using it would help us to understand a great deal more about our universe and ourselves than we could ever know through either science or religion, alone.

Chapter 1

Introduction

Knowledge in the Western world is defined and limited by what you can see, feel, touch, hear or smell and is only considered real or verifiable if someone else can have an identical experience and report the same results. Modern science defines and limits human knowledge to the physical outer world of measurable events. Rationality, observability, measurability, repeatability, and concurrence are the criteria which the scientific community requires. Physical evidence is all that science will accept as reality.

This book posits that the scientific method of inquiry sets limits on knowledge and that there are degrees of perception and other ways of knowing which cannot be investigated within the narrow confines of the scientific method. Science has helped thus far, but, it is a double-edged sword that can and has cut in the opposite direction. The scientific method can limit our knowledge, when we subject the study of all matter and behaviors to it. We apply this method of inquiry to almost everything in our universe that is observable and objective; a second method is needed for looking at reported subjective events. There is a need for an alternative method of researching or investigating when the subject matter does not fall within the physical dimension. Can we really afford to reject reports of subjective information and experiences simply because they do not meet the narrow confines of the scientific method? Many scientists, psychiatrists, psychologists and other practitioners are too intimidated by the professional consensus against the reporting of past lives, out-of-body experiences, clairvoyance and other psi phenomena to even look at the evidence. Professional consensus is very often rooted in religious beliefs which cause therapists and others to deny what they find. Perhaps many centuries of church dogma and scientific tradition are blinding us to other realities.

There is a spiritual vacuum of modern Western society brought about by this age of rationality and scientific inquiry. "What you see is what you get." is the creed which many live by. If you cannot see, feel, touch, smell or hear a thing, then it doesn't exist for them. Knowing for these people is certainly one dimensional; it is tied only to the physical dimension and therein lies the problem.

This book seeks to expand upon the scientific method of inquiry by exploring other ways of investigating non-physical evidence. It also explores psi phenomena of various kinds and it examines some types of mental illness in light of the theory of spiritual emergency put forth by Stanislav and Christina Grof and their colleagues (1989). Spiritual emergency is also explained in the DSM IV, the American Psychiatric Association's diagnostic manual. This book also examines the differences and similarities between people in cultures which include the supernatural in their religious ceremonies and consider it a "natural" phenomenon vs. people in cultures which hospitalize or institutionalize those who have similar "supernatural" experiences.

Dialogues with six extraordinary religious leaders, some of whom teach experiential spirituality, are presented, as well as the story of one deceased shaman whose teachings were grounded in orthodox Christianity. Also, included are the paranormal experiences of ordinary people and a survey of paranormal experiences among the general population of the Washington, D.C. Metropolitan Area.

A Brief History of Psi Phenomena and Psychical Research

Psi phenomena include but are not limited to: extra-sensory perception (ESP), psychokinesis (the movement of objects for no apparent reason), clairvoyance, clairaudience, precognition, telepathy, sightings of apparitions and more recently, experiencing the "missing time" phenomenon which people who claim to have been abducted by extraterrestrials experience. It is a common belief among researchers in this field (who are called psychical researchers or parapsychologists) that all of the aforementioned terms refer to the same general process which is called ESP (extrasensory perception) manifesting itself in different ways.

The Society for Psychical Research was founded in 1882 in Great Britain for the purpose of investigating psychical or paranormal events and it was to serve as a repository for information obtained from these investigations. Serious men and women, for hundreds of years wondered and guessed about how so-called psychics and mystics came by the information to which they were privy. Many researchers have attempted to answer the question, "How can the 'sensitive' do it? How can she obtain information which she just cannot have?" Lawrence LeShan (1974) stated that if serious people work for a long time on a question and do not get an answer, they are asking the wrong question. A more appropriate question, he posed is: "What is the relationship between the sensitive and the rest of reality at the moment when paranormal information is being acquired and what is going on when the paranormal event happens?" LeShan further states, "Deep within us all is the knowledge that we need the development of that other side of us, the part of us we have so neglected and undernourished, to be complete. We know that we have lost something of our heritage and potentiality and are thereby less."

World renowned psychiatrist, Carl Jung, according to Hall and Nordby (1973) in postulating his concept of the collective unconscious tells us, essentially, the same thing: that we have lost a link with our past; i.e., our evolutionary past. Jung called the collective unconscious a reservoir of latent images or primordial images. These primordial images are inherited from our ancestral past which includes our human as well as pre-human or animal ancestors. Jung felt that our psychological problems and social maladies stemmed directly from the alienation of humankind from our ancestral past (or primordial images).

Many of Jung's archetypes are found in mythology. According to the most prolific mythologist of today, Joseph Campbell (1970), mythology serves as a clarifying, unifying and authoritative vehicle for humankind to express our understanding of the universe and our relationship to the controlling force of the universe. It grounds our realities in the essences of prototypes upon which we rely for our guidance and "raison d'etre". In every culture the myths weave a common thread. The characters may be known by various names, but there is always a genesis, a falling from grace, an antagonist, a protagonist, a father figure, a mother figure, and many other symbolic representations of the archetypes about which Jung spoke.

Psychologist, William James, was one of the earlier pioneers in the field who expressed an interest in parapsychology. His interest was based, in part, on the experience of his father, American theologian, Henry James, who was relaxing by a fireplace in a rented house in Windsor, England, in 1844, when he was gripped by fear. He recounted that a vision of a squatting figure filled the room and manifested negative personality characteristics which were very frightening to him and which left the elder James in a state of "almost helpless infancy." This experience lasted for a full hour. For many years afterward, he was haunted by the memory and often spoke of it to his children, William and Henry, Jr. (the novelist).

The experience of the elder James had such a profound influence on the thinking of William James, that he became convinced that psychic sources supplied knowledge that cannot be traced to the ordinary sources of information. William James sought truth through trance mediums because he believed they possessed powers beyond the five senses. Also, like Jung, he thought that extrasensory perceptions were indicative of "a cosmic consciousness" which was much like a "mother-sea" or reservoir.

William James went on to become a leader in the scientific study of psychic phenomena. Around the same time that the Society for Psychical Research was founded in London by a group of prominent physicists, philosophers and others, James, then an eminent member of the Harvard University faculty, founded the American Society for Psychical Research in Boston in 1885 along with several other psychologists. The establishment of these two organizations marked a turning point in parapsychology. Their members were respected scientists whose goal was to objectively study the paranormal and attempt to explain it.

From the beginning, for both the American and British societies, there was a problem of separating truth from hoaxes. Sometimes the investigators were called to investigate occurrences and mediums; some of these investigations turned up seemingly authentic predictions and telepathic communications and some were outright fakes and magicians trying to make a name for themselves.

Sigmund Freud believed psychic research to be a legitimate scientific pursuit, but he declined to link his name with it because of the negative attitudes about parapsychologists. Even though they were striving to make their investigations into the paranormal as scientific as possible, still an air of mysticism surrounded the field and it was frowned upon by many erudite and hard-nosed physicists and faint-hearted psychologists who dogmatically demanded proof and objectivity from a new field which did not readily lend itself to the rules and steps of the scientific method. Subjectivity, rather than objectivity was the stuff of parapsychology. How then, could these pioneers harness the subjective nature of its investigations and lay the evidence before the scientific community so that it could carry out the next step in the scientific method, Repeatability? Ah, a formidable task it was, and the pioneers did not give up.

In the development of parapsychology since the 1880's, a question that has repeatedly been raised concerns the reasons for the rejection of this field by the scientific community as well as the general public. This rejection took the form of both angry dismissal of any possibility of truth to a bland ignoring of the data. This refusal to deal scientifically with the material gathered by parapsychologists and others is a phenomenon, in itself, which begs for an explanation. A wide variety of studies and carefully documented experiences have given us a wealth of unquestionable data, so that one would expect parapsychology to be an accepted and widely studied field of scientific investigation.

There have been a variety of explanations given for this lack of acceptance. Carington (1946) felt that there were two main reasons for the rejection by scientists: (1) that its introduction is perceived as weakening the status of causality and law in science; and (2) that the way will be opened for the introduction in another form of all the magic and superstition which they have fought against so hard and long.

Henri Bergson (1915) pointed out that each approach to science implies that certain types of data (which cannot be fit into its method) are invalid and unreal. Reality becomes a factor in most cases on non-acceptance because the data are subjective much of the time rather than objective. Bergson also believed that the modern approach, dealing with measurement as its prime dimension, had made the basic assumption that "mind" and "brain" are two terms referring to the same thing. With this assumption, science would automatically reject parapsychological findings and interpretation.

Eisenbud (1963) in his analysis of this problem hypothesized that the non-acceptance (as well as the assumption of non-repeatability of experiments in this field) is inherent in the general nature of the universe and of psi forces themselves. He sees psi as an aspect of the structure of the cosmos whose function it is to keep things running smoothly and lawfully - a sort of dynamic connective tissue. In his view, to try to bring psi out into the open and to harness it is to use it against its own structure and function.

There is a good deal of evidence that knowledge of the existence or possible existence of psi phenomena seems to produce anxiety in many individuals. Thus, Upton Sinclair (1930) quotes his wife Mary Craig Sinclair, who was the participant in their experiments, "I agree with Richet that the fact of telepathy is one of the most terrifying in existence."

Tyrell (1938) felt that the dissonant facts given to us by parapsychologists did not fit into our concepts of the world and its workings. This, he felt is why people reject psychical phenomena: they fear that the dissonant facts, if admitted would disrupt the scheme of the known and the familiar.

Dossey (1993) is in complete agreement with Tyrell. Cognitive dissonance is a psychological term describing the discomfort people feel when there is a conflict between their perceptions and their belief system. Looking at evidence of psi phenomena stimulates this inner tension in some scientists. Dossey feels that many scientists resolve this discomfort by derogating and rejecting the event without proper attention to evidence.

The concepts of "constancy and incongruity" also figure into this problem of non-acceptance of psi data and reports. Bruner and Postman (1958) explain, " For as long as possible and by whatever means available, people will ward off the perception of the unexpected, those things which do not fit their prevailing set. Most people come to depend upon certain constancy in their environment and except under certain conditions, attempt to ward off variations from this state of affairs." Bruner and Postman (1958) designed a study to show how people respond to a perceived breakdown of his expectations about the structure of the world. They used a tachistoscope to show participants playing cards and they measured how long a visual exposure was necessary before a participant could recognize a card. They, then, mixed incongruous cards in the deck; these cards had the suit and color reversed. They found that normal cards were recognized correctly to a standard of approximately twenty-eight (28) milliseconds. Incongruous cards took an average of one hundred fourteen (114) milliseconds. Verbal reactions of the participants to the reversal cards showed some sense of the stress they were under. The most amazing finding from this experiment was that the greatest percentage of their participants showed a pattern they called "dominance", a complete rejection of the incongruous elements. They actually suppressed all recognition of the incongruous element. Perhaps the greatest single barrier to the recognition of incongruous stimuli is the tendency for perceptual hypotheses to fixate after receiving a minimum of confirmation.

People tend to choose either the "mystical" view or the "mechanistic" view of the universe. There tends to be no middle ground for most. Either psi evidence is in error, a falsification, or it is true; the world takes sides. Some parapsychologists with clinical experience take the position that psi is inhibited by higher levels of cognitive and ego development. Ehrenwald, a psychiatrist (1971), holds that telepathy exists between mother and child prior to individuation. The connection between dreams and the paranormal and the importance of dreams in early development has also been noted by Tolass (1986). Tolass thought that telepathic communication developed in the womb to be used for emergencies prior to birthing.

The mystical traditions, on the other hand, acknowledge psychic phenomena and regard them as developmental milestones in human spiritual evolvement. They regard psychic abilities as by-products of development rather than end products or goals. They emphasize attunement to higher meaning rather than becoming overawed by the experience itself.

Anthropologist, Margaret Mead, was another eminent proponent of psi research. In her studies of primitive cultures, she had observed evidence of special paranormal powers. A bold pioneer, she risked scorn from many fellow scientists when she helped persuade the American Association for the Advancement of Science to admit the Parapsychological Association as an affiliate.

Healing

Edgar Cayce (1877-1945) who has often been referred to as the "sleeping prophet" believed in a "universal mind" which he frequently contacted in his work. Many books have been written about Edgar Cayce and much of his work has been catalogued by the Association for Research and Enlightenment, Inc. (A.R.E.). A.R.E. is a non-profit, open membership organization committed to spiritual growth, holistic healing, psychical research and its spiritual dimensions. Also, A.R.E. seeks to make practical use of the psychic readings of the late Cayce through nationwide programs, publications, and study groups.

Edgar Cayce was perhaps the most widely known psychic of his time. He was consulted by many doctors to diagnose and prescribe treatments for their patients. Cayce's treatments miraculously healed the most difficult of cases. Cayce's method was to go into a trance-like sleep and dictate therapies to his wife and secretary. A.R.E. has documented over 6,000 cases of healing through the aid of the "universal mind." Cayce explained that the knowledge gained while he was in a self-induced sleep came from his own unconscious mind which had tuned in to the "universal mind" or the "collective unconscious." He described the levels of an individual's unconscious mind and he discussed the collective unconscious in which the individual unconscious had its origin. Like Jung, he described the collective unconscious as a vast "river of thought flowing through eternity, fed by the collective mental activity of mankind since its beginning." Cayce believed that this collective unconscious is available and "accessible to anyone who develops his psychic faculties to such a degree as to be able to draw from, as well as feed into this river of thought."

Several others have claimed to either heal through psi techniques or have intimate knowledge of such healings. Healing with crystals and gemstones is a mantric art which focuses on the chakras of the body to bring energy or qui to the area(s) which needs healing (Chase & Pawlikm 2001 and 2002).

Carlos Castaneda (1993) apprenticed under a Mexican Yaqui shaman (or sorcerer, as he called himself). The shaman, don Juan Matus, helped Castaneda learn the art of healing. Castaneda claims to have received in his dreams, the answers to questions he was planning to ask don Juan.

Noted psychic and author, Sylvia Browne (2001), states that our past lives have an influence on our present healing. She asserts that our lives are affected through cell memory by the lives we have lived before. She relates many past life regression histories to support this position.

Healing through the laying on of hands is a tradition which goes back to the days of antiquity. It continues to be practiced today in many cultures. In this type healing, divine energy purportedly is channeled through the healer's hands and passes through to the "patient". One study tested the tactile sensitivity of healers' and patients' fingertips both before and after healing sessions (Maher et. al. 1996). They found that changes in healers' right hand fingertip thresholds were significantly different from changes in the right hand fingertip thresholds of patients, healer simulators and patient controls. Also, real patients' right hand fingertip threshold change differed significantly from that of patient controls. The before healing and after healing palm sensitivity tests done on patients and healers showed a significant difference with regard to time. There was significantly more change in the right hand thresholds of healers than in any of the other groups, suggesting that something other than mere chance was operating.

Psychic surgery originated in the Philippine Islands. This type surgery purportedly is performed by the Holy Spirit through the mind and spirit of the healer. The healer is usually in a meditative state or in semi-trance when his hands are guided by God. Energy is sent into the diseased area(s) of the body and healing takes place. There are reports of the healer's hands entering the body and pulling out tissue without leaving a wound or scar.

Larry Dossey (1993) has been involved in research into prayer and healing for several years. Much of his research that is well documented gives much credence to evidence of prayers being answered. Dossey has used human participants as well as plants and bacteria in his studies. His is the most compelling evidence to date which suggests that prayers do get answered. In one study, for example, using bacteria, two samples were used. One sample was prayed for and it multiplied and thrived while the bacteria sample which was not prayed for did not. The statistical difference between the samples was very significant.

Another study involved healing through prayer at a distance (Byrd, 1988). The participants were all Christians. Over 10 months, 393 patients admitted to a coronary care unit were assigned to either a prayer group or a non-prayer (control) group. Although both doctors and patients were informed of the purpose of the study, neither knew which patients were receiving prayer. The patients who received prayer showed significantly superior recovery compared to the control group, suggesting that factors other than chance were present.

Remote Viewing

With all of the debate going on between the believers in psi and the non-believers, a few bold and highly motivated researchers dared to try to prove, scientifically, the existence of psi. In the 1920s, most American universities were not very enthusiastic about psychic research. During those days, parapsychology was scorned because of its association with fake mediums and false claims. In the years following William James' death in 1910, several other serious researchers continued to conduct psychic research at Harvard, Stanford, and Clark Universities, even though the administrators at these universities were not very comfortable about it. In order for psychic research to gain a respectable foothold in the academic community, it needed a champion of stature and respect, someone who was well known and prestigious. William McDougal was just that person. McDougal came from England in 1920 and became chair of the psychology department at Harvard. McDougal had earned so much respect in the scientific community that he was allowed to devise his own curriculum at Harvard. He was openly interested in the paranormal and he is credited with coining the term "parapsychology." He used his position at Harvard to mentor several students who would one day go on to make names for themselves: among them were Gardner Murphy, a Columbia University graduate student who attempted to send mental images to another psychologist, Rene Warcollier in Paris; and George Estabrooks, a Harvard graduate student who conducted card guessing experiments between subjects in separate rooms. (This type of experiment is now called *remote viewing*.) However, McDougal had one student who went on to become the most famous psychologist in the field of parapsychology, Joseph Banks Rhine. Joseph Rhine is thought of as the father of modern parapsychology.

Rhine, a botanist by profession, was greatly influenced by author, Sir Arthur Conan Doyle, as well as McDougal (Rhine, L. 1967). Doyle was known to seek the services of Gladys Osborne Leonard, a well-known British medium. He shared with Doyle the belief that some kind of reality exists beyond the material world. He was further influenced by McDougal's book, Body and Mind, which postured that psychic research was needed in order to complete a full picture of human nature.

J.B. Rhine went on to establish at Duke University a parapsychology laboratory which is today in the vanguard of research in this area. He started with experiments in which he asked subjects to guess the order of a shuffled deck of cards. If they scored better than could be expected by chance, then he assumed that some unknown factor was operating. Karl Zener, an expert in the psychology of perception and Rhine's colleague, designed a set of five cards which consisted of a square, a star, a circle, a plus sign, and wavy lines. The Zener cards, as they were called, were used in many of Rhine's experiments. The deck of 25 cards consisted of five cards of each pattern. Chance decreed that a person would be able to guess five times correctly. Each correct call was considered a "hit." In one experiment Rhine tested a young economics student, Adam Linzmayer. Linzmayer was astounding! For the two years that Rhine tested Linzmayer, he defied the odds. In one session, Linzmayer hit nine in a row against odds of 2,000,000 to one. Others were tested and Rhine and his associates began to discern what they saw as a psychology of the psychic process (Rao, 1982). They found that both mood and motivation affected the psychic process; some subjects did better when they were encouraged or challenged. On one occasion, Rhine offered a subject, Hubert Pearce, Jr., $100 for every hit. Pearce won $2,500 in a 25-card streak at odds of 298,023,223,867,953,125 to one.

Rhine and his associates also found that there was a general tendency of ESP scores to drop over prolonged periods of testing. He called this trend, the "decline effect."

Other researchers today concentrate their research in areas such as psychokinesis, the movement of objects for no readily apparent reason, dream research, field investigations (of reported paranormal events), near-death experiences (NDEs), out-of-body experiences or traveling in the astral body (OBEs), clairvoyance, and Kirlian photography (photos of energy fields which surround objects) (Krippner & Rubin, 1975). Researchers at the PEAR Laboratory at Princeton University conduct many experiments investigating the phenomenon of psychokinesis. Around the world, there are scattered pockets of researchers who are engaged in parapsychological research of one sort or another.

Death and Near-Death Experiences

Underlying numerous philosophies and religions is the belief that the spirit and the body exist separately, and that the spirit or soul survives after death. According to Simon Bockie (1993) in Ba Manianga philosophy (a group in central Africa in the Congo-Angola region) a living person consists of three basic elements: "Nitu", the physical, visible body, "kini", the invisible body, a shade or reflection of nitu, looking exactly like it; and "mwela", the soul which has no bodily form. At death, when the visible nitu dies, kini and mwela exit from it to start their journey to the other world. Together, they form the life-body, that which continues alive, as opposed to the earth-body, which has been discarded and left behind.

But, what of the spirit during life? Is it possible for a spiritual form to journey outside the physical body and then return? If the spirit survives death, could it come back in another body? Throughout history, respected men and women have related their own experiences and answered yes.

Spiritual voyages are thought to take one of three forms. During an out-of-body experience, the spirit travels beyond the physical body for a short time and then returns. In a near-death experience, the spirit departs as if bound for the next life but is drawn back into the still-living body. Spirits who have survived the death of one physical body and then come back in another physical body as a newborn baby are said to have undergone reincarnation. Many religions and cultures believe everyone experiences reincarnation as many times as necessary for the soul to   develop enough to live on a higher plane.

Many people have said that they experienced out-of-body travel. One of the most well known persons to have made this claim was Charles Lindbergh (1978). During his 1927 transatlantic flight, around the twenty-second hour of his flight, the plane became enveloped in a dense fog. Lindbergh battled tiredness and sleepiness. He said that he felt himself leaving his body as he stared at his instrument panel. "I existed independently of time and matter. I felt myself departing from my body as I imagine a spirit would depart - emanating into the cockpit, extending through the fuselage as though no frame or fabric walls were there, angling upward, outward, until I reformed in an awareness far distant from the human form I left in a fast flying transatlantic plane. But, I remained connected to my body through a long-extended strand, a strand so tenuous that it could have been severed by a breath."

Lindbergh knew that skeptics would attribute his out-of-body experience to hallucinations and extreme fatigue, so, he responded to that line of reasoning by explaining, " My visions are easily explained away through reason, but the longer I live, the more limited I believe rationality to be."

Dr. E. Kubler-Ross (1969) worked with dying patients and learned many lessons from them as they went through various stages of dying. Her patients told of near-death experiences during which they traveled through a tunnel toward a bright light, were greeted by dead relatives and friends, and then had to return because it was not time for them to die.

Others who have communicated with the "other side" include mystics, shamans and psychics. Famous psychic, Sylvia Browne relates her tours of the "other side" (S. Browne, 2000). Her reports are of people who have died and who are busy working and playing after death.

Eadie (1994) gives a detailed narrative during a near-death experience (NDE). Her experiences on the "other side" were widely acclaimed and she was a guest on many talk shows telling us about her experiences which she feels are proof of life after death.

Others question the experiences of psychics who claim to communicate with the dead (Roleff, 2003). There are many who hold opposing viewpoints regarding the ability of others to communicate with the dead.

UFOs

Many people all over the world claim to have seen unidentified flying objects (UFOs). Accounts of these sightings exist as far back as 1290 A.D. when a group of monks in Yorkshire, England witnessed a large round silver disk which flew slowly over them. Some claim that there is evidence of UFOs in biblical passages.

While many UFO sightings have been reported and many people have made claims of being abducted, medically probed and released, evidence of these occurrences, which consist of healed physical wounds, implanted trackers and accounts given under hypnosis, has yet to be accepted.

There are those who say that the governments of the world have all conspired to hide the evidence of alien beings and UFOs, but this case has yet to be proven.

Popular Psi Interests

Other areas of popular interest include astrology, numerology, psychic readings, "colorology" and other ancient divinations. Many people are familiar with forecasting future events through the analysis of the positions of planets and our sun and moon. Many people, from the highest to the lowest in many cultures live by these forecasts.

Knowing your numbers is also a growing area of popular psi interest. Many people analyze their birthdates, addresses, automobile tags and other personal numbers associated with them.

Others use colors for their personal environment, energy, communication and healing (Mella, 1988). Some claim that colors affect mood and atmosphere.

Van Praagh (2001) claims to have psychic ability and he encourages developing our innate God-given ability. Everyone, he feels, has psychic ability to a greater or lesser degree. He also warns against attracting lower realm spirit entities when trying to make your own psychic connection. He calls these lower realm, earth bound spirit entities psychic vampires.

Sheldrake (2003) believes that everyone has psychic ability, also. He says everyone certainly has a sense of being stared at. If you stare at someone long enough, they will turn around to see who is looking at them.

Sheldrake also tells us that animals have psychic abilities that we have lost (1999). Dogs, birds and cats seem to somehow know when their owners are coming home. They have been known to make long migrations back home or trailing its owner to a new location it had never visited before. This phenomenon is called psi trailing. Animals have also been known to react to impending dangers or disasters such as earthquakes or floods.

Dog and cat lovers can tell us how empathetic these animals are during times of sadness or trouble. They are little "comforters" who snuggle, lick and try to help their human friends through tough times.

Young children have been cited as having spontaneous psychic experiences (Stevenson, 1974). Stevenson documents cases of children, mostly aged 2 – 4 who all reported spontaneous psychic experiences which is suggestive of reincarnation. Children have been known to display extraordinary talents and abilities at very young ages. Prodigies who can play the piano, solve high-level mathematics problems and other feats far beyond their age levels have been known for many decades. Reports of telepathic children are also common (Peterson, 1987). There are well documented cases of children having knowledge which they acquired telepathically or paranormally. Feng Shui is a very popular ancient Chinese practice in many parts of the world. It is the art and science of living in harmony with the environment. It involves placing furniture and other objects in positions within the home or at work to best attract peace, prosperity and good health. It is based upon energy fields created by the natural geomagnetic forces of Earth. People seek positive energy (ch'i). Feng Shui consultants are in demand in many parts of the world. They go into people's homes and offices and arrange the environment for the most positive results.

Physical acts such as fire walking, moving objects many times the weight of the person and other superhuman feats are well documented throughout the world. Acts of this sort are paranormal to most of us, but normal to those who can perform these feats.

Current Views of Mental Health Professionals

No study of Psi can be complete without including the work of Stanislav Grof and his wife, Christina. Stanislav Grof is a psychiatrist with over 30 years of research experience in nonordinary states of consciousness and transpersonal psychology, which includes spiritual experiences, meditation, mystical states of consciousness and other related areas. Stanislav Grof has conducted research at the Johns Hopkins University, the Maryland Psychiatric Research Center and currently at the Esalen Institute in Big Sur, California. He has published over 90 papers in professional journals and is the author of several books on altered states of consciousness. Grof and others (1989) have explored the concept of the emerging self. Some people who experience crises and some who actively seek spiritual knowledge sometimes undergo what Grof calls a "spiritual emergency." What happens is that those individuals experience metaphysical events and enter into nonordinary states of awareness, which to others seem strange and even psychotic. Grof and other psychiatrists who have often witnessed this happen to their patients want to see a distinction made between those people who are undergoing a spiritual crisis or emergency and those who are truly mentally ill. Grof views these crises as transformative breakthroughs which can hold tremendous potential for physical and emotional healing. He urges psychiatrists, psychologists, and the clergy to learn to recognize spiritual emergencies and to distinguish them from a state of genuine psychosis and to treat the patient/client accordingly.

The newly revised (1994) DSM-IV (American Psychiatric Association's Diagnostic and Statistical Manual) has included spiritual emergencies in the new manual as a non-pathological category of mental disorder in the new V Code. Both pathological and non-pathological manifestations of mental disorders are seen as contributing to the spiritual growth of the individual.

R.D. Laing (1965 & 1969), a controversial Scottish psychiatrist, delivers a scathing condemnation of modern psychiatry. Laing, as well as others, feels that the medical treatment model used by most psychiatrists is not scientifically justified since no specific biological causes have been found for the majority of the conditions which psychiatrists are treating. Laing is usually seen as a representative of "antipsychiatry." According to Laing, psychoses cannot be understood in terms of biological processes. They represent to him a reflection of problems in human relationships and with society as a whole. According to Laing, psychiatrists do not pay proper attention to the inner experiences of psychotics because they see them as pathological and incomprehensible. However, careful observation and study show that these experiences have profound meaning and that the psychotic process can be healing. Laing feels that special places should be provided where people receive the support and sympathetic understanding that facilitate the healing process.

Like Grof, Laing sees an urgent need to draw a clear distinction between pathology and mysticism. Like C. Jung, Laing states that we are estranged from the collective unconscious and he goes on to refine the concept of the collective unconscious and relate it to The Divine. Laing states, "I am not merely spinning senseless paradoxes when I say that we, the sane ones, are out of our minds. The mind is what the ego is unconscious of. We are unconscious of our minds. Our minds are not unconscious. Our minds are conscious of us. Ask your-

self who and what it is that dreams our dreams...our unconscious minds? The Dreamer who dreams our dreams knows far
more of us than we know of it. It is only from a remarkable position of alienation that the source of life, the Fountain of Life,
is experienced as the it. The mind of which we are unaware is
aware of us. It is we who are out of our minds. We need not be
unaware of the inner world." Laing recognizes an inner world
which is just as real as the external world. He posits that the
patient should be guided and helped through the inner world
by supportive and knowledgeable professionals who understand
spiritual emergencies and can distinguish them from psychotic
states. Laing , like Grof, believes that both working through a
psychotic state by using correct spiritual guidance and giving
support to a patient who is experiencing a nonordinary state of
consciousness can be healing and transformative.

Mythologist, Joseph Campbell (1972) tried to draw
comparisons between the world of the mystics and the world of
the schizophrenic. He stated, " The mystic...enters the waters
and finds that he can swim; whereas the schizophrenic...has
fallen or has intentionally plunged, and is drowning." He
thought that the mystic's transpersonal achievement might lie
in his ability to derive meaning from the experience, whereas
the schizophrenic does not possess that ability.

Much has been written and investigated about the
paranormal, but not enough factual information has been written for the masses. Many thought provoking ideas and concepts
have been put forth by researchers for other professionals and
researchers. I feel that this information and knowledge should
be shared with those who are not a part of the world of acade-
mia, as well. Therefore, this book contains non-technical words
whenever possible so that a lay person can understand it.

Since there is no suitable pronoun for God in the English language because God is neither male nor female, I have
used either he or she as a pronoun or I have substituted other
words to Describe God such as The Almighty or Our Creator,
among others.

Section One

Shamans, Mystics and Healers

Chapter 2

Chief Joseph Rain Crow: Native American Healer

Chief Joseph Neale (Rain Crow) keeps a very busy schedule for a man his age. Born in 1925, he has the stamina of a man half his age or less. Chief Rain Crow, spiritual leader of the Youghiogheny River Band of Shawnee Indians, Inc., is constantly on the go. He frequently goes into the mountains of Western Maryland with his Shawnee Tribe members to perform ceremonial rites such as the pre-planting ceremony, the spring bread dance or the green corn ceremony. When he's not doing that, he is ministering to the needs of those who call upon him for healing and special ceremonies and functions, such as weddings and naming a child.

Rain Crow is a man of two worlds, the world of his ancestors, the Shawnee Indians and a man of the today's cosmopolitan world. He skillfully blends the two worlds and he is in charge in both of them. Rain Crow , which means morning dove, has had more formal education than three or

four people combined: He earned a B.A. in engineering in
1953 from the U. of Steubenville; an A.B. in History and
Political Science from Bethany College in 1958; a B.A. in
Sacred Theology from Wesley Theological Seminary, and an
M.S in Divinity from Wesley in 1961; an M.Ed. from American U. in 1973 and he will earn a Ph.D. in Student Development and Higher Education from American U. if and
when he decides to finish his dissertation.

Chief Rain Crow combines his Christian upbringing
with his ancestral religion which is rooted in actual spiritual experience as opposed to beliefs. Raised in the Meth-
odist church by his grandparents, Rain Crow remembers
vividly the days of his youth when his grandmother used to
heal the people in the little valley off the Ohio River in Jefferson County. How valuable she was to the townspeople
there in that tranquil place many years ago. Everyone depended upon her for her herbal medicines. She delivered
the children of most of the people there, both whites and
Indians. Grandmother's hands were magical hands, healing
hands given to her by the Great Spirit. Rain Crow recalls
the night that Grandma sat up with a dying woman. The
doctor had said that she would not survive until the morning. Grandma replied, "Not if God and I have anything to do
with it!" She sent Rain Crow out into the woods to gather
rattle root. She had taught him well. He knew that the same
herbs look different during different times of the year. "Let
me tell you what it looks like now, Rain Crow," she said.

Rain Crow said, "I know what it looks like,
Grandma. You showed me what all the plants look like in
the different seasons." Grandma replied, "But, it won't have
leaves on it. It will be a stick now."

It was winter and he knew what to look for. Rain
Crow gathered the rattle root from the woods and brought it
back to Grandma for preparation. Grandma found some old
cloth, ripped it into strips and made a poultice from the rattle root and placed it upon the woman's throat. Throughout
the night she applied warm poultices to the woman's throat.
The poor woman was suffering from quinsy, a disease which
inflames and swells the tonsils to the point where they cut
off the air passage. The poor sick woman could be heard
breathing laboriously from many feet away. Grandma
prayed and tended to her needs throughout the night. In

the morning, Rain Crow remembers, the woman was well. The swelling was gone and she was able to get up from her bed. God and Grandma were an invincible team.

The townspeople who were healed by grandma's herbal medicines were grateful to her and they showed it, but not openly. Many times, late at night Grandma,

Grandpa, and Rain Crow would hear a thud on the porch outside or a noise that was very unsettling. Grandpa would go for his gun. There was no real law there in the valley then, just your gun...it was law. When they investigated, they would find no one. Instead, they would find, perhaps, a side of beef wrapped in sheets, or a ham, some fruit or vegetable preserves that someone had recently made, or cakes, pies...anything which they could either eat or use in some way. That was their way of saying "thanks" to Grandma because she never charged them a dime. Rain Crow explained, "When God gives you something, you're supposed to give it away. You share what you have with others." That was Grandma's and Grandpa's code of ethics and it is Rain Crow's code, as well.

"I have lost some of the remedies which my Grandmother taught me. It's a shame, but I have." He got up and headed toward the kitchen and brought back a large jar of a caramel colored liquid which looked like tea. He said, "Look at this...it's a cure for cancer. There exists a 200-page document full of medical testimonials about this medicine." On the jar, handwritten on a piece of paper and taped to the bottle was the word *essiac*. He went on to explain that essiac is Caisse spelled backwards. Rene Caisse, a Canadian nurse, first used the formula with terminal cancer patients. Rene Caisse discovered the remedy through a patient in the hospital where she worked who had been cured of cancer. This patient had been given this herbal remedy by an Ojibwa Indian herbalist. Rain Crow explains that Rene gave this remedy to patients who had been certified by their doctors to have terminal cancer. She administered essiac both orally and by injection. Some of her patients died due to prior severe damage to their organs but those who had no severe damage to life support organs were cured and lived 35-45 years after their cures. Many are still living today. Rain Crow said that the Canadian Ministry of Health and Welfare and the Parliament became involved. Fifty-five thousand signatures were collected on a petition for the right of doctors to administer essiac. Essiac came within three votes of being legalized by the Ontario government as a remedy for terminal cancer patients.

Recipe for Essiac Tea

Formula:
6 _ cups Burdock Root (cut to pea-size pieces)
16 oz. Sheep Sorrel Herb (powdered)
1 oz. Turkey Rhubarb Root (powdered)
4 oz.Slippery Elm Bark (powdered)

Supplies Needed:
5-gallon stainless steel pot
3 gallon stainless steel pot
Stainless steel fine-mesh double strainer
Stainless steel funnel
Stainless steel spatula
12 or more 16 – ounce amber glass bottles with airtight caps (*not* childproof caps)
2 gallons sodium-free distilled water
Measuring Cup
Kitchen scale with ounce measurements

Preparation: Mix Essiac formula thoroughly. Bring sodium-free distilled water to a rolling boil in 5-gallon pot with lid on. Stir in 1 cup of Essiac formula. Replace lid and continue boiling for 10 minutes. Turn off stove. Scrape down sides of pot with spatula and stir mixture thoroughly. Replace lid. Allow pot to remain closed for 12 hours; then turn stove to full heat for 20 minutes. Turn off stove. Strain liquid into 3-gallon pot, and clean 5-gallon pot and strainer. Then strain filtered liquid back into 5-gallon pot. Use funnel to pour hot liquid into bottles immediately, taking care to tighten caps. Allow bottles to cool; then tighten caps again. Refrigerate. Essiac contains no preservative agents. If mold should develop in bottles, discard immediately. All bottles and caps must be sterilized before reusing them. Wash and rinse thoroughly. They may be cleaned with a 3% solution of food grade hydrogen peroxide in water.

Directions for use: Heat _ cup sodium-free distilled water in a stainless steel pot. Add _ cup of Essiac. (Shake bottle first.) Mix and drink. Take at bedtime on an empty stomach, at least 2 hours after eating.

I asked, "Why do people not know about this? It sounds like a wonder drug which is desperately needed by the terminally ill."

Rain Crow went on to explain that cancer is the second largest revenue producing business in the world, second to the petrochemical business. "Money and power suppress this truth. I take it to ward off cancer", he explained. "It's also had some good results with diabetes patients. Ted Kennedy's son was cured with essiac. He had a sarcoma in his leg and he had it amputated. Dr. Charles Brusch, who was a personal physician to the late President John F. Kennedy, worked with Rene Caisse from 1959 to 1962. He also worked with the Presidential Cancer Commission and other Cancer organizations. Dr. Brusch, after ten years of research, presented his findings that essiac is a cure for cancer and the federal government issued a gag order and told him to keep quiet. Dr. Brusch helped Dr. Farber at the Farber Cancer Institute in Boston to save Ted Kennedy's son. "Quite an interesting story, eh?"

"Indeed! How else do you come to know about herbs and healing? Did you learn it all from your grandmother?"

Rain Crow replied, "I learned a lot from my Grandmother, but what you don't know, the spirit tells you."

I asked, "Do you talk to the spirit like you are talking to me?"

He said, "No. It's inward... you get the message inside your head. The spirit talks to you in your head. We have name giving ceremonies and when I prayed for a name for a child, the spirit (God) gave it to me inside of me."

"I see. Like a sudden insight or a hunch?"

"It is stronger than a hunch. It is like someone thinking inside your head, giving you guidance. You know the thoughts are not yours. You know they come from Kije-Moneto."

"Who?"

"We Shawnee call God... The Creator, Kije-Moneto. We have also a grandfather deity and a grandmother deity. During our ceremonies when the women take part in the singing and dancing, we listen for the voice of "Grandmother" to join in with the singing."

"Do you know Grandmother's voice?"

"Oh, yes! You know when grandmother is there.

Make no mistake about it. You know her voice."

"What's it like?"

"It is high-pitched and very distinct. Sometimes you see her and then she turns into the young boy. Sometimes you see her assume the form of the boy."

"So, would you say that Grandmother Deity is two in one?"

"That's right. She is two in one and then there is the Grandfather Deity. "

"Your experiences are both visual and auditory, then?"

"Yes, Kije-Moneto will show you things in many ways. Like, with healing, there are different kinds of healing. Spirits come to some and tell them what to use. Some people (healers) have only one cure that they might feed to some, rub on others or burn and pray in other cases. During one ceremony, we saw a child, an angel who came to us. Everyone in my band has had many experiences with spirits... my mother, too. My mother had premonitions of people dying before they actually died. She could tell by looking at someone's face if they were O.K. She once told someone about a man who was riding on the bus with her who lived in our town that he was going to die in three days. In three days, he died."

"My goodness, your mom was right on target."

"Yes. She was always right about things. She talked to the spirit. Kije-Moneto knows all, sees all and tells you what you need to know for healing and helping yourself and others. You know, some of us healers have been known to travel, too."

"Travel?"

"Yes...travel outside of their bodies. You know...come out and fly around."

"Are you talking about astral body travel?"

"Yes....yes."

"Can you do that, Rain Crow?"

"Well, I didn't know how to do it for a long time, but I wanted to do it. The old people talked about it when I was younger. I never experienced it until several years ago. I was at a medicine conference in Arizona. A group of Native American spiritual leaders were teaching doctors how to use Indian medicine. I went out by the pool to relax and I sat down in this chair and I let my head drop to the side...to my left side. The next thing I know, I'm flying across the city. I'm up real high. I passed Phoenix, went through a forest and I realized that I was several hundred miles from where I was sitting. I was in Nevada. I got scared and I asked, 'Oh Grandfather (deity), can I get back?' Grandfather answered me, 'Whenever you please, Joseph.' It was like flying with an eagle. I was up pretty high, but I could see so clearly. I could see small things on the ground even though I was hundreds of feet in the air. I wanted to go back. Next thing I know, I picked my head up and looked at my watch. Only four minutes had passed on my watch! I traveled across a couple of states in four minutes!"   Rain Crow smiled as he reminisced about his first astral trip. "I have done it many times since that day. I just do it whenever I please. Another time, when I was in Arizona, I did it. I dropped my head to the side and out I came. This time I think I went too far. I crossed over Nevada, Nebraska, and Illinois. When I got to the Illinois / Indiana border, I said, 'Grandfather, I think I went too far!'   Again, Grandfather replied, 'Go back when-ever you please, Joseph.' That time I was gone six minutes. It was wonderful...I could see where lizards had dragged their tails in the sand. I could see so much even though I was up so high."

"Rain Crow, from what you say, it seems that people in their astral form have better vision...telescopic vision!"

Rain Crow laughed and continued on, "I have trav-eled to cities far away...even in Europe. There is always a gold cast to these experiences."

"A gold cast?"

"Yes."

"What do you mean, Rain Crow?"

"The air...the air is misted with gold when I have these experiences."

"Oh, really?"

"There is a cast of gold around everything when I come out. I have been given this gift and other people want me to teach it to them."

"Do you teach them how to do it?"

"Yes. I taught one of my Indian friends, Big Bear. Big Bear flew with me. We went out together. We were both fly-ing high in the sky. We were at a big meeting when we did it and I knew we could not be out for long. I wished to go back and I did reenter my body. I looked over at Big Bear and he was not responding; he was still out. I got scared. I thought that he could not get back into his body. We shook him, but he did not respond. I thought, 'Oh, my goodness! He doesn't know how to get back in!' After a few more minutes, he opened his eyes."

I said, "Maybe Big Bear did not want to come back in."

"Maybe not." Rain Crow responded.

I asked, "Have you taught anyone else how to come out?"

He explained, "I do it for healing purposes only. I helped a psychologist from the National Institute of Health. I took her out with me and we had the experience together. It helped her to resolve something in her life. She told me afterwards, 'There is nothing in the world like that!' It helped her to heal. I am a healer. I help people resolve their problems in many ways. I am also a hands-on healer. I have cured people of various ailments. The spirit tells me and I share my gift with that person."

"Chief Rain Crow, what has been your most moving and spiritually revealing experience?"

"Well, two things. I took five men into the woods for a *blessed pipe ceremony* and one of the men told me that he found Jesus after that ceremony. This is a ceremony for men and one of the young men, a Caucasian, went with us. We take anybody with us. We are all the same. God made us all. We are not so different from each other. He was so deeply moved and overwhelmed by his personal spiritual experience that he wept and thanked me for the experience."

"How moving. That must have been a night to remember."

"The other time was the time when I was really low and I turned away from the church. When I was a young man, I met my first wife and she did some things that were real bad and all the time everyone knew, including my friends. She went off with another guy and I was devastated. I turned away from the church then and I vowed never to set foot in one again. Everybody tried to get me to go back, but I wouldn't." Rain Crow's eyes misted and his

voice cracked slightly as he told me about the disappoint-
ments of his first wife, the death of his second wife and the
death of his daughter who died when she was ten years old.
Rain Crow talked about how he found God again. After everyone failed at coaxing him back into the fold, he decided,
on his own, one day to sneak into church and sit on the
back row by the door just in case he should decide to leave,
so that he would have a quick exit. He did not want anyone
to see him. The next thing he knew, the most beautiful
young woman he had ever seen walked in after he was
seated; she headed straight for the front row and sat directly in front of the preacher. Whoa! It was love at first
sight!   The preacher announced that this young woman
would lead the congregation in song. She had the most
beautiful voice he had ever heard. She sang like an angel!
He returned to church and God after that long hiatus. That
beautiful young girl became his third wife. She was of German descent and Rain Crow recalls with mirth the time
when her family literally inspected him from head to toe
when he called on her to take her to a neighboring church
on their first date. Being a Native American, he did not
think that they would approve of him. There were some res-
ervations at first, but love won over racism. They had many
happy years together. Two children were born of that union.
His son, Crow, lives with him now.

   "My son, Crow, is spiritually gifted, too. I can see
auras around people from here to here." With a sweeping
motion, he indicated an area from the shoulder to roughly
the wrist or hand. "I can see in only one color, but Crow...he
sees auras in all colors. He can even see the bones in your
hand. He can see spirits in the house, too."

   "Are you saying he has x-ray vision?"

   "I don't have a name for it, but he can see through
the skin and muscles and see the bones in a person's body.
He is a very spiritual person, too. Four crows were flying
beside my son's car one day. They flew with him as he was
driving. That was a good sign. Four is a sacred number."

   "You and Crow have had many spiritual experiences,
Rain Crow."

   "I am totally experiential when it comes to religion.
We always have sacred experiences when we go to our
ceremonial sacred grounds in the mountains of Western

Maryland. My band of Shawnee Indians performs several ceremonial rites each year. Kije-Moneto (God) speaks to us all in many ways...many ways...and we must give away what we know....share it with others. We share with anyone. We do not care about race or class or anything like that. We are all the same. We are all human beings made by one God."

[Note: Chief Rain Crow passed away in October 1998, a few years after this interview.]

Chapter 3

Lazaro Galarraga: Yoruba Priest

He danced and played the drums like a man half his age or younger. As co-director of an up and coming Afro-Cuban dancing and drumming group, Lazaro Galarraga is considered a master of his craft. Lazaro was in his early sixties or late fifties. It was early June, 1993 and Lazaro and his group, Project Iroko, had come to Washington to perform at The Dance Place, recently converted group of dance studios in the northeast section of Washington, DC near The Catholic University.

Lazaro and his group of dancers and drummers came together from cities as far apart as New York and Los Angeles. His younger co-director was the spokesperson for the group since Lazaro's English was not perfect. The swirling and undulating young men and women who danced told a story through their dance of the Orishas or saints of the ancient Yoruba religion.

College educated, Lazaro is a father, grandfather, choreographer, entertainer, and Yoruba priest, and he is college educated. He spoke with pride about his children and his talented family. He is a highly talented man capable of bringing an audience to its feet with his rhythmic swaying and undulating keeping perfect time with the big conga drums. Last night, he was perspiring, and an inner feeling of total enjoyment shone on his face as he danced before the small audience in one of the dance studios which had been converted into a small auditorium. The crowd clapped and cheered as Lazaro did a sexy bump and grind down to the floor. One man from the audience ran onto the stage and slapped a five dollar bill halfway between Lazaro's forehead and his slightly balding crown. There it stayed as if glued to his head throughout the dance. His white ruffled shirt, white pants and white boots made him a striking figure of sexy masculinity. You forgot his age. The audience clapped wildly when he had finished. That would be his only dance number for the evening. Lazaro was lead drummer for Project Iroko. Again, he seated himself in the center of the other drummers and continued the show, beating the huge conga drums as the younger dancers took their turns on stage. The huge tiers of ruffles on the arms of his shirt billowed rhythmically as Lazaro beat his drums. Lazaro Galarraga's Project Iroko is a group of high energy, sensuous, and very talented Afro-Cuban dancers and drummers.

After the show, I approached him and asked for an interview, explaining that I was seeking interviews with shamans for my educational project and since he was a Yoruba priest, he would contribute to the diversity which I was seeking in my project. He agreed to the interview for the next day.

He slept late the next morning. The group had partied well into the night and he was exhausted. One of the dancers who had been in the show last night was sitting outside the two story townhouse were most of the group spent the night. It was a guest house owned by the dance studio. Lazaro had just awakened and gotten into the shower. One of the other dancers in the group was still asleep, or at least trying to sleep in a makeshift bed in the living room. The other dance troupe member said that

Lazaro would be downstairs soon. When he came down, a
few minutes later, he apologized for sleeping late and pulled
up a chair and sat down. The younger man who had been
sitting outside pulled up another chair, explaining as he did
so that he would interpret for Lazaro whose English, though
distinguishable, was not very good, and Lazaro agreed.

He hardly seemed like the sexy, uninhibited, hunk
of masculinity of the night before. He seemed smaller, almost shy and somewhat vulnerable. The expression on his
light tan, handsome face was soft and subdued, as con-
trasted with his face last night which was highly animated
and moist with beads of perspiration.

Lazaro wore ordinary street clothes, a cotton printed
shirt and coordinated trousers. He wore a gold chain
around his neck with a charm on it; the charm was intrigu-
ing.

"What is that?" I asked.

He replied with a heavy Spanish accent, "It is Laza-
rus. You know...in the Bible...Lazarus and his dog." The
charm was a slightly bent robed figure of gold which
seemed to be either leaning toward the dog to pet it or give
it something. The charm represented both his name and
what he stood for: an humble servant of God.

"I understand that you're a Yoruba priest," I said.

"Yes, I am. Forty-seven years ago, my grandmother
taught me.", he replied.

"Your grandmother?"

"Yes."

"Not your great grandmother?" He didn't look old
enough for a grandmother to have taught him.

"No, my grandmother. She was a slave and she
taught me how to be a priest."

Lazaro learned how to be a Yoruba priest from his
grandmother who had been a slave in Cuba. The Yoruba
traditional religion is very ancient, dating back many centuries. The religion is based upon the concept of one Supreme Being who works through many lesser deities and
saints or spirits who interact with humans to help and heal.
The lesser deities are called the "orisha". Each orisha has
its own following and priest or priestess. The dances which
Project Iroko preformed the night before told a story of some
of the orishas or saints. They danced the tales of Elegga,

the saint who guards the cross roads; Oshun, the orisha of fresh water and love; Shango, the orisha of thunder and lightning, and other orishas. Shango was once the oba or king of the ancient city of Oyo, presently located in Nigeria, Africa. My favorite dance was that of Yemaya, the orisha of the ocean. The dancers started out slowly and rhythmically and gradually built the tempo to a fast-paced whirling and gyrating spectacle that represented the calm waters of the ocean gradually growing into a full hurricane.

I asked, "Lazaro, what are your duties as a Yoruba Priest?"

He replied, "I teach people. I help them to be a good father, a good son. I teach people to respect each other."

"How do you teach these lessons? Do you have services?"

"Yes, I have services. People called on me to help them and I teach through the orisha. I teach everything that's in the Bible. Everything that's in the Bible is in Yoruba." What Lazaro meant by his last statement is well documented by some scholars of ancient religions. The slaves of South America and Cuba were not allowed to worship in the Yoruba tradition. They were indoctrinated into the Catholic faith. What they hid from the slave masters was an underground continuance of the Yorba religion within the Catholic Church. Each of the saints of Catholicism corresponded to one of the orisha's of the Yoruba religion. While the slave masters believed the slaves were worshipping in the Catholic Church and embracing Christianity, the slaves were, in fact, still keeping the Yoruba faith by mentally substituting each Catholic saint for a Yoruba Saint or orisha. The religions Candomble, Macumbo, Santeria and others all have their roots in the ancient Yoruba traditional religion. How clever the slaves were to have hidden their religion from their captors and passed on their own spiritual traditions. It has survived and flourished in spite of the bans on their services. Even today, those who worship in the offshoots of the Yoruba religion, as well as the traditional Yoruba, sometimes do so with much fear and trepidation. Some worshipers, mainly in predominantly Latino countries, will go to a Catholic church during the day and a "forbidden" African traditional church in the evening.

I asked, "Tell me, Lazaro, How do you teach others through the Orisha or Saints?"

"When the Saint comes down, I give a message."

"What do you mean by when the saint comes down, Lazaro?"

He explained, "The saint comes down and speaks through me. He gives a message. He says, 'What are you doing?' He talks about the family he's healing. He might say, 'The reason why you lost that job is this or that...do not do this any more', and then when the saint is finished, he leaves."

"Lazaro, are you saying that the saint enters your body and speaks through your mouth?"

"Yes. That's right."

"How does that happen? How does it feel?"

"Oooh, Oooooh!" Lazaro laughed and shook his head from side to side. "It's bad. I feel bad. It's not natural. It's very strong!" Lazaro explained that when the spirit enters his body, he is left powerless, because the spirit or saint is stronger. He said that the spirit stays for as long as it takes to complete its mission. The spirit or saint has stayed inside his body and worked through him for as short a time as a couple of hours and for as long as a whole day.

I asked, "Have you ever become ill after the saint leaves?"

"No. I'm fine. I never get sick. My body changes completely after the saint...after he leaves. It cleanses my body. It cleanses my system." he explained. According to Lazaro, the saint cleanses his body and he feels very good after the spirit has left his body.

"Do you know when the spirit has left?" I asked.

"Yes. You fly; you know...you feel good." He shrugged his shoulders and flapped his arms at his sides as if flying and chuckled, "You feel good!"

"Are you saying that in addition to healing others, the saint heals you, too?"

"It cleanses me... just cleanses my whole body inside."

"Lazaro, what about the period during which the Saint is inside you? How are you feeling? What are you thinking? Are you frightened?"

He answered, "I don't know what's going on. You can't control it. It controls you!"

I asked, "You don't have a clue as to what the spirit has done through you?"

He explained, "No. I don't remember when the spirit comes. People say, 'Hey Lazaro, the spirit say so and so and so and so'." Lazaro explained that he is unconscious during the time the spirit is inside his body working and healing. It is only when he becomes conscious again that he finds out what the spirit has done and said from people who were present.

Lazaro said, "I take no money. I get no commission. I love just helping people. I like to make their lives better...you know, help them to be better mothers and fathers, sons and daughters, husbands and wives."

Some of the members of Project Iroko politely interrupted us and told Lazaro that he did not have much more time for the interview because he had to perform soon. He kept a very busy schedule; the next audience would certainly enjoy this very talented man and his talented entourage. Soon, this dedicated Yoruba priest would become, again, the sexy performer that he was the night before and bring a new audience to its feet.

Chapter 4

Reverend Mother Mary Braganza: Mystic and Healer

Rev. Mother Mary Braganza's title was bestowed upon her years ago by her followers who describe her as "one who has lived an exemplary life and a person of the highest integrity". Rev. Mother Braganza is the founding president of the AUM Center for Holistic Health Alternatives of Washington, D.C., established in 1978. AUM (or OHM) is thought to be the sound of God and is spoken by many who chant during or before spiritual meditation. She has held many offices in both the church that she founded and the National Spiritual Science Center. She has also held public offices in the community and was recently appointed to a high echelon federal position. She is a widow, a mother of one son and grandmother of three.

Rev. Mary, as she is affectionately called by many, wears many hats. Among her many professional titles are: consultant, educator, healer, lecturer, therapist, mystic, philosopher, holistic health practitioner and ordained minister. Her outstanding work and contributions to the community and local and federal governments have brought Rev. Mother Braganza into the public eye with appearances on radio, television and newspapers as well as other media. She describes herself as a transpersonal psycho spiritual specialist who takes people beyond the narrow confines of conventional or logical wisdom and helps them to improve their destiny and lead a healthier and more positive lifestyle.

Her interview was taped at The Aum Spiritual Science Center and the following is an edited account of our conversation:

"Rev. Braganza, let's start out by telling me a little about your family background, whatever you want to tell us...the world about yourself."

"Well, I am one of nine children. My deceased father was the son of a minister. My father was a farmer who owned land but he had people tend it for him."

"Where was this?"

"This was in North Carolina. He had a store along the highway and he sold kerosene in those days; he had gas but in those days, you know, people didn't use as much. He sold sardines, cookies and candies... that sort of thing. It was like a 7-11 is nowadays. My grandmother on my father's side was the mother (first lady) of the church. My mother was a teacher of English and music. She had brothers who were teachers, as well as ministers."

"I see."

"I'm told that three days after my birth, my parents had what is known today as a baptism, but it was a special African ceremony. It was a ritual that offered me to the services of God by my mother and the officiators. I am the only one (of the siblings) who went into the ministry of the church." She went on to explain that she was a sensitive, gifted child from birth and as she grew older her spiritual gifts also grew.

"I come from a gifted family. All of them are pretty smart...pretty high I.Q.s. In fact, my brother next to me had almost a 99.9% photographic memory and I was pretty close behind him. I have always been a high achiever I have received all kinds of honors and degrees and awards and I have also received a lot of knocks and kicks and bumps because of who I am."

"Tell me about your degrees. You said you have several of them."

Rev. Mary told me that she was motivated to go back to school after an accident. She said, "I was in an accident in the mid-70's and the doctors told me I would never walk or talk again; but I changed that by going back to school. I got associate degrees in business, philosophy, and religion and the rest are bachelor's degrees in business education and philosophy."

"So, you have five degrees?"

"If you count them all I have seven. I have a myriad of certifications which are a composite of holistic health alternatives."

"My goodness, you have a lot of experience and you have been gifted since early childhood."

"I was born gifted."

"How did your gift manifest itself so that you knew you were gifted? Did someone tell you or did you just know it?"

"Well, when you go out to play with the other kids and they aren't where you are developmentally, you know you are different. Also, in school, you know your classmates are not where you are, academically."

"How did you deal with being different as a child?"

"The social structure was such that my mother knew who I was. She would always tell me to come to her when I knew something or saw something (for someone) and we were very close. I could tell her when someone was coming. I could tell her anything about my brothers or sisters."

"So, she wanted you to come to her before you said something to anyone else?"

"Yes, because, you see...she was psychic too and she knew the damage that could be done by people knowing that I could foretell the future. She was protection for me...and actually, I was pretty well protected until I came out in the open after I graduated from spiritual science school."

"Rev. Mary, how do you describe your gift? How does your gift manifest itself? I know you are clairvoyant, but are you also clairaudient and do you have a spirit guide? How do you receive your messages?"

"I do not receive messages in just one special way... I

receive all ways...mentally, physically, emotionally, materially...all aspects of it are alive in me and it comes in different ways. One time it may come one way and another time it may come another way."

"So, you may feel something or have a vision of something or an emotional feeling about something?"

"Yes, yes. All of these methods are described in the Holy Bible in Corinthians 12 by Paul. Now, he described all of the different aspects of the gift."

"So, your gift comes in many ways. I have spoken to several gifted people and some of them have one or two particular ways that their gift manifests. Now, you say that your gift manifests in many ways?"

"Yes. I have been blessed with just about every spiritual or psychic way that there is." She reads from her Holy Bible the passage in Corinthians 12, which describes the many gifted ways or *diversities of gifts* and *diversities of operations.* (Please see Appendix G.)

"So, your messages come in various and sundry ways?"

"That's right. One time it might come one way and another time, it might come another way. You know, just like when you walk into a place, you pick up a vibration."

"I see. Rev. Mary, would you describe your church services. What happens in your healing services?"

"Well, it's pretty much the same as the National Spiritual Science Center. The healing aspect of the service is the laying on of hands, but it's not touching. You work with the aura. The only thing you really touch, essentially, is when you hold the person's hand near the end of the healing process."

"So, you see auras also?"

"Oh sure, sure I see auras. I pick up the vibrations of whatever is manifested. When I heal, I pull the negative energy out of the person that I'm working with. It has a different effect on the various people that you're working with, but for me it feels like sticky bread dough". She rubs her hands together and continues, " When you do your hands like this you can feel it just sticking, like when you're making biscuits and that dough is in your hands...it's sticky. So, its different with individuals, you don't always have to touch or lay on hands. You do that in a church setting, but you could sit right here and heal somebody in Alaska. You don't necessarily have to have the person in your presence"

"So, you can heal people at a distance?"

"Sure, people can be healed at a distance, just as well as you can do it with the person being present."

"I see. Tell me about your most recent healing for someone."

"I haven't had anyone who was seriously ill lately. I have had some people to come in and say, 'I'm not up to snuff today, I need some fresh energy' or something like that and I work with them to give them fresh energy."

"How do you do that? Do you work with the aura?"

"Yes. You can work with the aura or you can hold the hands. Whichever way you are inspired to deal with it is the way you do it. My opinion is that people who work in this area of life, especially for as long as I have, don't have the same assistance...spiritual assistance with them all the time. You might have one angel or assistant, whatever you want to call them, work with you one time and they do it one way, and then the next time you heal somebody, another one (angel) is working with you and they work another way."

" So, you work with more than one angel?"

"Well, let's say different angels...or you might have a host of angels working with you at one time, depending upon the need and the case that you're working with at that time."

"I see."

"You could have a host of angels or healers working with you at the same time or you may just have one."

"I see. Now, there's a question that most people would want to know: do they talk to you and tell you what to do?"

"Yes. Yes they do. For the most part, it is not speaking as we speak. It is ...now that's hard to describe because we ministers also do that a lot in our delivery (spiritual readings), also. It is telepathic. The first time I experienced telepathy, I was about to graduate from the National Spiritual Science School and I got a call from a church down in South Carolina. They were having a big program and they wanted me to deliver the message. Now, this was the first time that I was to deliver a metaphysical message. So, naturally, I prepared just as a student would prepare to make a speech before a class. So, I had my speech ready and I went down with my speech to deliver the message. Well, I got there and I was called upon to deliver my speech. I got up and went up to the rostrum and I got through the introduction and spirit took over and I didn't say another word that was on that paper, just the introduction. The introduction was an introduction of me, for the most part. I told them that I had come to talk to them and how nice it was to be there. But, when I got ready to go into the message, I said not one thing that I had written on that paper! Spirit was speaking to me telepathically and I was speaking behind spirit and that is the way that I have delivered my messages since then.

"Now, Rev. Mary, when you say 'spirit', are you referring to an angel or to God?"

"I am referring to the spirit that Paul is talking about here in Corinthians 12...and in this chapter, Paul identifies spirit as one and the same. There is no separation here, it (spirit) is one and the same."

"One and the same means the Universal Spirit of God?"

"Yes. It's one and the same. There is only one Spirit; there is only one God and that's what Paul is saying here."

"O.K. I just wanted to make that clear."

"I, myself, can say nothing; I know nothing. It is the spirit of God that induces me to do whatever I do ...to say whatever I say."

"Rev. Mary, when you work with the sick, do you go to the hospitals to visit them? Do you do any healing on that level?"

"Yes. Now, it used to be that you could go to the hospital and lay on hands, but we never really touch because in order to touch we would have to have a doctor's license, so we cannot touch. But, we are trained to focus healing energy on anyone short or long distance."

"I know you have had many, many experiences in your work, Rev. Mary, but what are some of the most memorable highlights of your ministry?"

"Well, I'll say that some of the most memorable highlights have come from visitations." She went on to explain that she had experienced astral projections or out of body travel with her spiritual mentor/teacher whom some people might call a guardian angel or spirit guide. She said, "He has taken me all over the world. He would come and take me to all of these places. I'd never know anything about where they are and I couldn't go back to them either." She explained that for sixteen years, at various times, her spirit mentor would come to her and take her to places and teach her about what was going on in each place.

"Rev. Mary, what would you be shown?"

"Aspects of spirit. Sometimes it would be classes in a higher aspect of something that I might need to deal with here. She went on to explain that these classes were not on Earth, but on a high metaphysical plane of life which some would call Heaven or The Hereafter."

"Rev. Mary, tell me about those classes."

"Well, I don't know anything else I can say except people were sitting in classes, in a temple. It was a religious atmosphere. Paintings were all around the wall and that sort of thing...a very antique-like, old but rich place. People were there in classes doing different things. All of it was a learning environment. I could see that it was different aspects of learning...different aspects of reaching higher levels of something you already know."

"I see. So, your learning was increased at higher levels when you would travel through the astral planes."

"Yes." She further explained that these experiences would always happen at night when she was supposed to be asleep. She stated that these experiences were out-of-body experiences, not dreams or flights of imagination.

"That's very interesting. A lot of people have described out-of-body experiences, especially near death experiences and they have often said that they see a light and they go through a tunnel."

"Well, now, I've had that experience with this accident that I had when they said I'd never walk again. I died and went to Heaven."

"Did you?"

" Yes. I went to Heaven and I was sent back. I was told, 'You have more work to do'."

"Who told you that?"

"I went through two gates. Now, this is a time when I was surrounded by angels and one step would be about as far as from here (Washington, D.C.) to Silver Spring, Maryland (approx. 15 miles). You take a step and it's like you are springing...and I'm surrounded by angels."

"So, you're saying that covering a long distance did not take time...that it was instantaneous?"

"Yes! Yes! We went through two gates and when we got to a third gate, that's when we were turned around. We were told to turn around ...that God was not ready for me yet, 'You've got more work on the Earth Plane to do', they said. I died...I died in this accident and I came back and I could hear what the doctors and interns said. I was one of the subjects or teaching cases for the medical students at this hospital. In the mornings, my room would be filled with students and this doctor was teaching them different things about my kind of accident."

"Rev. Mary, were you in a coma?"

She was not really certain if she was comatose or not. She said, "I could hear and see, but I could not talk." When I asked whether or not her doctors had described her condition afterwards as a coma, she had not had a conversation with them about that. She replied, "I can't ever remember anybody telling me that I was in a coma, but I could hear the doctors telling the students that I would be a paraplegic for the rest of my life."

"So, you heard all this, but you couldn't speak?"

"I couldn't speak. I could hear everything and I could see, but I couldn't speak."

"Were you in your physical body or out of it when you could see?"

"I was in my physical body...as a matter of fact, when I was going to Heaven in my astral body, I could see. I could see the angels and the blue sky."

"How did that experience make you feel?"

"It was like when I was a child again...when I was walking on the clouds ...they were like a sponge. You know, you step on one sponge and you bounce all the way over to another one. It was terrific!" I told her about the out-of-body experience which I had when I was almost overcome by carbon monoxide. I described the sensation, which I felt at the back of my neck upon reentering my body at that point and she said that her experience was remarkable, also.

Rev. Mary said that she finally left the hospital after a lengthy stay and how she helped herself through prayers for healing. She said, "I believe that my call to God was answered. I was able to get up on crutches. I had one under each arm." She indicated that she was determined to prove to herself that she had beaten the odds and that she was academically astute. She enrolled at a local university and began a course of study that garnered her several degrees in various related fields. She stated,   "The first semester, I did so well, they put me in the honors program....and that's where I remained while I was there. So, I was assured that my brain and my thinking were as good as anybody's. People try to criticize you and low-rate you and bring you down because you're a little quicker and a little smarter than they are and so I had to prove it to myself. The doctors had said I would be nothing the rest of my life; that's what the doctors said in front of a roomful of students!"

"I see. You know, Rev. Mary, sometimes people say awful things about other people because of ignorance. You had a miraculous recovery and I'm sure you proved your capabilities both to yourself and to others. You have had many experiences. Are there any other experiences that you would consider very revealing or significant...any particular healings or other experiences?"

"Well, now, when it comes to healing, I have been healing tumors and growths. People have been coming to me for growths and when they go back to the doctor, the doctor can't find the growths. I've had women who have come to me who want to have babies and doctors have told them they couldn't. Some have been told they couldn't get pregnant, some have been told that if they got pregnant they couldn't carry a baby for nine months and God has proven that it can be done regardless of what the doctor may diagnose. Even I, myself, have cancelled the doctors' diagnoses. Look at me! They said I'd never walk or talk again! I've been talking for years now and the doctor couldn't stop me. I have made a lot of people happy through the power of God."

"Wonderful! Is there anything else that you want to say about yourself or your ministry that we haven't touched upon?"

"I can't think of anything right now, but I certainly plan to continue on the pathway which I am on." Rev. Mary said that she would continue in her service to God, healing and delivering God's individual and collective messages to others.

[Prior to this interview, Rev. Mother Mary Braganza, another spiritually gifted minister and two gifted laypersons spoke to a group of doctoral students whom I had convened for one of ten peer days (one day learning experiences) as a part of the requirements for our doctoral program. The topic which all had agreed to explore for that day was Learning How to Channel the Safe Way.

All of the gifted ministers spoke to the group about their gifts, their spiritual or psychic experiences and each imparted a wealth of information and advice to us. One of the gifted ministers prophesied about the sudden, unexpected hospitalization which would befall the boyfriend of one of the doctoral students. An account of this peer day is given in The Experiences of Ordinary People section of this book.]

Chapter 5

Nana Kwabena: Akom Priest

Time of Interview: May 1994

Nana Kwabena is an African-American man who was born in New York City and raised between the Bronx and New Rochelle, New York. ` Nana' means priest or reverend in the traditional religion of the Akan people of Ghana. Nana Kwabena is the divorced father of four. He is well educated, having received his undergraduate education at both Howard University and The District of Columbia Teachers College (which subsequently merged with two other institutions to form the University of the District of Columbia). He earned two master's degrees: one from Antioch University in Community Education in 1976 and a second one from the Howard University School of Divinity in Religious Studies in 1983.

Nana Kwabena is a tall, broad-shouldered, bronze-hued man with finely chiseled features. He is strikingly handsome. His sharply defined features would have landed

him a job in anyone's modeling agency or film if he desired
it. His youthful appearance belied his forty-nine years. He
could have taken at least fifteen years off his age and gotten
away with it.

I asked, "Tell me, Nana Kwabena, what got you interested in the earth religions?"

He replied, "Most of my training has taken place in
Ghana in West Africa. I got involved in the Black Consciousness Movement of the '60's. I got interested in this
religion because I began to look at whatever it was that God
had given Black people. I thought, since everybody else has
an indigenous religion, then God must have given Black
people something, also. Then I began to investigate and
read about African religion. (I use that in the overall sense.)
I did readings on various ethnic groups and I began to see
that as you looked at them, the same kinds of mystical concepts and themes that one would find anyplace else , such
as within mystical Christianity or within the mystical aspects of Hinduism or Buddhism exist within the African religion."

"Is that right?"

"Yes. I had begun to do readings on Eastern religions, since I was about thirteen years old. So, once I began
to see the same things I had been reading about within African religion, I realized that within the development of this
particular kind of cultural expression were all the things
you would find anyplace else."

I said, "I was just talking with someone the other
day about Catholicism and how the slaves were brought
over to South America from Africa and how they managed
to hide their traditional African religion within the Catholic
religion without it being detected by the slave holders. Each
one of the Yoruba saints or deities corresponded to one of
the saints in the Catholic Church."

During the 1960's, Kwabena's mother introduced
him to an African Priest and Kwabena, along with others,
used to sponsor bus trips from the Washington, D.C. area
to New York City to his temple. This priest went to Ghana in
1967 and converted from the Yoruba priesthood to the
Akan Priesthood. The Yoruba religion is the traditional religion of Nigeria, and Dahomey; it is also found in Cuba and
Brazil.

Kwabena said, "I also became a priest at the same time that the priest from New York converted to the Akan religion; that's how I became involved in the Ghanaian religion."

"Is your religion called the *Akan* religion?"

"Yes, it is really the traditional religion of the Akan-speaking people. I guess that is the most accurate way of describing it. However, there are people in Ghana who don't speak Akan...who practice a religion which is very, very similar, if not exactly the same."

"If you had to give it a name, what would be the name of the religion?"

"Over there (Ghana), they just simply call it *Akom* which means power and each person has their own way of plugging into it."

"I see."

"Each shrine has its own collection of spirits that plugs into it, so any four shrines may share maybe one or two spirits amongst them but have different ones that are there."

"How many spirits, all totaled, would you say are involved in Akom?"

"Oh, I wouldn't even try to guess."

"More than a hundred?" I asked.

"Oh, goodness!"

"More than two hundred?"

"I wouldn't even try to guess."

"Really?"

"Because...on my last trip to Ghana...they must have introduced me to maybe fifty, at least, that I hadn't even heard of...which, I had no knowledge of."

"Whoa! Fifty that you never heard of?"

Nana Kwabena explained, "Now, I'm not saying that a Ghanaian, born in Ghana, wasn't aware of a whole bunch of them because I wasn't aware of them. There are many, many, many more."

"Is that a fact?"

"The Gods of India are the same...the Hindu pantheon...is the same. There are so many spirits, as well as aspects of Shiva, aspects of Rama and aspects of Krishna."

I asked, "In Akom, there is the notion of a supreme deity working with other deities. Would that be correct?"

He replied, " To understand African religion, things are different . Things interrelate as opposed to being put into boxes. Everything is related. It's one organic interrelationship of spiritual forces. And the Akom call the one supreme force *Inyame*, or *Udamonkoma*, and *Yonkape*."

"There are three (Gods)?"

"Oh, yeah"

"Then, there's the trinity concept."

"Yes, this comes out of Egypt." Kwabena explained how the Bantu and the Yoruba traced their origins from the Nile Valley and Arabia through the pottery styles of various regions in Africa.

"Most of the ethnic groups included the Bantu who trace their roots to the Nile Valley. It's part of their oral history." He cited this fact as a reason for finding a concept of the trinity in the Akom religion . He went on to explain, "Christianity has had some influence upon the religion." He talked about the Holy Spirit as being the female aspect of God in the Christian trinity of the father, son, and Holy Ghost. "Additionally, one of the things that's in Christianity but is not readily identifiable by the lay person is the elevation of the female as a concept of God. Inyame is the female aspect of God in the Akom religion . Like, within Christianity, the thing that you hear talked about the most is the Holy Spirit, and it is considered by scholars to be the female aspect of God. This is a very, very old African paradigm. In Akom, Inyame would be the female aspect, Udamonkoma would be the creation or the son aspect of God, and Yonkape , the father aspect."

"What role do lesser spirits play, Nana Kwabena?"

"If you were to take any religion as a paradigm, regardless of what the practitioners tell you about a religion, you'll find that all of these concepts can be broken down in the same way: belief in a supreme being, reverence to the ancestors , and an acknowledgement of other spirits, whether you call them angels, fairies, deities, saints, divas, etc. There is not a religion that you can look at that does not have some kind of breakdown, whether they call it monotheism or polytheism. African religion is exactly the same way. They acknowledge a supreme being and have saints or angels or what have you."

"Tell me a little bit about your ceremony. How does it go. Do you heal? What do you do?   What happens?"

"The thing about it ...the way that Black people practice religion around the world, and the way that Europeans used to practice it before they got involved in Christianity, is that spirituality always included the immanence of deity...the closeness and presence of God here on earth...and everywhere. Within the European tradition, God is far away...remote."

"Yeah. Up in the sky."

"Up in the sky (he nods in affirmation)...remote."

I added jokingly, "And, God can't see what we're doing down here on earth." We laugh.

Kwabena said, "You know, within the Black experience, something which has been inherited and carried over from Africa is the very, very close intimacy to Deity in all the songs. Within African religion, the deities are very close and very personal. They come down. They joke. They play. They interact with people. They do healing. They do prophecies. They tell people what they should be doing in terms of God's law, or cosmic, or universal law."

"I see. Go on."

"They say, 'Hey, you shouldn't do this. You shouldn't steal. You shouldn't commit adultery, you shouldn't work witchcraft because it disrupts the social order.' So, when the deities interact, you see people walking up, talking to them and asking them things. So, that's what you see when you go to Africa."

"Really?"

"That's what you see. It's pretty interesting."

I asked, "Is it like a ceremony with rituals or just a lot of visitors who come to see the deity?"

"It's all of that. There are some sacred shrines. There are a couple of things that you see when you come to visit. A traditional ceremony, be it in Africa, Cuba, Puerto Rico or Brazil, would be similar. There are some shrines that you would go to in order to see the deity possessing on the priest there. The people would come there and that deity wouldn't do much of anything except advise people and give suggestions for healing if there is a sickness; or, if there is a legal case or domestic case, give some advice for the restitution of that situation."

"Nana Kwabena, do you work with one deity or are there several deities that you work with."

"Well, I have several deities. Some priests are just priests with one deity. It depends on the priest as to how many deities he or she works with."

"Tell me, how do you call the spirits? Is it through a prayer or what?"

He answered, "It's a process. Suppose I just want to invite people here for the sake of calling the spirits. We would simply pour libations and pray to whichever deities you want to come."

I said, "Wait just a second. Do you call specific deities and do you actually know who's coming?"

He replied, "All of the above."

"You ask for certain ones to come?"

"Yes"

"Then you do know who's coming?"

He explained, "You never can be sure who's coming. There are reasons why you call the spirits. The deities or spirits who help with whatever type problem or problems you are having would be the one or ones who come down."

"O.K. You don't call just one. You call just the spirits you work with. Right?"

"Umm-hmmm."

"Did you say there were four deities you work with?"

"More than that."

"More than four?"

"Um-hmmm. Each deity has a holy day. So, on that holy day, you fix food for that deity. You feed that deity. You pour libation for that deity, and you drum and sing for that deity. Then the deity will come. But, suppose it wasn't that deity's holy day and you just wanted to call the spirits. You pour the libation, drum and sing and the spirit or spirits will come."

"Usually, how long do they stay?"

"No fixed amount of time."

"A couple of hours, maybe....a day?"

"Some stay for hours. They can stay for more than a day."

" Have you ever had an occasion where one stayed for more than a day?"

"No. Not me, personally."

"Oh, but you have seen it?"

"Uh- huh. In Africa."

"Normally, yours stay for how long?"

"A spirit can stay (he snaps his fingers together) for as short a time as a moment or two or he can stay for hours."

I asked, "What is your experience during that time? What are you feeling? Is it a possession when the spirit comes into your body and are you aware of anything?"

He replied, "Well, there are certain things I can't tell you because you are not initiated. But I will tell you as much as I can tell you. If you were in the religion, then I could talk with you more freely."

I said, "This is positive. O.K.? I'm not going to say anything derogatory about you or anything like that."

Kwabena unflinchingly said, "These are some of our secrets. I can't tell you."

"O.K."

"But, basically, I'll explain what we call possession by a spirit so that you can understand it. First of all, when you become initiated into the religion, there are certain deities which are given to you or, in a parallel sense, are attracted to you because your personality and their personality are similar. Either way, that deity is given to you or comes to you of its own volition; it becomes attached to you because it likes you. It begins to live within your aura. It begins to live within the electrical body or the spiritual body. Under the stimulus of drumming and singing, or rhythm, it begins to march from the outside of your aura to the center of your aura which is you.... your consciousness. And, when that happens, your consciousness and your personality gets pushed aside so that it's either not detectable or barely detectable. And, the personality that you see is the personality of the deity because it has marched to the center. It has moved the personality of the owner of the body out of the way long enough so that you can see the personality of the deity. You would be able to tell what deity is there; and, by a process of elimination, what deity is not there. Do you see what I'm saying."

"Yes. Yes, I think so."

"Let's say, we know it's not this one...we know it's not that one, but we know it's not the other one. So, this is how possession takes place. From most of the reading I have done, there seems to be a propensity amongst people with melanin (people of color) to possession. People who

have done research in this area, both scholarly kinds of research and just basic observational kinds of things have
concluded that people with melanin have a greater propensity toward possession than those who do not have melanin. That does not mean that..."

I interrupted, "Why? Why do they think that?"

He explained, "Just by observation. They noticed
that people who have melanin tend to go into possession or
are inclined toward possession and, of course, (He names a
prominent African-American female psychiatrist) and all of
these other people have their own theories about the pineal
gland and neuromelanin and all this stuff that deals with
an altered state of consciousness. But, to make a long story
short, Europeans can and do possess but it seems as
though there is a greater tendency toward possession
amongst people with melanin."

I responded, " That's some theory. I'd like to see
some data."

He replied, "Now, I don't know how scientific all this
is but this is what I read in anthropological books and
what I have gotten from various other books. So, to make a
short point, if you put an average Black person in an environment with the spirits and with rhythm, then you can
look for something to happen to them...even if they don't
believe it. You see it happening when people get up in
church and shout or speak in tongues ."

I said, "Right. Right! That's when people say that
the spirit 'came on' someone or he/she 'got the spirit' this
morning. Yeah! I can remember very vividly, the days of
my childhood in church. There was a man in my Baptist
church who used to get up and shout up and down the
aisles regularly...and a woman, too. She used to say things
no one understood or speak in tongues."

He added, "Some of them even dance up and down
the aisles."

"Yeah. Nana Kwabena, do you think that you will
only find this spiritual expression in a Black church?"

"Well, no. The hill people in Kentucky and West Virginia do it. They possess. I've seen them. They handle
snakes and..."

I interjected, "Oh, yes! I know. I saw them on TV
doing that."

He continued, "So, the average Black person, whether he or she believes it or not, is subject to having this phenomenon take place on them."

I asked, "How do you feel when the deities have left. Are you aware?"

He replied, "Now, remember the explanation I gave you for possession?"

"Yes."

"If you think about the explanation I gave you for possession, then you can answer the question for yourself...because if you think about how far in your aura the deity is and how far displaced the personality is, then you have the answer."

"Is your personality displaced totally or in part during a possession, Nana Kwabena?"

"Those are things I can't tell you."

I said," Let me tell you why I'm leading in this direction. I did talk to a Yoruba priest and for him the experience was an unconscious one. He was totally out of it and the deity did possess completely. His personality was completely pushed aside."

"Umm-hmm."

I added, "He did not know what was going on when the deity possessed him completely. Other people told him what had transpired during the possession of the orisha as they call saints in the Yoruba traditional religion. So, I was wondering if your experience was the same as his or if it was different."

He explained, "If your personality is completely pushed to the side, the possession is what you call a 'deep possession', or 'complete' or 'full possession'...and that phenomenon takes place sometimes but not all the time with most priests. O.K.? When you get priests who have achieved a very high level of initiation, then many times you see *full possessions*. There is really no way of telling how deep his possession was other than what he told you. Right?"

"True. He said he feels really bad when he comes out of it. Do you feel alright when you come out of it?"

" Well, it depends upon the deity that possesses you. Each time that you are possessed, you may or may not have your personality totally removed and that determines how much a person will remember, know, and be aware of. Do you understand what I'm saying?"

"Yes."

" And, the intensity of the possession determines how much he or she will or will not know or be aware of. O.K.?"

"Um-hmm."

"And so, I can't tell you the veracity of this man's statement because I don't know."

I said, "Oh, it's alright. I was just trying to draw some comparisons between the two of you. I'm sure he had no reason to say anything untrue. It would not profit him one way or another." Kwabena replied, "The comparison is that the nature of possession is exactly what I said: the degree to which a person is deeply into the possession is the degree to which that person's personality has been pushed aside."

I said, "O.K. And, that could be a little bit, a little bit more, or complete?"

" Yes. Now bear in mind that the difference between an Akom priest and a trance medium is that we are taught how to control our possession. Maybe they're trained mediums but they're not priests. There's a difference because we're trained to understand the nature of our deity and the personality of our deity. We're trained so as not to be a danger to any other human being that's around with that amount of power that is on us...and that's part of our training. In all of these things , we are trained."

"How long was your training program?"

"It's continuous."

"Continuous?"

"What you do is go to another level, and then you go to another level and so on."

"Is there a ceiling on the number of levels to which you can go?"

"No."

"And, you started your training in the Akom priesthood twenty years ago?"

"Yes."

" Do you go to Africa for your training every year?"

"No. No I do not . I've been very busy with family responsibilities. I've been three times. There's lots of training."

"Nana Kwabena, you seem to know a lot about things of the spirit world that many people just guess about. You also seem to have no fear of these things. Many people would be afraid to attempt what you do...I mean lending your physical body for a possession by a deity. You seem to have a broad knowledge and a deep faith in God."

He replied, "I do. The nature of how things are in the spirit world is that our deities will come to us while we're asleep...in our dreams. They will show us how to do stuff in our dreams. That's how it works. Once you have a deity, that deity will show you how to do things. In the training that you get in the African religions...and...In the Native American religious training, there is a great emphasis on dreams. Once you have been initiated and have crossed the threshold into the dream world or into the spiritual world, then all of the spirits that you have can be called upon to interpret for you."

"So, your deities will interpret your dreams for you?"

"Yes."

"O.K. Tell me more about when a deity possesses you."

He said, "Each time I possess, sometimes it's total and complete and sometimes it's not total and complete. And, even that is an oversimplification."

I asked, "Do you receive reports back from your church members about your healing and things that were very significant?"

"What do you mean?"

"I mean, things that have gone on during the visitation (possession) of a deity that were significant for you?"

He said, " Let's emphasize something else. We are taught in our training, how to control the deity and we are also taught , during our possession, how to go deeper and deeper and deeper into possession. If the deity comes and the deity has not come on us strongly and our personality has not been displaced, we are trained how to go deeper and deeper into the possession. You need to know that. Some of the things are of a personal nature...and, I always feel uncomfortable with discussing things like that. I'll tell you some of the things that I have observed during services. Deities who know nothing about your friends or loved ones at all would tell them everything...tell them everything about themselves, about their personalities , about their situations at home, and give them suggestions, and they also give you warnings as well as guidance about what you're doing. This is why God Almighty created the deities. It's not a happenstance thing. The gods were created to assist us with our daily lives and there are deities who have specialties. For instance, there are deities who are protectors, and deities, like my deity, *Tikaray* who is against witchcraft. My deity's purpose is to catch that person and arrest him just like a policeman would arrest someone. My deity will travel around and stop that person from doing that or put them in a state of very , very depressed health until they confess or stop doing what they're doing. There are some other deities whose specific function is domestic affairs. Suppose , for instance, that there is a problem with your husband or one of your kids. The deity will tell you what to do to rectify the condition of someone in your family. That same deity controls the female reproductive organs, so any problem that you are having like fibroid tumors, prolapsed uterus, or any of those problems, will be taken care of by the deity. Do you see how it works?"

"Yes, I think so."

" So , if you are having a problem at home you would come and see me . If you are having a problem with a court case , you would come to see Nana (He names another priest) who has another deity who deals with that problem. Do you see how it works?"

"Specialties! Right?"

"Specialties. So, the way that the whole thing is organized is that The Creator bureaucratized the whole cosmos and we human beings reproduced that in paradigm and we bureaucratized our whole society. You can approach God at any time, but God has already delegated to deities, angels, or saints the task of helping us with everyday problems that we face. But, if you want to bypass them, you can. Just like if you want to bypass your supervisors and go straight to the top, you can!"

"You can?"

"Yes. The fact of the matter is that there are people who have been put into the bureaucratic structure where you work and this is how and why the deities were created. They have certain kinds of things they tell us to do and not to do. They have food taboos. I have seen and performed healing. Cancer goes into remission all the time. You know, I have seen people who have been diagnosed with cancer and put up on the (examining) table and brought down off the table because it has gone into remission. I have seen people who had serious legal problems come out of situations which they (normally) would have gone to jail for...for a long time. Prophecy is something that all deities do. I have seen people who wanted to have children come to the deity and get helped. Not all the healing work is psychic, though. The deities have a repertory of herbs that they use and they would tell someone to take something or put something on his or her body."

"They would have you drink something or put it on your body?"

"Yeah."

I said, "This reminds me of Edgar Cayce, the sleeping prophet. When he went into his trance or dream state, information came to him about cures for various illnesses. Much has been written and documented about Cayce's cures. It really sounds like the same sort of thing."

Kwabena said, "It is similar. African religion is very, very structured. It is such that you would know that there are certain deities that you would go to if you needed them, or if you needed a job interview. There are certain deities that you would go to who would assist you with any problem. So, I'm not knocking Edgar Cayce, but our religion is so ordered and so structured, that whatever you have a need for, there is a particular deity you would go to."

"Nana Kwabena, let's say, for instance, that someone is having a serious problem. Would that person have to wait until you called the deity or could he or she come to you that same day for help?"

"We call the deities every forty days. People don't have to wait until I call the deities. For example, we started about five o'clock this morning. We started because today is a working day for my deity, Tikaray. He works on Wednesday, Friday and Sunday. If someone comes on Tuesday, I would take them to another deity I have. If I didn't have a deity that worked on Monday, I would tell them to come on Tuesday."

"Does Tikaray have a specialty?"

"His specialty is witchcraft (stops evil witchcraft)."

"And, the others?"

"Tikaray is a healer; he specializes in eliminating harmful witchcraft. Suppose someone is being adversarial and really being unfair, just really trying to mess you up. We know how to take care of them. But, not just Tikaray, we have other deities, too, who can do the same thing. Tikaray is the kind of deity who is about balancing things. Anyone who disrupts the social order and brings unwarranted and unnecessary pain to others, like people working black magic...he is vehemently against that. But there are other deities who have other specific kinds of things that they work on."

"Nana Kwabena, I certainly appreciate the information you have given me. And, in closing I'd like to ask you if there is anything which you would like to add which I have not asked?"

"Yes, I have something to add. You referred to it (Akom) as an earth religion. It is an earth religion. The earth is energized by the sun which is why people around the world revere the sun. Because it is the physical embodiment and the channel through which God's energy gets to us here on earth. As the sun goes out, everything goes out. Energy comes to Earth from the sun and gives life to the plants and, consequently, other life forms. And, if you know which herbs go with a particular deity, you can use them for healing. In other words, if I were going to give you a bath for a particular deity, then I would have to go to the herbs for that particular deity. (Bathing of females before calling the deities is a ritual of the Akom religion.) The power for that deity comes from the herbs."

"I'm just thinking, Nana Kwabena...it really takes a lot of courage to go back to your roots as you have done. It takes courage to be so interested in your ancestral spiritual roots that you would actually go back to Africa, study your spiritual roots and actually incorporate this knowledge into your life. I think it's admirable and it takes backbone... because, many times, anything which emanates from people of color is thought less of or denigrated, and I think it's admirable and I commend you for having the courage to follow your spiritual pathway."

He responded, "Whatever denomination that Black

people are in...It is very important for them to investigate African religion. If they are comfortable with the religion they are in, then they need to look at their frame of reference. If they are Christian, they need to look at it and see what Africentric ideals are set forth in that religion and they should investigate to see what originally was there."

"I see."

"And, I stop and say, first, and...this is a little bit of proselytizing at this point, it's very important to go back to our source of power. White people are flocking to this religion in droves."

"Really?"

He said, "In droves! There is a White man in Chicago who was on the Donahue or Geraldo Show who has five hundred followers there."

"Is he an Akom priest?"

"He is a Yoruba priest.

" How did he learn it?"

"He learned it because a Liberian *Babalaou* taught him and it's very interesting to see what's going to happen. They're going to be learning it but..."

I said, "I hope he's sincere. I hope he's sincere"

Kwabena added, "My (family member) who lives in New York is heavily involved in the religion and she has so many White friends who are involved in it with her. And, when I was in Ghana, I saw letters coming from all over Europe asking for help. I'm only saying this to say, while we as a people are debating, they're already on the bandwagon."

"I see...I see. Well, again, Nana Kwabena , I want to thank you for your time. I have certainly learned a lot and I appreciate your taking the time out from your busy schedule to talk to me."

"You're certainly welcome. We will be calling the deity in a few more days. Perhaps you can come and sit in on our services."

"That would be very interesting. Let me know the exact date and I'll see if I can fit it into my schedule. Thanks again."

"You're very welcome."

(Warning: For those who are interested in try-ing to call spirits or deities, please do not do so. It is reportedly very dangerous when done outside of a spiritual or religious context.)

Chapter 6

Nana Kwabena's Temple of Nyame

Time: August 1994

I accepted Nana Kwabena's invitation to attend his service. The following is an account of that day. Nana Kwabena was very animated about his ceremony today. This was the day when he would call down the saints. This ancient Ghanaian religious ceremony which occurs every forty days is one in which the priest or priestess calls upon the Ogun (saints) to come down to earth and guide the affairs of humans. This centuries old religious ceremony is also practiced by the Yoruba as well as some other so-called "earth religions", which seek God in nature and through ancestral ties.

Preparations for the ceremony began around ten o'clock on a very warm and humid August morning which was typical of the weather for this time of year in Washington, D.C. It was sticky warm already. It felt like eighty-five or ninety degrees. The afternoon was sure to be a blistering, muggy day.

The huge Victorian corner house, which was the center for the *Temple of Nyame*, was abuzz with activity. People were entering two by two, alone, or in groups. Some were dressed in African garb and some were dressed in western clothes. Men, women, and children entered the Temple of Nyame, located in the Anacostia section of Southeast Washington, D.C.

The neighborhood was just off a busy thoroughfare in a working class neighborhood. The homes were neatly kept: the lawns were almost perfectly manicured and many of the homes had beautifully landscaped front yards full of lush green bushes and a rainbow of flowers. There was a mixture of both old and young residents. The neighbors were mostly twenty-something to middle-aged Blacks with a remaining few older white residents who had not fled to the suburbs to escape the social changes in their neighborhood during the sixties and seventies.

People entered through the wrought iron gate, onto a short walkway which led up to a very large wooden porch. Nana Kwabena warmly greeted his congregation and guests at the door; he asked them to take off their shoes and proceed into the living room. Shoes could not be worn inside the temple for reasons of sanitation.

The living room was huge, with a high ceiling. It was a large, well-lit home with lots of windows and greenery inside and out. Plants filled the living room. There was an antique mahogany upright piano in one corner of the living room and a wood burning stove near one wall.

In another smaller room off the main shrine room, where the ceremony would be held, were several women who were dressed in white garments which covered their entire bodies. They were assigned to give other women herbal baths in a large tin tub. This was done in order to cleanse the spirit or soul in preparation for a new year.

The "new year" begins at a different time in the Akom Religion. There are nine forty-day cycles in the year (360 days). Kwabena had compared this number of days to the same number of degrees in a circle. The circle has a place in Akom (and other religions) which is mystical and sacred.

The day was also set aside for the Yam Festival which celebrates the renewal of spirit and soul, the leaving behind of negativity and the forgiveness of past wrongs. The oguns (saints) are called down from heaven or the astral planes to participate and give guidance, blessings, heal and prophesy for the Yam Festival.

In the small kitchen off the living room, a huge pot filled with yams bubbled on the stove. The yams would be served later, after the ceremony, along with other African dishes. Some members of the congregation had brought various African foods with them to share with the others.

As people were filing into the shrine room, which was just off the kitchen and parallel to the living room, Kwabena asked women who were on their periods to sit in the outer room. Women on their menstrual cycles were not allowed inside the shrine room. Some religions, including Akom, consider women to be "unclean" during this time. Women were not allowed to wear pants into the shrine room; only traditional female garb was allowed there. Also, people who wore gold jewelry were asked to sit on one side of the shrine room because some of the Oguns disdained gold ornamentation.

Kwabena was both relaxed and animated. He wore his priestly medicine shirt, which was a tan short garment which reached just below his hips. The sleeves were short and flared, and the shirt hung straight from the shoulders to just beneath the chest where the inverted pleats made it flare. It was woven of coarse threads similar to sackcloth but woven much tighter. It almost had the rough, rich texture of raw silk. Sewn onto the shirt were several very small leather patches of various colors and a larger leather medicine pouch. There were also several charms sewn onto the shirt at various places. Kwabena explained that medicinal herbs were placed in the pouch and on the patches for healing ceremonies. He explained that the charms served to protect the priest from being supercharged by the possessing deity as well as to strengthen the priest and protect him from malevolence.

More people filed into the shrine room where the ceremony would be held. There were several children present, ranging in age from a toddler around two years old to teenagers. Fifteen or sixteen adults were present. Kwabena requested that women wearing pants sit outside the shrine room with the women on their periods.

The shrine room was not as large as the living room, but it, too, was bright and welcoming. A yam was hung at the door of the shrine in keeping with the Yam Festival tradition. Wooden folding chairs had been placed around the room in a semi-circle, two and three rows deep. On two walls which were the length and width of the shrine room were the eight altars dedicated to individual deities or oguns.

Nana Kwabena, as his flock addressed him, explained that there are eight shrines to eight different deities in the shrine room. (*Nana* means priest.) Each ogun (deity) has his or her favorite foods, pastimes, likes and dislikes just like us. Each altar was approximately three feet wide by three or four feet deep; some objects belonging to a particular ogun were hung on the wall space behind the ogun's designated floor area.

There was another priest there with Nana Kwabena as well as two priestesses. The nanas were never sure which ogun or oguns would come, so they prepared favorite foods for each ogun and placed them at each shrine.

Nana Kwabena had said a few weeks before that he had recently brought over a new ogun from Africa (Ghana) for his shrine room. He meant that the new ogun or saint could be entreated to aid whomever he was trying to help. On the floor in front of some of the shrines were small bowls of boiled eggs, fruit, a bowl of yams at one, pots of water with herbs in them, smaller bowls of water with trinkets in them. There were statuettes, large and small. Some shrines had candles placed on a small table. At the first shrine by the entrance were several African gourds made from various shapes and hues of squash which were hung on the wall along with the skin of what looked like a wildebeest. At the base of this particular shrine, on the floor, were tributes to the Ogun: a pack of Camel cigarettes, a bottle of bourbon, fruit, and other small bowls of food which were pleasing to him.

At some shrines, there were large plates of food. At one of the shrines was a statuette made entirely of light blue and white lace. It was made in the image of a female and there was a small pearl necklace around the neck area. This shrine was obviously that of a female ogun. Next to the lace figurine was a small box containing a pair of medium-sized pearl earrings. At another altar, a couple of white sheets had been used to cover the floor and bowls of food and other objects had been placed on them.

At another shrine were very old framed photographs. One of the larger photos was that of a woman, and the others were smaller pictures of several other people. The large photograph of the woman was the brown and white type which had been taken before color photography was invented and the photographer had colorized the lips and cheeks. These photos were of people in Nana Kwabena's family, his ancestors. There was also an old-fashioned hot comb at this shrine of photos. It was the type with slightly curved teeth which were widely spaced; this type was used prior to the nineteen forties to straighten Black women's hair.

The Ceremony

Some people were milling about in the other rooms and others took their seats in the shrine room, as the group awaited the arrival of the drummer. Drumming, chanting, and dancing are all a part of the ritual of calling down the spirits (or saints). The drummer arrived and took his place on the side of the room facing the shrines, behind the chairs. He had two very large conga drums which were made of light colored wood and animal skins. The ceremony was about to begin.

Nana Kwabena began the service by calling the group to attention. He explained that when you call the saints, you do not know which spirit (ogun or saint) will come, nor how many. He further explained that when the saint comes down, he or she would not necessarily possess him, but the Ogun might possess anyone who was present that day and speak or heal through them. Nana Kwabena poured a libation of spirits (usually bourbon or vodka) into a glass and then he poured some on the floor. In Africa, the ceremony is performed outdoors and the libation is poured onto the ground. Next Nana Kwabena put the glass to his mouth and then spat it out three times toward the animal skin on the wall of the first shrine.

The drummer began to pound rhythmically on the two large congas, one of which was shorter than the other.

He was a tall light-skinned African American man with a neatly trimmed mustache. He wore all African garb. His dashiki and loose-fitting pants both matched his African hat which was shaped like the military hats worn by soldiers during World War II.

Nana Kwabena, the other priest, and the two priestesses walked to the center of the room and began a slow step-dance in time to the drumming. The shorter priestess was a petite, medium brown-skinned attractive woman whose natural "afro" hairstyle framed her face perfectly. She wore a strapless African dress which wrapped around her down to her ankles. The other priestess was taller, dark-brown skinned, medium build and also attractive in her western garb. The other male nana or priest was bearded, light-brown skinned and he wore a dashiki and slacks. He was shorter in stature than Nana Kwabena and he had some kind of relationship with the shorter priestess, since they appeared to have arrived at the shrine together and they had been talking to each other most of the time before the ceremony began. As they step-danced around in a small circle they would pause intermittently to chalk their faces. They used baby powder to whiten their faces. The whitening of the face is thought to heighten the spirituality of the ceremony. It is a way of preparing the body for the saintly possession.

Nana Kwabena had placed a ceremonial leg band around one of his legs, just above the calf. It kept slipping down, and as he danced, he motioned for various participants to push it up on his leg. He never spoke, he just motioned. The nanas chanted in an African tongue and some of the flock responded in the same language. In most churches, this exchange is known as "call and response": the leader says something and the congregation responds back to him or her.

The drumming continued and the four nanas danced around the circle singing and chanting. The congregation sang and chanted with them. The group became more and more spirited. The level of energy in the room rose by degrees. A few of the members of the congregation entered the circle and began dancing with the priests and priestesses. They, too, chanted and sang; they invoked the oguns to come down to guide and heal them. Nana Kwabena apparently tried to summon the ogun of the first shrine by the door. He picked up the pack of Camels on the altar, tapped out a cigarette, lit it, and continued to step dance as the cigarette dangled from his lips. Occasionally, he would motion to one of the group to put out a cigarette ash or to push up his leg band. Once he motioned to someone to pick up a penny which had fallen to the floor. He called some into the circle and gave them a hug.

Nana Kwabena seemed to be going deeper and deeper into another state of consciousness. He seemed aware of everyone and everything in the room because he would occasionally motion to someone to do something without actually speaking. His eyes were more fixed and his facial expression less animated. His step-dance had become a bit slower in pace than before. He stood more in one place and in one position as he stepped to the drumming. His eyes were half shut as he danced and his head moved slowly from side to side. The two priestesses, the other priest, and another man and woman in the group were still chanting and dancing in the circle. Nana Kwabena motioned to a pretty woman on the front row to join him in the circle to dance. He offered her a puff of his cigarette and she drew the smoke into her mouth and blew it out. He hugged her and she danced around the circle for about five minutes or more, before she sat down. He motioned to one of the younger boys to come into the circle. He hugged him and then the young man danced a while and sat back down.

The drumming, chanting, singing, and dancing had been going on for well over an hour. Sometimes Nana Kwabena led in the chanting and singing and sometimes the priestesses led. The group was well into the second hour of the service when the shorter priestess held up her hand to silence the drummer and the group. She said, "I want to let you know that we have a visitor. *Ogun Asuogyebi* is here with us today and he wants you to know how happy he is to be here." Asuogyebi is the river deity who specializes in healing the body. He is the physician in the Akom faith. Her voice became a whisper as she spoke to the other priest who acted as her interpreter for the group. Everyone had stopped dancing and the drumming had stopped so that all could hear the message of the ogun, Asuogyebi. The priestess rocked from side to side and barely whispered into the priest's ear. It was as though something or someone had taken away her voice. Could it be that there was a spiritual entity who had taken control of her body? Was this the possession of which Nana Kwabena had spoken? She seemed to be experiencing a physical state in which it was difficult for her to speak above a whisper; she seemed unable to move about as she had been doing. She merely rocked from side to side and whispered. As she whispered to the priest, he, in turn, told the group what the ogun was communicating through her. A message of guidance was directed to one of the women in the congregation. A message of good will and admonitions regarding healthful habits were given to the group. The male priest called various people into the circle and gave them a message from Asuogyebi or a healing. The priestess indicated to her interpreter that the River Ogun, Asuogyebi was preparing to leave.

Next, she twirled rapidly around and around within the circle. This act of twirling rapidly, according to tradition, was to assist in the dispossession of her by the saint or ogun, Asuogyebi. Two men with outstretched arms waited for her to finish. She began to collapse, but the two men caught her before she hit the floor and they led her out of the room; she could barely walk. Her knees buckled at every step. The men had to carry her around her waist with her arms outstretched across their shoulders. Who or what took away her strength and her voice? These questions are always in the minds of the onlookers of phenomena which are called paranormal.

About three or four minutes later, the priestess walked back into the room on her own, as if nothing had occurred before. Her face had been washed clean of the white powder and she was very calm and poised. She took a seat on a small stool inside the circle.

The energy in the shrine room was high. The drummer resumed his rhythmical cadences; the other priestess and Nana Kwabena continued to dance in the circle along with a few members of the congregation who felt the spirit and spontaneously joined in or who were beckoned into the dance circle by Nana Kwabena. Kwabena continued to smoke the unfiltered Camel cigarette from the first shrine by the door as he beckoned to others in the room to join him in the circle of dancers. One inspired man got up from his seat and walked to the outer ring of the circle where the drummer was furiously beating the large drums. The drummer's hands moved rapidly without missing a beat; his handsome bearded brown face was aglow in the rapture of the moment. The man slapped a couple of dollar bills on the drummer's moist forehead. The bills stuck there until he reached up and took the bills from his forehead and put them in his pocket seemingly without missing a beat. This was the man's way of telling the drummer how good he was; that single act served as his applause and praise of the talented drummer.

The ceremony had been underway for over two hours with no signs of letting up or ending. Nana Kwabena had said at one time that the ceremony could last just a few hours or it could last all day. The length of the ceremony depended upon when the saint or saints came, how many came, and the length of their visitation. A couple of the children in the group who had grown a little restless left the circle and sat on the steps in the living room, just outside the second entrance to the shrine. There, they sat quietly observing the ceremony, but at a distance which allowed them to leave unnoticeably, if they desired.

The taller priestess asked for quiet, stating that she had a message from all the Ogun. She stated that they were happy to be there and that they blessed the event. There was one saint in particular who gave a message to one of the women in the room concerning a problem in her family. The taller priestess did not collapse like the shorter one. She seemed to be in another state of consciousness which did not affect her voice or her ability to walk. Kwabena had mentioned earlier that there are different stages of saintly possession and that some possessions are not as *deep* as others.

I knew that they would be there for a while longer than I had anticipated. I quietly excused myself and left by the second entrance.

Reflections

Due to the influence of mass media such as movies, fiction novels and plays, possession is a concept which has long been associated with horror films, satanical cults, and evil doings. The people at the Temple of Nyame were anything but evil-doers; rather, they were seekers of divine guidance in their own unique way. The roots of this religion go back centuries before the advent of Christianity and many modern religions. What I witnessed was a deity possession, according to the Akom faith. Visitations by angels, archangels, saints, Mary, mother of Jesus, and other religious beings are a part of most of the world's religions. To act as the conduit of the messages of one of these beings is considered an honor and the conduit is considered an "anointed one" or messenger of the word of God.

It was clear to me that the priests and priestesses were undergoing changes in their levels of consciousness and that there were actual physical changes taking place within them right before our eyes. Some may say that chicanery was a part of what we saw. But, that begs the question, "For what purpose?" Money? They didn't ask for any. Control over others? There was not a hint or suggestion of a desire for it. Those who received messages seemed to accept what was told to them, both joyfully and gratefully. Whether you think tricks were involved or not, clearly all who were there saw the presence of a phenomenon which was both paranormal and deeply spiritual for some.

Temporary possession of a person's body by a saint, deity or emissary of God for spiritual reasons, may be the good side of the issue of spirit possession. Do we really know enough about the forces, seen and unseen in our universe to say that these kinds of things do not happen and that people in spirit do not exist just because we cannot see them with the naked eye?

Science cannot explain many things today because the scientific method is limited in its scope of what it is able to investigate. Every observable event or phenomenon in our universe cannot and should not be subjected to the narrowly constricted rules of the scientific method which totally ignores subjective experiences in favor of objective data and consensus.

We cannot see all of the matter and energy in the universe. Electromagnetic energy exists, but we cannot see it. Sounds and images are transmitted through the air constantly into our radios and televisions, but they do not in-

terfere with our daily activities because they are unnotice-
able to us until we turn on a receiver which matches the
frequency of the sound or picture which is sent; only then
do we see the pictures and hear the words. We are receivers
too; only, we see and hear a small range of frequencies out
of a broad range of electromagnetic frequencies that are
present in our daily environments. We humans are limited
by our physical makeup. Suppose, like bats and dogs, we
were able to hear above the frequency range which now limits our hearing. Could we hear spirits? Suppose some of
us in a spiritually exalted state can hear voices and see visions of things which others cannot see. As a receiver who
is not limited to normal human frequencies, you would be
considered an anomaly, a "freak", or just plain "crazy" by
some. That was yesterday. Today, the mental health field
recognizes that temporary spiritual emergencies or awaken-
ings are not pathological events and have stopped labeling
them as such. What is normal in one culture (i.e., spirit
communication) is considered pathological in another. Ethnicity, culture, and race have been found to play a role in
the experiencing of paranormal events. The acceptance or
non-acceptance of these events is directly tied to one's culture and expectations. The issues of observable vs. non-
observable phenomena and spiritual emergencies are discussed in more detail in the final chapter of this book.

Chapter 7

Brother Andre: Miracle Worker

(1845-1937)

Brother Andre is included as one of the Shamans even though I did not interview him. I only witnessed the apparent results of his healings. When I visited Montreal, Canada during the early 1990's, I took a tour of the city. One of the most beautiful sights was that of St. Joseph's Oratory, a Catholic shrine which sits high on Mount Royal, which rises, majestically over the city of Montreal. Once inside the Oratory, we were guided to a chapel, which contained the remains of Brother Andre.

There were votive candles burning, lit by those who entreated either Brother Andre or St. Joseph to intervene on their behalf. When you looked up, on the walls of the chapel hung hundreds of prosthetic devices: canes, crutches, leg braces and even some antique walking aids. People had left them at the Oratory after being healed through the prayers of Brother Andre. I stood in awe of the sight, which I witnessed. I looked at the tiny marble tomb, which held his remains and wondered about Brother Andre. Surely, he was a true servant of God, and God had given him the power to heal the sick and minister to those in need. Who was he? I wanted to know. At the time I visited the Oratory, Brother Andre had been nominated for sainthood. The process of his beatification began in 1940 and in June 1978, Pope Paul VI declared Brother Andre worthy of the title "Venerable". He was beatified in Rome by Pope John Paul II on May 23, 1982.

Even though Brother Andre is no longer with us, his legacy remains. His story is worthy of being told. His is a story of struggle against many odds, perseverance, faith in God and an overwhelming love for his fellow man, and a heart so full of love for God that he wanted to serve God above all else in the world. If the words "pure of heart" fit anyone in this world, they fit Brother Andre best.

Brother Andre was born on August 9, 1845 to Isaac and Clothilde Bessette in St. Gregoire d'Iberville, a farming village thirty miles from Montreal. Brother Andre was given the name Alfred and he was the eighth of ten children born to the couple. The Bessettes lived in a one-room home, which was filled with love, joy and faith in God. Each of the children did his or her part in helping with the family chores and little Alfred, the frailest of them all, was sickly much of the time. Alfred was born with a severe stomach ailment which left him frail and weak for many days of his childhood. He was unable to eat solid foods like his brothers and sisters. His mother, Clothilde, loved him dearly and she nurtured little Alfred, making certain that he ate the foods that he was able to digest.

Little Alfred's strict Catholic upbringing prepared him mentally and spiritually for the challenges of his life that were to come. He was, truly, a devout man who yearned wistfully to become a servant of God. His heart was so full of love and adoration for the Holy Family that he could think of no other desire than to serve the Lord in any way that he could. His heart was bigger and stronger than the frail body, which held it.

When Alfred was nine years old, his father was felled by a freak accident: a tree in the forest fell on him and crushed him to death. His mother was determined to keep the family together after that and she did so for a short while, but she came down with tuberculosis and was forced to give up her children, with the exception of Alfred. She kept little Alfred with her and they both went to live with her sister, the wife of Timothy Nadeau, in St. Cesaire, a neighboring village. Alfred watched his mother grow weaker and weaker as the disease ravaged her body. He was in such pain and agony because he loved his mother dearly and wanted her to live. However, at the age of forty-three, she succumbed to the disease two years after their move. Alfred was devastated by her death and he clung to his Bible for daily strength to keep going on. His source of strength, love and nurturing was gone. The words in the Twenty-Third Psalm of the Holy Bible sustained him: "The Lord is my Shepherd, I shall not want" were the words which he turned to again and again for strength and faith. Alfred meditated daily on the Passion and he became increasingly devoted to St. Joseph.

Alfred remained with his aunt and uncle, the Nadeaus, after his mother's death. There he had already begun to pattern his young life around the church and St. Joseph. He was a frequent little assistant at the parish church, helping Father Andre Provencal with Mass.

His uncle owned a lodging and coach business and expected little Alfred to do his share of the work to earn his keep. However, Alfred, still being frail and weak could not control the coach horses and met with the ire and derision of his stalwart uncle. His uncle persuaded him to become a shoemaker. But, this work also proved to be too demanding for Alfred because of his physical problems. Alfred, being a very sensitive and intelligent young man, was deeply wounded by the constant nagging and ridiculing of his uncle. Sunday was the only day of the week that Alfred could do what he wished. It was the only time he had to play with other children in the village, but he chose to stay in prayer for most of the afternoon. He yearned deeply to serve God and his early childhood sacrifice of his playtime was an indication of the seriousness of this desire. During his canonical proceedings, his sister once told Father Henri Bergeron, "Ah, if you only knew my brother in his youth! On Sunday he passed the greater part of the afternoon in the church."

Young Alfred often practiced severe penances and his aunt sometimes had to take away instruments of mortification from him. His severe penances included a leather belt pierced with tacks and worn around the waist, an iron chain and sleeping on the floor. He never disobeyed his aunt when she ordered him to stop. She was trying to protect his health. Alfred would stop, but he would invent some other form of penance as a substitute. These penances continued throughout his lifetime. His inability to perform strenuous tasks continued to be a sore spot between him and his uncle. Alfred felt inept and useless as a laborer. His self-esteem suffered mightily and due to his low self-esteem, his flagellations continued and caused much consternation on the part of his loving aunt, Madame Nadeau.

Little Alfred was, in a sense, rescued by the mayor of St. Cesaire, a very kind man, who offered to adopt Alfred. His aunt and uncle readily agreed and at age fifteen, Alfred became a hand at the Ouimet farm. After a year with the Ouimets, Alfred tried various trades. He was an apprentice baker, tinsmith, and blacksmith; but he, sadly, failed at all three trades because of his physical frailties.

Alfred migrated to the United States in his late teens to work in the factories of New England. He worked for four years in the United States in the textile mills. He later said, "Despite my weak condition, I did not let anyone get ahead of me as far as work was concerned."

Between 1863 and 1867, while working in the United States, Alfred learned to speak English   He did not know, at the time, how well this skill would serve him. He grew no stronger, physically, while working in the factories; in fact, some days it took all the strength in him just to get up and get dressed in the morning. Many days, Alfred would take frequent breaks, causing the supervisors much consternation at his condition, but he was a likeable, pleasant man, and he found friends who helped him during those times.

Alfred's devotion to St. Joseph grew more and more. It was during those roughest of times and days that Alfred prayed and asked for The Saint to intervene on his behalf, and St. Joseph came to his aid. Alfred would tell those who would listen of the many blessings bestowed upon him by God through St. Joseph. His faith grew stronger; his love for St. Joseph was a mighty source of power and strength upon which Alfred relied. His yearning to serve God grew more intense during those trying times.

Years later, Brother Andre told about a spiritual experience which he had while working in the United States. One day while he was working in a field, he stopped for a moment to rest. His eyes became filled with light and he experienced a dizzying sensation. He stood there for a moment and wiped his eyes thinking that he had had too much exposure to the sunlight. Then suddenly, he witnessed an apparition of St. Joseph. The Saint smiled at him and showed him a building on a hilltop and said, "Build this in the name of God and I will be its patron saint. I love you and our work will be there." Just as suddenly as he appeared, The Saint disappeared. Alfred Bessette had seen his future work. God had answered his fervent prayers to do God's work and sent St. Joseph to deliver the news. However, the vision, which he witnessed, was not to be for many years to come.

In 1867, Alfred returned to his homeland along with thousands of other French-Canadian migrant workers. After their return, they witnessed the dawn of the Canadian Confederation. Shortly after he returned to Canada, Alfred went to visit his longtime friend and mentor, Father Andre Provencal. Father Provencal and Alfred had communicated during all of his travels and travails. This strong guiding hand was the one whom Alfred turned to in this time of indecision and renewal.

Across the street from Father Provencal's church was a new school where eighty boys were taught by six brothers who were members of a new religious congregation, the Congregation of the Holy Cross. Father Provencal encouraged Alfred to dedicate his life to God because he believed that Alfred belonged there. Alfred, even though this would have been his greatest joy in life protested by saying, "But Father, I can neither read nor write!" At age 25, Alfred had not received any formal education. Father Provencal replied, "No matter, there are brothers who dedicate themselves to other works, Alfred, that require neither reading nor writing. You do not need to know how to read and write, young man, to pray!"

Two years later, after much consternation and hand-wringing, Alfred decided to join the brothers. The Holy Cross Brothers at St. Cesaire knew of Alfred's physical condition and did not encourage him in his religious pursuits.

Father Provencal, however, continued to encourage and support him in his efforts. Alfred entered the Holy Cross Novitiate in Montreal in 1870. He entered the combined novitiate and school for boys called Notre Dame, which sat on the city's highest mountain, Mount Royal. Father Julien Gastineau was both principal of the school and master of novices. Father Provencal had sent Father Gastineau a letter of reference for Alfred. In the letter he wrote to Father Gastineau, "I am sending you a saint."

It was at the Holy Cross Novitiate where Alfred received his first religious habit and changed his name. He, officially, became Brother Andre in honor of his beloved mentor, Father Andre Provencal. The brothers of the Holy Cross were not really enthusiastic about Alfred joining them. There were concerns about his health and whether or not he would be able to function at the level that they desired. Nevertheless, they neither did nor said anything to discourage him. Alfred's excitement was apparent to all who came into contact with him. His eyes, his voice, his whole demeanor seemed to change. Alfred's self-esteem was higher now than it had been during all his years before. He was fulfilling a lifetime dream to serve God. The constant derision, which he endured from people who ridiculed him about his frailty and size was no more. Here, he could flower and become the man of God which he was determined to become.

During the novitiate year, Brother Andre learned to read. After learning to read, he memorized whole sections of many spiritual books. He was assigned to the laundry and linen supply for the novitiate and school. He swept and mopped floors, tended the sick at their infirmary and was at the beck and call of everyone. At the end of this year, Father Guy, the novice master, told Brother Andre that his future as a Holy Cross Brother was in serious doubt. Heartbroken and upset by this news, Andre sought the intervention of Bishop Ignace Bourget who was visiting Notre Dame. Bishop Bourget said to André, "Do not fear, my dear son, you will be allowed to make your religious profession."

Bishop Bourget's intercession on Brother Andre's behalf helped him to become admitted to the profession on August 22, 1872. Andre wrote his first temporary vows which he read as he knelt before his community. He vowed,

"I, Joseph, Alfred Bessette, Brother Andre, unworthy though I am, rely nevertheless on the divine mercy and, earnestly desiring to devote myself to the services of the Adorable Trinity, make to Almighty God the vows of poverty, chastity and obedience, according to the sense of the rules and constitutions of this congregation, in the presence of Our Lord Jesus Christ, of the Blessed Virgin Mary conceived without sin, of her worthy spouse, St. Joseph, and of all the Heavenly Court, promising to accept whatever employments it may please my superiors to entrust to me."

Brother Andre's first assignment was as porter of Notre Dame College. As a porter, his duties were to answer the door, welcome guests, find the people they were visiting, wake up the boys (age seven to twelve) in the school, and deliver mail. Brother Andre jokingly told someone, "At the end of my novitiate, my superiors showed me the door, and I stayed there for forty years." The porter's room at the door of Notre Dame contained a narrow wooden couch, which Brother Andre used for his bed. Uncomfortable as it was, that mattered very little, since he spent most of the night on his knees in prayer. What food and sleep do for most people, prayer did for Brother Andre; it revived and sustained him. He kept a small statue of St. Joseph turned backward on his windowsill, which faced Mount Royal. When he was asked why the statue was turned backward, he replied, "Because some day St. Joseph is going to be honored in a very special way on Mount Royal!"

Along with his duties as porter, Brother Andre continued his laundry and sacristan work. In addition, he was a messenger and he did maintenance work. Sometime when he was in another building and the front door rang, he would have to shuffle between buildings, answer the door, go find whomever the visitor was there to see and then return to his maintenance work. Interruptions of this sort would have exasperated a less patient and willing person, but not Brother Andre. He bore all in good humor and with a willing heart. His superior at Notre Dame, Father Louage, did not take kindly to Brother Andre and he often disciplined him in a seemingly unfair manner. Because of this, the other brothers nicknamed him "lightning rod" because they said, "He receives the bolts of Father Louage." Brother

Andre compared his persecutions to the suffering of Christ and he endured without protest.

Shortly after his assignment at Notre Dame College, the supernatural phenomena, which marked the remainder of his life, began to occur. Sometimes, when Brother Andre was going about his errands for the College, he would receive word that someone was ill. He would visit the sick person to cheer him and pray with him. He also rubbed the person with oil that was taken from a lamp burning in front of St. Joseph's statue in the chapel. The health of some of these people improved after Brother Andre prayed for them. Word began to spread about his healing powers and people began to call him "Good Brother Andre". People began to seek him out to pray for their sick friends and relatives. He cured so many of the students at the College that he developed a reputation as a gifted miracle worker.

The Miracles

Brother Andre had been a porter at Notre Dame College for about five years when his gift of healing was first noticed. Once he visited one of the boys at the school who lay ill in the infirmary. The boy had a very high fever and he was ordered to rest by the school doctor. Brother Andre took one look at him and said, "Get up, you lazy bones! You're not sick. Go outside and play with the others." At first, the boy did not want to go, but he got up, went outside and started playing with the other boys. Word immediately got back to the College authorities on what had transpired. They were very angry with Brother Andre for going over the head of the doctor and getting the boy out of bed. Andre said to them, "Please permit a doctor to examine him. You'll see that St. Joseph cured him." The doctor came and examined the boy and, sure enough, he had completely recovered.

Shortly after the infirmary healing, there was a smallpox epidemic at the Holy Cross College of St. Laurent, which was not far from Notre Dame College. The epidemic struck both students and members of the religious community. Some of the ill died. Brother Andre volunteered to nurse them. When he arrived at the school he knelt and prayed to St. Joseph to protect the sick. From that moment, no other people died from smallpox.

Another miracle healing occurred one day when Andre was scrubbing the floor in the parlor of the college. A woman who had heard of his reputation came to see him. The woman was suffering from crippling arthritis and she could walk only by being assisted by two men. She asked Brother Andre to heal her. Brother Andre continued with his scrubbing, not looking up from the floor and he said to the men assisting her, "Let her walk." The woman walked out on her own volition.

Again, and again, healings were reported and Brother Andre was given credit for the miracles. He, nevertheless always told the sick, "It was not I, but the Holy Father through the bountiful healing arms of St. Joseph." He would even perform miracle healings from afar. Once day he saw the father of one of the boys at the school. The man had a sad, strained expression on his face. Andre asked the man what was the problem and the man told him that he was worried about his sick wife. Brother Andre replied, "But she is not so sick as you think. At this very moment she became better." The man was very cynical about what Andre told him because his wife had been ill for many years. The man went home, still not believing that his wife was healed. However, when he arrived at his door, his wife had risen from her sickbed and greeted him at the door, perfectly healthy, in good spirits, and asking about their children who attended the school. Later, when the man had a conversation with his wife's nurse, he found out that his wife had asked to be taken out of bed exactly when Brother Andre pronounced the words, "At this very moment, she became better."

A Holy Cross priest, Father Henri-Paul Bergeron, knew Brother Andre and wrote a book about him, The Wonder Man of Mount Royal. In his book, Father Bergeron recalled an event that happened one day when Brother Andre was making his way along Bienville Street in Montreal. Someone brought a sick woman to him for healing. Brother Andre prayed for the woman and she was immediately healed. After this healing, word spread like wildfire throughout the neighborhood. People poured out of doors bringing with them their sick and infirm and the curious came just to catch a glimpse of the, by now, renowned man of God. The whole street was filled with people, healthy and sick. Brother Andre tended to the sick with patience and love. As everyone rushed forth to beg for favors and cures, Andre's chauffeur, in making his way through the crowd, remarked, "How wonderful; it is like a scene from the life of Our Lord." Brother Andre responded in his usual self-deprecating fashion, "Perhaps so, but God is surely making use of a very vile instrument." That one statement tells so much about the heart and soul of the man. He was humble and obedient; never arrogant, boastful or vain about his gift of healing. He gave credit to St. Joseph for the healings, never taking any credit for himself. There were those in the church who envied him and wondered why a person of higher rank and ordination was not chosen for this work of The Lord. He was reviled and ridiculed by some church authorities and made to perform menial tasks, which no one else wanted. But, he always did so with a willing heart. All he wanted to do was serve God and humanity, however he could.

Word spread far and wide about the little gifted brother. People came to visit him and be healed from many places around the world. Brother Andre's desire to build a shrine to St. Joseph grew stronger with each passing day. His dream to build the shrine received reinforcement one day when one of the brothers told him about a strange phenomenon which transpired in his room. This brother had a statue of St. Joseph which he placed facing his bed. Whenever he left and returned, he found the statue of St. Joseph turned around, facing Mount Royal, where the shrine now sits.

Brother Andre asked for permission to build the shrine. He was granted permission to build St. Joseph's shrine, but given no money to do so. He was told to use whatever resources he could find to build it. He used the money, which he earned giving haircuts to the students at the college, to begin construction of the shrine. The first structure, which he built atop the mountain, was a one-room structure with no heat. He spent the next two decades building the shrine to St. Joseph. What started as a fifteen by eighteen foot chapel in 1904 became a large basilica, which was completed in 1966.

Brother Andre traveled to many places healing the sick. Testimonies of those who were present at the healings were many. He once healed a baby who had a brain tumor by rubbing his head. When the doctor examined him, he found that the baby's tumor had disappeared. There were many miracles to follow. St. Joseph's oratory holds testament to the many afflictions, which were healed by God through Brother Andre and St. Joseph.

Brother Andre's health remained poor throughout his lifetime. In late December, 1936, he suffered from an attack of severe gastritis and was hospitalized. Shortly after the New Year began, he had a stroke. He suffered greatly; but, even though he suffered, he managed to stay in good spirits. While hospitalized, he whispered to a friend, "How good God is... how beautiful... how powerful. He must indeed be beautiful since the soul, which is but a ray of his beauty, is so beautiful." He soon lapsed into a coma and died on January 6, 1937 at the ripe old age of ninety-two. He lived long for one so ill throughout his lifetime. Upon his death, about a million people climbed up to St. Joseph's Oratory to pay tribute to this humble soldier of God. He was a savior to many who sought his intervention and he was repaid with a tremendous outpouring of love and respect, not only from those whom he had cured, but from many around the world who had heard of his miracles.

Chapter 8

Reverend Chloe: Auras Healer

Time: Circa November 1995

Candles were everywhere...on the fireplace mantle, on the low table in the front of the living room which had been converted to a room of worship, on each window sill, and even on the steps leading up to the home-based Spiritual Science Church. The healing service was just beginning. There were four rows of folding chairs on each side of the room. Several people were sitting and meditating silently as soothing music played softly in the background. Reverend Chloe and another female minister were accepting people to be healed at the front of the room. Whenever either minister finished with a person, anyone who needed healing could go sit on one of the two stools in front of the ministers and allow them to perform their healing rites.

Reverend Chloe is an ordained minister who works with the *aura* in healing others. The aura is defined as an electromagnetic force field which surrounds every living being and which is a multi-status indicator of sorts because it mirrors the emotional, spiritual, and physical state of the person by changing both colors and force field direction. The aura is also capable of opening, closing, expanding, contracting or spinning. The status of the aura depends upon the person's activities and mental status.

The ethereal sounds of the music and the candles give the room a warm energy which is both calming and spiritually uplifting. Rev. Chloe who is dressed in casual pants and a sweater is around forty-five years old; her long blond hair is pulled back into a ponytail. Her bifocal glasses are attached to a glasses holder and they rest on her chest along with a very long - to -the-waist chain with a Christian cross on it. It is a Sunday evening around 5:00 P.M. and almost everyone is very casually dressed, some in jeans, others in sweat pants and athletic shoes. Visitors rarely dress up for church here. Three other ministers are present, a man and two other women; the man and one of the women are wearing traditional ministerial robes.

A young woman walks to the front and sits on the stool in front of Rev. Chloe. Not a word is spoken. Rev. Chloe steps around to the front of the stool so that she is facing the young woman. Silently, she begins her aura heal-ing. She raises her hands above the woman's head and without actually touching her body, Rev. Chloe moves her hands around the woman's entire body, head to toe, back, front and sides as though her hands are searching for something. Next, she moves her hands through the air as if she is hand sculpting something around the woman. She moves around the woman and she appears to be smoothing the air space surrounding her. When she has finished, she steps back from the stool and the young woman returns to her seat. One by one, those who wish to be healed take their seat on the stool in front of the ministers for their healing rite.

In her everyday world, Rev. Chloe is a mature college student, a loving sister to her brother and a mother. Since grade school she has been able to "get answers" to any-thing. When other children were stumped about a problem or an issue in class, Chloe would always know the answer. During that time, even she did not know that she was spiri-tually gifted.

When she was thirteen years old she observed her dad playing with a deck of ordinary cards. He was reading the cards like people read tarot cards. "After I saw my dad read the cards, I started reading them too. I got so good at it that when I would visit my girlfriends, their moms would meet me at their door with a deck of cards in hand. They always wanted me to read cards for them. I got tired of it, so I stopped."

Rev. Chloe revealed that she really did not know exactly what she was doing with the cards until a palmist told her that she was reading things psychically. It was normal for her, and as a child, she did not realize that others, except for some family members, did not perceive psychically and intuit in the same way.

"As a child, I used to drive my eye doctor crazy. I used to see these little round things and I would tell him because I thought he saw them, too. He always thought I was joking, but I wasn't!" said Rev. Chloe as she laughed heartily.

Rev. Chloe comes from a family of psychics. Her father's mother was part of a group of psychics who healed through exorcism rites. Her mother had a sister who was psychic. Rev. Chloe said, "Mom told me that her sister always knew when their dad was coming home. My brother and my cousin were both psychic. Once my brother and I knew of a friend who had his car stolen. My brother did a reading for him and told him that his car was burned up and that it was in Philadelphia, Pennsylvania. Sure enough, shortly thereafter, the police found his car in Philadelphia. It had been burned!"

Even though Rev. Chloe is spiritually gifted, she took a class on learning how to read auras. She took the class through her church's training program for ministers. Some of her classes centered upon the psychic healing arts.

Rev. Chloe explained, "Some people see auras in colors. I see auras in white. When I pass my hands around a person's body, my hands get pulled to a spot on the body that is affected and needs healing. What I do with my hands when it looks as if I am sculpting is that I am moving the white stuff around. It may be bunched up in one area and very thin in another area, so what I am doing is smoothing it out and fluffing it up."

Rev. Chloe explained that the aura has healing properties. The aura is a protective shield which guards us against negative spirit entities which try to possess our bodies. One of the mental illnesses people experience is a direct result of the aura being open and spirit beings who are evil being able to penetrate the shield and communicate with the person. Who or what controls the direction of the force field and allows them inside the aura? God controls the aura and, if it is open, the person is experiencing negative karma or being punished by God. People who have attempted suicide or who have tried to contact the spirit world have often reported hearing voices which torment them and try to influence them. Those who do not accept that explanation would say that the person is hallucinating or schizophrenic.

According to some experiential religions, other physical or emotional maladies can disturb the aura. We have a personal, small atmosphere surrounding our bodies which is similar to the greater atmosphere that we all experience. When our personal atmosphere is disturbed by anger, grief, fear or any emotional state, the aura becomes unstable and can be compared to an atmospheric thunderstorm sometimes. Compare the aura's little lightning bolts and silent thunder to that of the larger atmosphere and personal atmospheric disturbances is easier to understand. Healers who work with auras do so with the permission of God and their healing hands help restore this shield to a calmer, more normal state.

"I sometimes work with a healing sister who comes to me." Rev. Chloe explained that the sister is in spirit form and that she once was a nun when she was incarnate. "My sister sometimes comes with a broom and she waves it around. Her broom always means she's cleaning house...spiritual house, that is. She comes to help me in my healing work sometimes."

Rev. Chloe talked about how she once had two spirit helpers who were American Indians. She said that they would dance around as a part of their healing rite. She has had many spiritually revealing and moving events in her life, but the one that she recalls with much excitement and elation was when she saw a *harvesting angel.*

"I saw a harvesting angel one night before my sick friend died. I was sitting in his bedroom while he slept when, suddenly, a tall, shiny, slightly bent over, beautiful figure came through the wall, through the bookcase. He looked at me as if he was surprised that I was there, and I looked at him, equally as surprised. The harvesting angel had come for my friend. After looking at my friend for a moment, the angel turned around and left through the wall. He was so beautiful and luminous! The next day, my friend died. I know that the beautiful harvesting angel came for him after I had gone."

On the surface and at first glance, Rev Chloe looks and acts like any average middle-aged woman you would meet on the street. What is it that sets her apart from the rest of us? It is her ability to see things which others do not see. Most of her life , she has hidden this fact from people because being psychic meant either you were overburdened by friends and family with requests for readings or you were made to feel that you did not belong. Rev. Chloe, still, feels the need at times to hide her gift from others because of the problem of non-acceptance of psi or the rejection of intuitive information in favor of scientific rationality.

Chapter 9

Reverend Clarence: Prophet and Healer

Time of interview: August, 2001

> *[Rev. Clarence chose to be anonymous since he has*
> *two other occupations in addition to his ministry. He*
> *felt that his contribution, being counter to orthodox re-*
> *ligious beliefs, might be detrimental to his livelihood.*
> *His real name has been changed.]*

"I attended church practically every Sunday since I learned how to walk!" explained Rev. Clarence. He continued, "My parents raised me and my siblings in the Christian faith. I served my church from the time I was a pre-teenager until I graduated high school and went away to college. I was a very devout young person. I had as one of my goals to read the Holy Bible and The Complete Works of William Shakespeare in their entirety before I graduated and left home for college. Needless to say, my very socially engaging teenage years left me little time for extracurricular reading. There was too much fun to be had, too many parties to attend. Life was a sweet bowl of cherries for me."

Rev. Clarence is a tall, thin Caucasian man with thinning, straight, medium brown hair mixed with gray that he wears parted on one side and combed over to the other side to cover the thin areas. He has a sharp nose and a strong square jaw. His mouth is fuller than most Caucasian men of his generation and it gives him a very handsome appearance. He looks to be about sixty or sixty-five years old. He has a decided air of authority about him, which commands your attention when he speaks. His light brown eyes look into you as if he is seeking a connection to your inner being, the real you, minus the mask. He is warm and articulate and sometimes funny in the way he talks about life and people.

"I dearly loved going to church when I was growing up; even as a teenager, my friends and I attended church every Sunday. I even went to Sunday school through my senior year of high school." He explained that when he was around eight years old, he received Christ into his life. He said that he felt the minister was looking directly at him each Sunday when he called for people to come down and accept The Lord into their lives. He said, "I was a shy kid, and naturally, I did not want to get up and walk down the aisle in front of a church full of people; but one Sunday, I did. I felt guilty, and those penetrating eyes of our minister seemed to be signaling out to me, 'Christ wants you...you....you. Come on down.' So, I did. A couple of weeks later, I was baptized in the baptismal pool and the guilt ended then and there. I was 'saved'...no longer a sinner.

Rev. Clarence said, "I maintained my Christian faith throughout my childhood and teenage years; but, my faith was challenged and I allowed it to be destroyed when I went away to college."

I asked, "How did that happen?"

He replied, "Well, in my sophomore year of college, I took a humanities course, which covered the arts, religions, various ancient and modern cultures, and the usual stuff covered by undergraduate humanities courses. "He explained that his professor, a very scholarly Ph.D. informed the class that what they were about to learn might shake their faith somewhat, but that he wanted everyone there to maintain whatever faith they had when they entered the class. My professor forewarned, 'These are the facts, ladies and gentlemen, I do not want to upset any of you, and I would like for you all to leave here with the same faith in God that you came in here with'. I never figured out what he meant by that statement until after I completed the course. He must have known that some of us, if not all of us, would leave there with broken faiths, growing agnosticism in our bellies and atheistic nihilism shaking the ground under our feet like individualized made-to-order earthquakes in our lives."

"What do you mean, Rev. Clarence? What did he say that shook your faith in God?"

"The section on religions covered discrepancies in the Holy Bible, questions which no believer would dare ask anyone.   There were questions which both confused and angered me at the same time. I felt duped by all my religious teachings. I felt that I had been brainwashed, lied to, and fed a diet of fairy tales and myths in church. I was very, very angry at orthodox religions. I had nowhere to turn. There was no one who could answer those questions, so I began to doubt...first the authenticity of the Bible, then the existence of God. It was painful. It was dark and frightening. I felt empty inside and the emptiness and anger at, what I felt was society's biggest lie, fueled my slide from agnosticism to outright atheism."

"What questions did your professor pose? What was so discrepant that it led you to become an atheist?"

"I would rather not say, specifically, because I would not like to cause anyone to question his or her faith like I did. I will say this, generally...when I learned that some of what has been passed down to us as truth is mixed with a biased reporting of history, as well as civil laws, which have been handed down as God's laws, I was disillusioned. I did eventually get answers to those questions, but not from any person. I got answers directly from GOD...straight from the source. It took me many years of doubt, disbelief and spiritual anguish to get to that point, though. But, I'm getting ahead of myself."

"Rev. Clarence, how did you turn all of that around? How did you get to the point of regaining your faith?"

"God."

"God? But, I thought you had stopped believing in God."

"Let me explain...God has a way of bringing you back to his bosom when you go astray. I was first an agnostic, then an atheist for many years before God brought me into the light. It all started with troubling times in my life. When trouble comes, it sometimes comes in duplicate and triplicate doses. Ol' Man Trouble moved in with me and camped out in my living room!"

"What happened, Rev. Clarence?"

"Well, to make a long, sad story short, I lost my wife whom I had been with for twenty years; she died of breast cancer . I lost my job as an accountant due to cutbacks, and I lost many of our friends all at the same time. I was having emotional woes, financial problems and my life was filled with a terrible loneliness. She had always taken care of all the major household tasks and I had few skills as a homemaker; but, I did learn to cook for myself with some help from my sister.   I drew unemployment while I looked for another job...but bills don't wait. I had hit rock bottom financially , emotionally, socially and spiritually."

"But, what about your friends and family? Couldn't they help?"

"Yes, but you can't ask them to pay your bills every month and they certainly could not stop my heart from breaking!"

"So, what did you do?"

"Nothing."

"Nothing?"

"That's right. I did nothing. But GOD did something!"

"What?"

"One of my neighbors, a nice elderly lady with whom I used to exchange pleasantries, approached me one day as I was leaving the apartment to look for a job. She said that she noticed I seemed a little 'down' lately and she slipped something in my hand and said 'Try this. It will help. It always helps me'."

"What was it?"

"It was something that I almost tossed in the trash, but I was polite and put it in my pocket. It was a prayer for spiritual understanding (Appendix E). You know, I was still an atheist and prayer was the farthest thing from my mind at that time. But, I thanked her and went on my way."

"Did you pray, Rev. Clarence?"

"No, not right away. I tossed it on my dresser and looked at it for a while, thinking that there was no way I was going to pray. For me, God didn't exist. Only science was real, tangible and could explain the universe. I reflected back on those discrepancies and unanswerable religious questions that my humanities professor had posed and I sank deeper into darkness and despair. My bills were mounting and my heart was still not mending. I was a mess."

"What did you do to pull yourself together?"

"I was still too blind to pray, but God knew that; so, one morning when I got up, God spoke to me. I had forgotten that the prayer was on top of my dresser along with my bills. Somehow, during the night it had fallen to the floor and I had to either pick it up or step over it on my way to the bathroom. I picked it up. I actually read it for the first time. Much to my surprise, the prayer was challenging the reader to pray for understanding about God and life. What did I have to lose? I accepted the challenge. I prayed for the first time in many years."

"What did you pray for?"

"I prayed for understanding of God and life. I asked God to show me a sign if he really existed, because that's what I needed. And I said, 'please let me know for a certainty that it's you'. I had an aunt who always used to say that she asked God for signs. I guess that's why I asked for a sign. I also prayed for a job. That was the beginning of my road back to God."

"So, go on, did you get your sign?"

"Yes. I got many signs, but the first one which I got brought joy to my heart and peace to my aching soul...I saw her...I saw my wife."

"What? I thought she died?"

"I mean...I saw her spirit. I was lying across the bed one afternoon feeling very sad and lonely when something that I can't explain compelled me to look at the walk-in closet that was open. When I looked in the closet, I saw her. She paused for a moment and then she seemed to pass through the left wall of the closet and into the hallway by the bathroom . I felt both joy and sorrow at the same time. She had survived death! She had survived it! I had seen what I was hesitant to tell anyone for fear that they would think that I had completely lost it...but, I know what I saw. It was she."

"Rev. Clarence, had you been drinking or taking anything when you saw her?"

"No. I'm not a drinker...never have been. I tried it once in high school and it made me so sick, I never tried it again...and I certainly was not taking any drugs, not even prescription drugs."

"Rev. Clarence, were you frightened by what you saw?"

"No. I felt a loving presence there in that room. I felt...hope...for the first time in many years...I felt hope...in the possibility that God really did exist! I continued to pray for spiritual understanding and other things started to happen."

"Like what? What happened next? What other signs did you receive from God?"

"Well, one sign which I call my 'awakening' came to me just as I was waking up one morning. You know... the stage of sleep between sleep and arousal is a very peculiar state sometimes. Your dream can be just ending and you can be awake and still remember it...or at least how it ended."

"Yes, I know. I have experienced that myself."

"Well, this particular morning, I was in that stage of sleep and I heard music...an angel chorus singing a song to me that I had never heard before. It went something like this...(He sings.) 'Earth life is a game of survival--a game of survival-a game of survival. Earth life is a game of survival and you must learn God's rules. You don't know the rules.-- You don't know the rules.-- Ask God.--Ask God.--Ask God.' I will never forget it! I became fully awake and I still heard the angel chorus!   Their voices were melodic, rhythmic and wonderful...baritones...sopranos...basses. There were even piano and guitar sounds! They played instruments! They sang it twice as I lay in the bed fully awake and totally in awe of what God was showing me. It stopped and all was silent again. I knew for certain, at that moment, that God had personally answered my prayers to let me know for a

certainty that He existed. He sent his angels to tell me to
ask for guidance. I was overjoyed. I cried tears of joy and
relief and even grief for my years of being away from God
and for my wife being alive in spirit form. I had such a mixture of powerful emotions; I must have gone on like that for
an hour before I decided to meditate. I had several meditation visions that day and in the ensuing weeks."

"So, Rev. Clarence, you were certain during that
time that God was letting you know that he existed beyond
a shadow of a doubt?"

"Absolutely! I knew, then, that a supernatural force
was operating in my life and that it was good! Whatever we
choose to call him or her...God, Allah, Yahweh, The One, or
whatever we call God, the truth of the matter is...he's real!
I was convinced by my experiences that God was helping
me. Three days after I heard the angel chorus, a former co-
worker called to ask if I had found a job yet. I had not, so he
said that he would put in a word for me at the accounting
firm where he was working. He did. I got an interview the
next day and I got the job. Some people might say, that was
just a coincident, you know...I prayed...he called...I got the
job. I felt it was not a coincidence. I continued to pray. I got
the job on a Thursday and I was to report for work on the
following Monday."

"That was lucky!"

"Maybe you call it luck, but I have since learned that
there is no such thing as luck. You shape your own
luck...there's karma...good and bad; it depends on what
you do as to how you get repaid. Most of us don't know
what we do to deserve bad luck, but that's a whole different
story. We sometimes march to the beat of a different
drummer who is not beating out God's message...maybe
your society's message or your culture's message or your
religion's message...but, I digress."

"Yes, your sign...what about your sign?"

" You know, I seldom used to dream, but that entire
weekend prior to going back to work, I kept having the same
dream. There I was...sitting in a lovely , well-furnished office
and this gorgeous, tall , blonde walks in, takes my hand,
kisses it and sits down in the chair beside my desk. She
gazes into my eyes and I can see that she has the most
beautiful green eyes and beautiful teeth. She says nothing,

just kisses me on the lips and exits. I woke up and my heart was pounding and I was full of excitement, if you know what I mean."

"Yes, I think I do know what you mean...eroticism in dreams is as common as any other type of dream."

" Let me finish. When I went to work on Monday, I was led into an office that looked exactly like the one in the dream. I sat there for most of the morning dumbfounded. Was this my sign? I was almost sure it was, but I still had some doubts. When our lunch break rolled around, my friend, Benjamin, and I went to lunch in the cafeteria that was located downstairs in our building. We got our food and we were eating, when Benjamin's friend came over to our table and asked to join us. I almost choked on my food when I looked up at her. It was she! It was the exact woman I had seen in my dreams! She was tall, blonde, green-eyed and terrific! I could hardly speak or carry on a conversation with them. She kept looking at me while she was talking to Benjamin. She told me that she worked in an office one floor above us and wondered if she could be of any assistance to me in getting settled in. I told her that I had a few more boxes to unpack and that I was going to do that after work. She offered to help! We started dating after that evening."

"So, was she your sign?"

"Not just her...the job...the office and her. I was cer-tain that there was a force moving in my life that was su-pernatural. At that time, I still didn't call this force God. I had received a prophecy...through a dream. I had neither seen this woman nor the office before that Monday! But, there they were...exactly as I had seen them in my dreams. Was that not a prophecy?"

"Perhaps."

"I thought so. I was hot on the trail of finding God, again, and every opportunity I got, I visited the library to get books on religion...all of them...I knew that Christianity did not have all of the answers for me...maybe some...but I was on a search for the truth. I wanted no more lies, myths and fairy tales. I wanted the truth. I still used my prayer for un-derstanding...daily. God led me to the answers to some of those unknowable questions that had caused me to lose my faith many years ago. God directed me to two religions that had some of the answers that I was seeking. I don't want to say which ones because I'm not about promoting or bashing anyone's beliefs. One of them is a religion that explains about the rounds of creation. It teaches that our universe was created in stages and that each stage represents a growth period in our lives. Now, this made a lot of sense to me and it was compatible with the scientific evidence of evolution. This religion introduced me to the synthesis concept of religion, science and philosophy. It made more sense to me than anything else I had read or been taught. The only exception I took with them is that they seemed to espouse racial superiority in their teachings. I couldn't deal with that, knowing that there are geniuses and intelligent people of all races."

"How can they get away with espousing racial superiority?"

"Well, they do it a way so that you have to think about it real hard before you realize what they're saying. They believe that all humans belong to a 'root race' and the 5th root consists of white people, the 4th root, of Asian people and the 3rd root, Black people, and that there is a 6th root evolving who will be more enlightened, intelligent beings. Can you count up from the bottom?"

"Oh, I see what you mean. I suppose you never joined that group."

"No, but their explanations of science and religion were good and made me curious for more knowledge. So, I investigated another religion that I had read about and was very curious about. This church was one of the experiential churches, and I truly think that they have a lot of information that the entire world can use. They had sermons that they called *channeled readings*. The messages are supposedly from a higher plane than Earth, messages given to them by angels or spirit guides who speak through them. Some of the ministers of the church are what we might call psychics although I hate that word. 'Gifted' is a more appropriate word for the real ones because there are also fake psychics. We are all psychic to a degree. The fact that we dream, have hunches and intuitions means we are all psychic, but some people use more of their intuitive faculties than others."

"So, you think the experiential churches have all the answers?"

"No. I didn't say that. I said that their information is valid because it is coming directly from a higher source. They do individual spiritual readings in their church, if you want one. The first time I had one done, I was amazed. The elderly, white-haired woman minister had never seen me before, nor had I ever seen her. When she came to me, after giving several other people a spiritual reading, she told me some things about myself that only I knew. Why, she even told me about a job offer letter, which I had received, and exactly where it was in my apartment! She was so accurate in her reading of me, that I joined their development circle, as it was called then. I wanted to know how they knew what they knew!"

"What did you learn, Rev. Clarence? How did they know things?"

"They prayed and asked God for guidance and information and they meditated and waited for answers to be given to them."

"Is that all they did?"

"Pretty much, in a nutshell. I learned to ask God questions, too. I learned to meditate in a spiritual way and wait for God's answers to come. Let me tell you, the more I prayed, the more I learned and the angrier I got with other religions for not teaching people that we have a direct line to the Creator. But, many religions just teach centuries old doctrines that are based in believing instead of knowing. These experientialists don't proselytize, though. They think that when a person is ready for the truth, it will be revealed to them. But, first, people have to question religious authority. They have got to stop accepting everything they're taught about God without question. People listen to others teaching them but God will guide them, personally, if they would just ask God."

"So, is that what you teach your flock?"

"Yes, I do. I teach people how to get information directly from their creator."

"Rev. Clarence, tell me about some of your other revelations."

"Okay. Well, One day during one of my meditation sessions...I meditated daily, you know...about fifteen to twenty minutes a session. I usually started my session during the early morning hours when I would not be disturbed by a lot of noise and telephone calls...or, if I didn't start then, I'd do my meditation session at night when most people were asleep. I don't need a lot of sleep, so I stay up late. Sometimes I meditate with chants and sometimes I don't. This particular morning I had been using the *ohm* chant. Are you familiar with that one?"

"Yes I am. As a matter of fact, I have taught it to some of my friends and other interested people. I find it very calming and it puts you into a meditative state faster. It's very helpful for beginners."

"Right. Well, I had been chanting 'ohm, ohm, ohm' over and over and meditating for about ten minutes when I felt a tingling in my forehead about where the third eye is located. It felt like a very gentle vibrator that was raising my consciousness to a higher level. I started seeing a faint color that started out as a pinpoint and grew outward until my inner visual field was saturated with red color. Next, I saw a white light that emanated from a source that looked like a star lighting the darkness. After that, I saw a beautiful silver fish, flapping its tailfins. I didn't know what those visions meant at the time, but I have since come to learn that the fish represents spiritual food. And the light represents understanding of God and life. God was telling me, symbolically, 'I will prepare your spiritual food; I will teach you everything you need to know'."

"How wonderful!"

"Yes. It was wonderful, exhilarating and enlightening. I felt like God was giving me the keys to all of the so-called mysteries of our existence...just for the asking. Prayer is you talking to God; spiritual meditation messages is God talking back to you. I asked for knowledge of God and proof of his existence and God was answering me, personally. I was filled with joy and spiritual ecstasy. Who knew that all we have to do is ask? We're not taught that in our churches. We're taught to listen to religious authorities who try to tell us right from wrong, but they're just repeating what they have been taught...by other men who said God said something. People are taught to just believe and not ask questions. But, God gave us a brain and She expects us to use it."

"She?"

"Yes. God is neither male nor female. There are no equivalent pronouns in the English language, so I alternate genders or I just say God."

"I see. So, go on, tell me about your other visions, Rev. Clarence."

"Okay. I digress a lot. It's because I'm still angry about what I call religious brainwashing by many churches. A few days after the fish and light visions, I had another that was so profound. I was walking up some golden stairs above the clouds. It was an unusual staircase. The bottom part of the stairs was made of small steps and the steps became larger and larger toward the top of the staircase. Beneath the stairs was a locked golden door. The door represented the separation between heaven and earth. The graduated size of the stairs represented heaven and the astral planes or levels. The lower steps represented the lower planes and the higher, larger steps represented the higher planes of heaven. Simply put, the rewards are greater the higher up you go. Of course, the rewards are directly related to your deeds and accomplishments on earth. Revolutionaries graduate from earth to the highest planes of heaven."

"Revolutionaries? Really? Most people think that they are the real troublemakers and the cause of a lot of mayhem and grief."

"They may, indeed, think that. But, I'm not talking about people who go around blowing up buildings and shooting up places for no good reason. I'm talking about people who contribute knowledge, inventions, ideas and innovative methods to improve our world. I would not discount the warrior revolutionary, either. There is always a just cause to be won in battle. But, God is the judge of what is beneficial and good for the world versus what is done in the name of selfishness, vanity, fame and power."

"I see. Did you have other meditation visions which you can tell me about which will shed some light on your marvelous transformation from atheist to a true believer?"

"Ah. Ah. Please don't call me a believer. I hate that term as it relates to my knowledge of The Creator. I know. I am not a believer. I am a knower. Let those who do not ask questions of God call themselves believers. They will always be just that when they rely on the information and misinformation, which has been passed down to us by religious authorities for centuries. Just because it's old information doesn't mean it's the truth. We all need to ask God what is really true in our holy books and what is not."

"Sorry. I won't call you a believer since you say you are a man of knowledge. Is there anything else that you want to say about the meditation visions?"

"Well, I had many revealing meditation visions since those early days when I first started. I have also had visions of other kinds, which I will share with you. Let me ask you...have you ever heard someone say they had been in an accident and there was no other vehicle there but suddenly they had a collision and they didn't know where it came from?"

"I have heard news reports of people who make statements of that sort. Why?"

"Once I had what I call a change of scene vision. I had gone to the grocery store one day. After I bought my groceries, I got into my car and headed for the exit. The street that I had to enter was a four-lane street with two lanes of traffic in each direction. I looked both ways to make certain that there was no traffic coming. The street was completely empty, so I proceeded to make my exit and wham! A car in the oncoming heavy traffic broadsided me. Where had all those cars come from? The street had been clear and straight, no curves or bends to obscure my vision, but all of these cars appeared instantly after I entered the street. I was supposed to have that accident. God was warning me about something, which I had not been heeding in my previous signs God showed me, so I got my message the hard way. God always warns you many times before you get a spanking."

"Rev. Clarence, are you saying that God substituted one scene or environment that you were in for another?"

"Not actually. It was a vision, which masked the real scene. The change of scene vision is a scene that masks the actual environment that you are in. God changes your visual field so totally that everything in it looks as real as this chair I'm sitting in and as real as you sitting here. God has the ability to do anything, including cloaking people, scenery, or anything that God wants you to see or not see. I have had several change- of- scene visions since them, none resulting in an accident since that first time, however."

"You have? Tell me about the other change of scene visions."

"Alright. Now, remember that the change of scene vision is always a message from God or a spanking by God or protection by God. God can protect you by cloaking you right in front of someone. If God does not want that person to see you, they surely will not. Speaking hypothetically, for whatever good reason you need cloaking, and if you ask God to cover you, then God may do so. But, I digress again. The story I'm about to tell you happened about ten years ago. I was helping one of my church members, Bob, move some things from his apartment to a house he and his wife had purchased. He picked me up in his full-sized van that morning and one of the other church members was with him. The van was large but there were only two seats in the front because Bob had converted the back into an area, which contained two small bunk beds on the wall behind the driver's seat, and the rest was open space. When I got into his van I noticed his two children playing in the bunk beds. One was a little girl with curly black hair. She wore a frilly pink blouse and a red pleated skirt with suspenders. She looked to be about two or three years old. She was playing with her little brother, who resembled her in appearance, but he looked about four or five years old. They played and frolicked in the bunk while we men were discussing sports. We arrived at his apartment shortly after he picked me up and we moved several items into the van for transport to his new house where his wife was waiting for the telephone man. We were pulling off when I noticed that the little girl was missing. I said, 'Stop! You forgot your other child. She's not in here!' Bob stared at me in an incredulous way and asked, 'What little girl?' I told him about the little girl whom I had seen playing with his little boy. He looked at me again and said, 'I only have one child...my little boy here.' It was then that I knew I had had another change of scene vision. I asked them both if one of their wives was pregnant. Bob gave me a long, surprised look and said, 'Yes. My wife is expecting. She is due to have our baby in about six months.' I told him that I had seen his child and that they would have a girl."

"Did they actually have a girl?"

"Yes, they did. She looked exactly as I had seen her in my change of scene vision. Moreover, the colors of her clothing were a message about why God was returning her to Earth. A red bottom and a pink top* were both indicative of developmental weaknesses, which of course everyone has. That change of scene vision was a prophetic one! God masks things and people for our own good. It's just one way that God informs and protects us. I have been given many other prophecies by God; some are for the world and some are for the individuals whom I pastor."

"Rev. Clarence, that is an amazing account of your visions and other spiritual experiences. I am truly in awe about what you have just told me. You were learning things directly from God. Right?"

"Absolutely! We can all do the same thing. But, we allow our religious authorities to come between our Maker and us because they claim to be anointed or chosen or whatever they say to make us think we cannot go directly to God and learn truths for ourselves. We can....we can! God is living and wanting us to stop listening to others and pray for direct guidance. Too many of us go astray listening to the religious misguided teachings of others. If we would all pray and ask God questions, there would be only one religion in the world because we would all get the same answers."

"There are so many religions in the world, Rev. Clarence. How can anyone know who has the truth and who doesn't. Do you mean that if we all asked God, there would be one worldwide religion?"

"Yes...one religion...the truth...unaltered, unfiltered, uninterpreted...straight from God. God is the only one who can tell us which religions have the truth and which ones do not. All we have to do is ask God in prayer: ask God if what you're being taught is really the truth. I've done it and I've gotten answers! Without banging and bashing any-body's religion, let me say this. There's a lot of cultural , non-spiritual stuff in our holy books... all of them...not God's word, but man's word...and it's up to us, individually and collectively to ask God for the truth. Our religions are all limited because they are based on truths, half-truths and some outright lies. But, just because the religious information we are taught is ancient, we do not question it. But, old information just could be old lies passed on for centuries. One particularly disturbing misconception in Christianity that I take issue with is that people cannot enter Heaven without going through Jesus. Now, I'm not against Christians or anything like that because I teach many Christian concepts. But, to say that is to negate every other God-worshipping religion on earth; and, what about the people who lived before Jesus was even born? They *couldn't* go through him. So, what did God do with them when they died? Does that mean that all life was damned before Jesus' advent?   If there were people today living in remote areas of the world who never heard of Jesus, would they be condemned to Hell, no matter how good they were? I don't believe God is that narrow. There are many pathways to God; Christianity is just one of them. God is greater than all our religions. None of them has the whole truth. I suspect, though, that many people would not accept the truth even if it were handed to them on a silver platter."

"Why not?"

"Have you ever known someone who could not live with the truth because it was so horrible that they had to make up stories and excuses to maintain their very existence?"

"No, but I've heard of people like that. Why?"

"Some people do not want to accept the truth about their lives so they learn to live with lies. They are able to function only in their own little fantasy world. Many people are like that. The truth is too ugly to bear. It's unthinkable for most of us to accept that we are in Hell. None of our brilliant, arrogant leaders, scientists and movers and shakers would think that they were worthy of such a place."

"Are you saying we are all in hell now, Rev. Clarence?"

"As we live and breathe! The last plane in our spiritual hierarchy of locations is Earth Plane. It is where we must work off our bad karma, improve certain aspects of our character, learn to love, and we all have other more specific ways to develop, depending on our progress in our last life and previous lives. Karma is cumulative...it adds up from lifetime to lifetime. Earth is more hell for some than for others. It's all fair. Life is fair. We just don't understand why

God would let someone be born in a slum with raw sewage flowing through the gutters of the streets and where people have to drink the same water they bathe in. We don't get it. Why is someone born rich and someone else born poor? Is it because God is playing favorites? No. It's all about karma. Even if we do things that are culturally legal, they may not be keeping God's laws and God will punish us for doing those "perfectly legal" things. All over the globe, we legalize immorality. Some places have legalized euthanasia; same sex marriages; selling harmful drugs like alcohol and cigarettes; and female subservience. These things are all legal, but very immoral. But, in the end, we will pay a heavy price for not keeping God's laws and legalizing or institutionalizing our weaknesses. We don't understand the rules of the game, so most of us play it backwards or not at all."

"Game, Rev. Clarence?"

"Game. Life is a game called 'survival'. It's about staying alive and mating...those are the two basics we need to accomplish in our lives. We have to conform to the same natural laws as other life forms. We're no exception to the number one rule. We just do it a little differently. Most people don't know what they are supposed to be doing with their lives. That's why we keep coming back to Earth. People keep aborting their missions because they don't know what they are."

"Wait a minute, Rev. Clarence. The greatest good is supposed to be to help others even if it means you must make sacrifices. Right?"

"Wrong. God does not require a sacrifice of any kind from us...never did...never will. God's laws are about staying in the game called survival, not dropping out because you're trying to help someone else stay in it. Many people mistakenly believe that. They've believed it for centuries, even to the point of sacrificing animals and even their kin to God. What does God want with a roasted lamb, goat or human? God doesn't want us to kill for His sake. Ancient man got it wrong, passed it on to us and we've still got that sacrifice thing wrong. God's rules are about self-preservation. We should help others if we can but not to the point of making ourselves martyrs for whatever cause or reason. That will not get us through the pearly gates. It will get us a round-trip ticket back to earth plane after we die, though. We don't know God's rules; therefore, we don't know our mission."

"Well, how can people find out about their purpose or mission here?"

"My dear, there are many pathways to God's wisdom...and prayer for spiritual knowledge is at the beginning of each pathway. God will answer everyone according to their level of understanding."

"Rev. Clarence, how can everyone get the same answers if everyone is not even speaking the same language."

"I mentioned that God speaks to us symbolically as well as directly. There are universal symbols and signs through which God speaks to us...they are colors, geometric shapes, numbers, animal signs, body parts, planets and their movements, directions and polarities, physical functions and other ways. The late psychiatrist, Carl Jung, had a lot of insight into these universal symbols when he talked about the *collective unconscious* and his archetypes. Are you familiar with his work?"

"Oh, yes. I have administered the Myers - Briggs Type Indicator, a personality inventory many times. That instrument is based upon his work."

"Then you know that universal symbols such as the warrior, the clown, the mother figure and the father figure, and others are present in every culture. God talks through symbols like these as well as others. Sometimes, God just talks to us straight, no symbols, but that might be disconcerting to some, so we get symbolic messages ...daily...but many go unheeded because most of us have turned off our intuitive sense and use only our other five senses. Too bad...we miss a lot when we do that."

"Okay. But, how can everyone get the same answers?"

"Let me answer that by telling you about one of my guided meditation sessions. In my meditation group, we have both guided and unguided meditation. Guided meditation means that you are seeking the answer to one question...one thing and everyone prays about it and meditates on it. Unguided meditation means that you pray for enlightenment from God and God guides you in whichever areas of your life that God so desires. The members of the group meditate silently for about twenty minutes or so during which time, a tape is running so that any waking visions or clairaudient messages revealed during the session are recorded as various people receive them. Usually the group consists of no more than ten people. More would be a bit unmanageable. But if we have more people, we simply break up into smaller groups. This particular evening, the meditation group was doing guided meditation on the color, blue. What does it mean? Well, I had already received several signs from God about what the color means, but several of the new people in the group had not. God revealed the meaning of the color to each person in the guided meditation group. Some received their revelations clairaudiently, while some received them through symbolic moving visions. The crucial point is...all persons received the same answer...the color blue means improvement, healing or getting better."

"So, if everyone prays and meditates on the same question, issue or problem, everyone gets the same answer?"

"Yes. The same essence of the answer is present in everyone's message, regardless of the way that it is received. That's why I said that there would be only one religion in the world if everyone asked God for the truth and stopped relying on so-called religious authorities."

"But, Rev.Clarence, aren't you being contradictory? You are a religious authority...why wouldn't you want people to listen to you?"

"I am a religious authority simply because I was misled by religious authorities, all of whom swear they have the real truth...God's word. Well, nobody has all of the truth and when we turn to God instead of to our authorities, we will all be better off; but, they say you need an intermediary, minister, saint, this and that before you can talk to God directly. That's a lie! People need to come back to their roots in the bosom of The Creator. Once they have learned to communicate one-to-one with God, there will be no need for any religious authorities; my job will be over. I would be happy to hear one of my followers say, 'why am I listening to you when I can get the truth straight from God?' My mission will have been accomplished and I would happily wave goodbye to a follower and become her friend instead of her leader."

"Is that right? You would welcome people leaving your fold?"

"Yes, because I would know that my teachings opened their eyes to real, true knowledge."

"I see. God gives you knowledge and when you know that you're getting it straight from God, you have no need to listen to others. Right?"

"That's right! God will tell you all you need to know and then some. I asked God to use me as a tool in his work...and God did! I started receiving so many messages in many ways...dreams...wide awake visions...clairaudient messages...symbolic real life messages...many messages. I received many messages about why God returns most of us to Earth plane."

"Why do most of us come back?"

"Well, like I said before, we all have negative karma as well as good karma. Most of us need to work on our negative karmic debt to God; some of the weaknesses of man on Earth which I have received revelations about are about man being a follower and a listener. We listen to or follow wrong religious and cultural teachings which God holds us accountable for, no matter what you have heard or been taught. That's why good people suffer. They think they're doing what God wants them to do, but they're following what they have been taught by their church or society, which just might not be God's way. We don't know God's rules for this plane of life. We only think we do. Other reasons why we are returned to Earth are: subservience, especially female subservience. That's not God's way. We should have no master but God and that baloney about male dominance being ordained by God...you can throw that one in the trashcan! We are also returned because of power lust, placing our love in things and not in people, self-sacrifice."

"Self –sacrifice? But, that is supposed to be a virtue."

"Well maybe in some religions it is taught that way, but God's rules are the rules of survival...staying alive and nurturing yourself and others if you can, not destroying yourself. Self-sacrifice is one of the greatest sins. It is not a virtue. God wants us to love life and love ourselves. If you don't love yourself, how can you love another? Yep. Sacri-

ficing our lives is a great big no-no. Martyrs don't graduate
to the high planes of heaven. They have to come back and
learn how to love themselves more and not sacrifice their
lives for the sake of others. God's first law is survival. That
means love yourself first and help yourself first, then help
others if you can. Many other people have to come back to
Earth because of *face problems. Saving face* or being overly
concerned about what others think about you is a serious
character flaw which many get sent back here to correct."

"You know, Rev. Clarence, what you said about saving face brings to mind the behavior of gang members and
people who endure awful situations in life because they do
not want others to say bad things about them or think ill of
them. I know several people like that, myself."

"So do I. I'm working with several men now whose
wives earn more money than them and they do not want
other people to know. They even pick at their wives out of
jealousy. They're my hard-core bunch. They will have to
change in order to enter into the Kingdom of Heaven and
stay. Why, I even had one fellow come to me complaining
that his wife was unfaithful and that he was thinking of
leaving her. We prayed and meditated over it; the message
which we received from God was essentially this: she belongs to God and she had done no wrong. 'She is mine, nòt
yours' was the core of the message. Possessiveness in love
is punished by God. Even marriage is not God's law. It's
man's law. There were people before there were churches
and people mated" (At this point in the interview, Rev. Clarence expounded about marriage and God's natural laws.
Please Rev. Clarence's Revelations, Chapter 11 for more details.)

"I see. What about some of your other signs? You
said you have several kinds of messages. What were they?"

"Well, I continued with my prayers for spiritual understanding and my meditation even after I left the development circle."

"Oh, so you left the development circle? Why did
you leave?"

"I left because I am not really comfortable with spirit
communication. I don't want to knock anyone who does it,
but I am not comfortable with it. You must be absolutely
certain that your intentions are of the highest spiritual na-

ture. I know some mediums who go into trances and allow a spirit guide or assistant to take over temporarily. They do good work and most of the people who use spirit guides in their work have a clean spiritual house."

"Rev. Clarence, what do you mean by a clean spiritual house?"

"Simply put, my dear, there is a dark side to spirit communication. People who play around with it can and have gotten possessed or they have been under spiritual siege by one or more discarnate entities who pretend to be sent by God to help them. I call it a spirit con game."

"But, how can that happen?"

"People who play around with ouija boards, who call upon spirits in séances, who try to escape from life through drugs or alcohol, who attempt suicide or have serious death wishes, and those who practice satanic rituals or other evil-based rituals which seek to control others will be opened to the evil discarnate people who walk the Earth. Let me add to that people who do automatic writing and drawing. Any activity that is not God-seeking is subject to God's wrath. God reverses the electromagnetic field of the aura that surrounds that person. When that happens, a person is *open game*. Everyone has an electromagnetic aura that protects them from the evil ones, except when God opens it. When the aura is open, evil people in spirit can speak to the person and try to con him out of his body. They hunt for people whose auras are open so that they can speak to them and begin their con game. They are stalkers of the most horrible sort."

"How can a person be conned out of his body?"

"Every confidence game has trust as its major objective. Okay?"

"Okay."

"People whose auras are open can hear them and they can mentally or verbally respond back to them. They always pretend to be sent by God to guide the person, or they can read a person's *thought forms* which are pictorial representations of our thoughts. They can only be seen in the spirit dimension of our world. These evil spirits know which people and what things are important to a person. They push buttons. They know who to pretend to be. If your relative has died or a good friend who had influence over you or just someone you admire and respect, like a public figure has died, they pretend to be whomever you might obey; they are impostors and master psychologists who have studied an ancient con game of the spirit world. They pass it on and teach newly dead evil people how to do it. They get points for getting you to do various things, even small things like eat this or that. Wear a hat today, anything that they tell you to do and that you actually do."

"Okay. So, how do the points figure in this game?"

"The points count as time that they get to stay inside your aura and work toward entering your body and actually moving it and eventually taking over control of your body; it's the spirit con of identity theft. They pretend to be that person if they are in control of the person's body. They study the friends and family of the victim so that they know a lot of her history and work habits. Possession doesn't happen all at once: it happens in stages or at different levels of their evil game. God is the scorekeeper. This is the most severe punishment that God metes out to us for being unfaithful to Him and breaking His rules."

"What do they want with a person's body?"

"You see, they are in a physical environment without a physical vehicle. Our bodies are pleasurable. We enjoy food, sex, drinking, and other pleasures of the flesh, but they cannot. This is the ultimate Hell. It's Hell for us, more or less; but, it's more Hell for them. They want to indulge in the pleasures of the flesh and if they are electromagnetically bonded inside a person's body along with that person, they can taste and feel everything that the owner of the body can experience."

"How do you know this, Rev. Clarence? Have you ever experienced anything like that?"

"No. I have not. God has revealed these things to me and I have done spiritual work with four people who were under siege by these evil discarnates. Some people call them demons or devils, but they are really just evil people whom God did not allow into Heaven. They are serving jail time on earth plane until they have to return or be reincarnated. God showed me the purpose of their game in several ways so that I could help the people with whom I was working."

"Why does God allow it to happen to people?"

"God is very, very sad whenever God has to punish someone in this way. But, remember, God is running a universe and God is firm, fair and square. God does not want us to listen to any other being for spiritual guidance except HIM. Okay?"

"Yes, but why that punishment?"

"When people call upon spirit forces for guidance, then God let's them have exactly what they're asking for. God knows our intentions you see. And if we aren't seeking God, then we must be seeking someone other than God. God doesn't like for us to do that. 'Thou shall have no other gods before me.' is a true statement. People who attempt suicide often tell doctors they hear voices. They do. God punishes them because self-destruction is a major sin. We cannot hear what they hear because our auras are closed to the evil ones. It's like the difference between different frequencies of radio waves. You can't hear FM on an AM station and vice-versa. They're on a dual frequency when they can hear spirit voices, except, they hear the evil ones, not the angels or God's true assistants. What doctors and scientists don't know about is a whole new world. We live in a dual or parallel universe at this level. It consists of both the spirit world and the physical world. They cause one type of mental illness. Schizophrenia is one illness that doctors will never cure. It is a spiritually based illness. It is a subjective illness; that's why no one else can hear what they hear. God has opened their aura to the frequency at which they can hear the evil ones. This universe is based on frequencies. Everything that we see, hear, feel, taste and smell is a variation of frequencies. God revealed the Law of Ascending Vibrations to Me. (Please see Chapter 11 for more details on this law.) All physical and spiritual manifestations abide by this law. Man couldn't see pictures flying through the air or hear words flying through the air just a few decades ago. But now, we have radio and TV among other electronic wonders. If you had said that these phenomena existed back in the 1800's they probably would have said you were crazy. It's the same with the afflicted people hearing the voices. Doctors can deaden the person's senses and calm them with drugs, but salvation is the only cure for it."

"Have you ever cured anyone of schizophrenia, Rev. Clarence?"

"God cured two people through me. I don't have the power except as God gives it to me. I am working with the other two people now."

"What happened to these people? Can you tell me what led up to their illnesses?"

"Well, I am bound by a sacred trust not to reveal the identities of anyone whom I counsel. However, without telling you their names, I will tell you a little about them. There was a gentleman whom we will call Martin. Martin was in love with a young woman and she left him for another man. Martin tried to jump off a bridge, but someone saved him before he jumped. It was immediately after that when Martin started hearing voices telling him to go back and jump. The voices were telling him that he was a loser and that he had nothing to live for. Martin was directed to me by one of my church members who knows that I deal with this sort of thing. God opened Martin's aura to the evil ones because he was trying to self-destruct. For a week, Martin was hearing voices at work and at home. They were telling him to do various things and to go to various places. I told him to ignore them and do nothing that they said do. I also prayed with him and for him in an exorcism ritual. Prayer is the only answer for this illness. The evil ones had just started with him. If he had not come in when he did, he might be afflicted to this day and be confined to a mental hospital. But, he did not allow them to accumulate any points toward their next level of possession. The voices continued for about three more weeks, taunting, teasing, trying to ridicule him and even pretending to go away and come back as a dead relative, his grandmother. There is a way that they can imitate our loved ones voices. It has to do with our thought forms and how we respond to a perceived loved one. There is a scientific correlate as well as a spiritual one in this evil game that they play. Gradually, the voices became fainter and then one day, they were gone. That was about three years ago. He is fine now."

"My goodness! Nobody will believe this can happen!"

"Truth is stranger than fiction, my dear. We don't know God's rules, so we get into big trouble with Our Creator. Now, the second person whom I worked with and whom

God cured through me was a female whom we will call Miriam. Miriam had recently lost her fiancé through an automobile accident in which he perished. She was heartbroken and she went to a séance to try to contact him. During the séance, Miriam called upon the spirit world to come to her and bring him back into her life. Now, this gets real, real strange. Miriam started hearing voices, too. These voices claimed to be her guardian angels sent by God to be the doorkeepers for her fiancé's visits to her. They imitated his voice and Miriam believed that she was, indeed communicating with him. Now get this...they had a spirit wedding and she agreed to allow him to enter her body to consummate the marriage. Of course, it was not he, but an impostor evil one. However, he got inside her and their bodies are like elastic...they can contract and concentrate in any area of the physical body to induce pleasure or pain. She thought that he had made love to her and she continued to move deeper and deeper into other levels of the game. In earlier days, people called that kind of experience *a visit from the incubus or succubus.* Miriam was taken to the hospital one night. The evil impersonator who was inside her had caused internal adhesions in her intestines and blocked her bowels. That was another tactic to get her to give him total control of her body. She did not. It was at this point that she came to me. It was a difficult exorcism. As I prayed for her, I watched various expressions on her face, which were not hers, but the evil person inside of her trying to frighten me into stopping the prayers. They frowned at me and grinned at me, and widened her eyes and blinked them rapidly, but I was not afraid of them. I knew that God protected me and that no harm would come to me. I worked with Miriam for two years. She had let the evil ones gain too many points for her to come out of it quickly, as did Marvin."

"I'm sorry; but, please explain again why this happened to her. She was not trying to kill herself."

"Remember, now, not everyone gets into it by attempting suicide. What was Miriam doing? She was trying to contact the spirit world herself to get in touch with her boyfriend. Her intentions were wrong. They were not God-seeking intentions and we engender God's wrath when we seek guidance and solace from spirits and not from Him. I will quote again, 'Thou shall have no other gods before Me.' God is not playing with us when it comes to that."

"But, Rev. Clarence, you make God seem mean and vengeful. Most people learn that God is a god of love and forgiveness, comfort and our Shepherd."

"Yes. God is loving, kind, forgiving and comforting...all of those things and more, but God is not mean; God is firm and rules his universe when needed with tough love. You see, most people are uncomfortable when we speak of God as our punisher. God does punish us for our wrongdoings. God is our Parent /Creator and as our parent, God "spanks" us or corrects our behavior through our bodies. Illnesses, accidents, and all other forms of negative karma are God spanking us for something that we have done. But we get warnings many times before we get the spanking, but who on Earth is listening to God? Not many...hardly any. We go by whatever we are taught from the cradle, which may or may not be in keeping with God's laws. We don't know God's rules. You'd be surprised at how much cultural trash is in all of our religious teachings. God didn't say half the things that man says God said."

"Much of what you are saying is so new to people. People, especially ministers, don't usually challenge the scriptures...but you do."

"I do because people need to pray and ask God to separate the fact from the fiction in their scriptures because there are mistakes and stuff in scriptures that God did not say."

"I see, can you tell me about the other two people with whom you are working who are, as you say, *under siege?*"

"Both cases are very sad. The other two are females. One is an older woman whose husband died and she tried to contact him through a Ouija Board. She called upon him daily to talk to her through the board. There were messages through the planchette that moved across the board. Next she started hearing faint humming noises, and then she stared hearing voices. The evil one who talked to her pretended to be her husband and he got her to do a lot of things. He got her to sell her car, move into a new house, take a vacation and numerous other things. One of their most successful tactics is *impoverishment*. They get the victim to give up their worldly possessions by saying things like 'God will provide.', 'Take what you need.', 'Rich people cannot enter the kingdom of heaven.', 'The root of all evil is money.', and things that will get the person to give away his or her money and starve or be at the mercy of the guides or spirit. These evil people are ever present, morning, noon and night...they don't need sleep. They are constantly talking and working on the victim, so that the victim becomes totally dependent on them to tell him or her what to do. Why? Because the victim thinks they are angels, a wiser loved ones or famous role models."

"So, are you saying that all of those thing which she did counted as points toward the evil one taking complete control of her body?"

"Yep. You got it! She had done so many things that he had accumulated a lot of points. At one time, before she came to me, she said her hands just started moving like she was playing the piano. He had control of her hands at that time. She asked him to stop and he wouldn't. That was when she finally realized, that he was not her husband. I am still working with her now. He did not fully possess her; little by little we are gaining ground on the evil one. She doesn't hear him as loudly as she used to, just faintly but he continues to send her dreams to try to influence her behavior. So, you see, he has at times some privileges in her brain, but not on a perpetual basis. Some churches, including the Catholic Church have known about possession for centuries. Some theologians explain possession in three stages: infestation, obsession and possession. Infestation is the mildest form of diabolical activity. Demons, as some call the evil people in spirit form, stalk the victims hoping for a chance to talk to them. Obsession is the next stage. This was defined by theologians in 1906. The evil ones torment the victim and may leave wounds and scratches on the body. According to the most widely accepted theological position, the last stage is possession, when the victim loses control of his own body and the possessor uses the body, totally. The victim is powerless and trapped inside with someone else whose astral body energy is much stronger. It's a horrible tragedy."

"That's absolutely, unbelievably scary!"

"Yes, it is scary. Think about what it must be like for the person under siege! Some of these people chose not to go to a doctor because they did not want to be hospitalized and drugged. Do you know what a psychiatrist or psychologist would have done if these victims went to them and said, 'I hear voices.'?"

"Sure. They would have diagnosed them as schizophrenic and followed through with the proper treatment."

"Exactly! These people knew that they had been dealing with the spirit world and knew that no one would believe their stories except perhaps a Catholic priest or someone who is knowledgeable about possession and who knows what to do."

"I see. What about the other person? What did she do?"

"The other person was a young lady, fifteen years of age. She had been ice-skating on a lake near her home in another state. She and her friends had not gotten permission to do so because the ice was too thin at some points. One of her friends fell through the ice and drowned. She was so distraught that her mother sent her here to stay with her grandmother thinking that a change of scene might help. The girl lit candles every day for her friend and wrote notes to her friend and left them on her dresser every day. She would tell her friend that she wanted to join her wherever she was in the universe and that she wanted to end it all. She began dabbling in the black arts to try to reach her friend."

"Do you mean that she was dabbling in Satanism or black witchcraft?"

"Satanism. She was angry with God for taking the life of her friend and she turned her back on God and sought whom she thought was God's enemy. Needless to say, God opened her protective aura and turned up her hearing to the frequency at which people can hear voices and she got just what she was seeking. She heard an evil one who claimed to be Satan and who promised her visits with her friend and all kinds of power over others. She did many things that the voice told her to do because she thought her friend wanted her to do all those things. Well, the dark side gained many points and she has been under siege for many months. She is my worst case, yet. She is so young and so full of anger. We had to deal with her anger toward God first, and then with the fact that her invading spirit was not who he said he was."

"Not Satan?"

"No. They always claim to be Satan, God's angels, dead queens and kings... never anyone ordinary. Who would listen to an ordinary person in spirit form and do his or her bidding?"

"At what stage of possession was this young lady when she came to you?"

"I'd say she was almost fully possessed. She had gone too far for a short exorcism. They had accumulated too many points toward taking over. When two or more are working on a victim, they share the body. They take turns eating, having sex or whatever they want to do with the person's body."

"But, she was just a child! How could that happen to a child?"

"Well, the age of adulthood is constantly shifting in our society. But, maturation is when a person goes through puberty. *God* considers them adults, fully capable of knowing right from wrong and judges them as *adults*. We keep our children in *the nest* for many years past puberty, but God doesn't judge them to be children, we do. Like I keep saying, we don't know God's rules. We just think we do, based on what our churches and societies teach us. They teach some truths; they also don't have all the answers. We all need to pray and ask God for guidance in our lives and for truth and understanding."

"Rev. Clarence, these stories of possession are just too unreal for most people to even believe. I have a few more questions about possession...what about mediums who say that a spirit enters their bodies and talks through them? And, what about people who say that they have heard from or seen their 'dearly departed'? Are they in spiritual danger?"

"No. Absolutely not. These are isolated spiritual events, which God allows to happen to guide people and bring comfort to them. Like I said before...intent is everything when it comes to matters of this nature. There are good mediums who regularly contact the spirit world to bring messages of comfort to others. They are in service to God. The truly gifted ones are protected by God."

"Did the two people who were healed by you ever find out who, exactly, was trying to possess them?"

"Yes. The angels are sent by God to warn a person before it happens to them and if they do not heed the warning, then they have a battle to fight. After it was over for the two people God healed through me, God allowed an angel to do a reading for them. One person had a teenage ruffian who had died several years prior. He had killed lots of innocent people, robbed for a living and done all sorts of things to earn him Hell. He had two cohorts with him who would have shared the body if they had won. They still like to hang around in gangs, even after death. The other person had a female and a male together trying to take over her body. The female was a madam who ruined the lives of many young women. The male had been a Nazi under Hitler. They, of course pretended to be very learned people and they tried to teach them various things. They always like to sound super intelligent. They make up a lot of spiritual garbage trying to sound like angels, but they are evil to the core. They will be punished by God in their next lives. We received readings that the woman would be reborn into a life of extreme poverty. She would be born to a life in a third world country where she would have to live with the 'garbage heap' people and scrounge for scraps to stay alive. Such places exist, you know. The teenage ruffian will be returned to a life which will be most horrible. He did the most evil. His life will be far removed from modern society. He will be in a remote area in southeast Asia, in a mountainous or hilly area and he will be a young male concubine for a group of pedophiles in a Third World country. According to the victim, this evil one constantly blasphemed God many times by saying 'I wish there was a devil god. I would worship him. I hate you God. I wish Satan was real!' I guess he'll be getting what he deserves; the pedophiles are the devils on this earth. We also got a reading on the Nazi. He will be reborn into a life of poverty also. At some point early in his life, he will be blinded and have to rely upon the kindness of others. He will not find many kind people in his environment. He will be physically and verbally abused, robbed and taken advantage of by others."

"So, God revealed their future lives to you?"

"Yes. They did horrible things to the people they tried to possess. Life is fair; God does repay...the good and the bad. Through the ages, some of their evil teachings have seeped into our holy books because some of the authors were clairaudient and under siege. That's why scholars are needed to interpret some of the contradictions."

"Do you really think so?"

"I know so. I asked God to tell me what was true and what was not true in our scriptures and God has taught me a lot. There is lots of truth in the scriptures but the lies are very dangerous if we believe in them and follow them. God holds us accountable for what we do...regardless of what we are taught."

"Rev. Clarence, you must know that science will never accept your explanation for schizophrenia, don't you? They will say that it's superstitious gibberish, to put it mildly!"

"Science and religion can be happy bedfellows, you know. Just because there are mysteries in religions, doesn't mean that there are no scientific correlates to explain them; spiritual and physical concomitants can be glued together into one big whole. You see, we humans love to compartmentalize things. If something...an idea, a concept or fact is multidimensional, we don't like to deal with it. We like our science to be science, our religions to be faith-based only and mysterious, and never the twain shall meet. That's wrong! God created a spiritual and a physical universe and they interrelate; not only do they interrelate, but also they are intricately interwoven in a schemata that is in a sense symbiotic and catalytic. Spiritual growth and development in an area of life stimulates growth and development in the corresponding physical body part. Do you understand?"

"I think so. You mean that no spiritual growth takes place without something taking place in our lives on a physical or emotional level or both. Right?"

"Yes. But, more than that, God interacts in our lives and talks to us in so many ways and most of us fail to comprehend; and when we fail to comprehend, we set ourselves on a course that is unsafe, hazardous and wrongheaded. Some of us grow, while some of us regress. Regressions are physically punished and the body part or function which corresponds to the problem is affected or afflicted."

"Who do we listen to or follow besides God, Rev. Clarence? All major religions claim to follow God's teachings."

"Yes, they do. But, God is the only one who can tell us which one is right and which ones are wrong."

"Have you asked God that question?"

"Yes, I have. The answer is that most religions have lots of truth in them , but most also have lots of ethnic and cultural customs mixed in with the truth and passed on as God's word. That's the bad part. The good part is that most churches are doing a good job of helping people on an everyday basis with the problems that confront them in their everyday lives."

"Isn't there one religion which is better than all the others?"

"Look, I don't intend to 'knock' anyone's religion, except those that do not seek God. You must remember that man has handed down the words in most holy books and man is capable of making mistakes as well as mixing the truth with his own opinions. Cultures and kings have used some of the major religions as tools to further their own ends. Why, King Henry the Eighth was so angry with the Pope for not granting him a divorce from one of his many wives, that he separated from the Roman Catholic Church and started the Church of England; he even wrote his own Bible, The Great Bible."

"So, are you saying that churches are political in nature?"

"They are political as well as spiritual. Some are more political than spiritual. In my opinion, when churches try to limit the individual's God-given free-will (and some of them do) then they are not spiritual entities, but purely political, controlling bodies, hell-bent upon establishing a power base upon the backs of the naïve and the weak , or as they like to call them...the unquestioning faithful."

"But, Rev. Clarence, many people are taught by their religions not to question God or His Word. They believe that He gave it to us and we're supposed to accept his word on faith. That's what many believe."

"My dear, that is one of the biggest lies that has ever been told on God and man has told so many lies on God as a means of controlling us. *God gave us a brain and he expects us to use it.* The reason why I lost faith in the first place was because of just believing everything I was taught about God and when I was confronted with other facts and discrepancies, that made my beliefs look and sound like a scam artist had been at work in my holy book, I completely lost it! What I should have done is prayed to God for my answers, personally, privately and sincerely. I didn't then, but I do now. I get answers to each and every prayer I pray. God always answers prayer, even if the answer is 'No'. I ask God questions about everything...finances, personal relationships, scientific matters, health, sexuality...e-ver-y-thing and anything. I get answers to questions scientists should be asking. Many of our diseases could be conquered if more scientists were spiritually oriented instead of religiously oriented. I even had a vision one time about the AIDS virus and how we could stop it!"

" You did! Tell me about that."

"Now, mind you, I'm not a virologist, so what I'll be describing will be purely in a layman's terms. One day during one of my meditations, God showed me how this virus rotates into a cell. It penetrated the outer wall of the cell like a drill boring into a piece of wood. Then, I saw that there were small cilia or hairs that helped them to rotate at a high speed. If the motion of the cilia could be stopped, then the virus could not penetrate the cell. Chemical compounds could do the job. Just which ones, is up to us to determine through research and through prayer. Many of our famous inventors and scientists have been spiritual men and women. When they rely totally on science to answer questions, they may or may not get answers. Science with God involved is a sure win!"

"I know. George Washington Carver to name one had visions and created many inventions and helpful compounds to help people."

"Yes. But, the main thing about a disease...any disease is that it has a spiritual concomitant. Fix what's wrong spiritually and you fix or get rid of the disease. Man on Earth will never be free of diseases because we have major spiritual flaws to work on. AIDS is a disease, which is a punishment for sexual flaws. It first started with the homosexual community and spread to the heterosexual community. But, homosexual or heterosexual, it speaks to sexual or gender weaknesses, such as female or male subservience, male dominance, and/or living the wrong sexual lifestyle. God doesn't play politically correct when it comes to correcting our behavior. Let me show you something."

At that point Rev. Clarence got up and went into his bedroom, he came back with a shoebox full of papers. "Look at these answers. The small sheets are my prayer sheets. I wrote down questions which I wanted God to answer and I prayed every day for the answers." He handed me a small stack of sheets and I could see questions on them and dates after each question.

"Why are these dates here, Rev. Clarence?   Are these the dates you started asking your questions?"

"No. Those dates are the dates that God answered my questions."

I could see that the questions were both of a personal nature as well as general questions about life and a couple of questions about the universe. "Are you telling me that you actually know the answer to global warming and the ozone layer problem?"

"Yes, but I'm not an astronomer or a physicist, so who would listen to me? We need to take better care of the environment, but a certain amount of global warming and ozone layer depletion is going to happen naturally, anyway. It's been happening for thousands of years in accordance with God's gradual creation. It has just accelerated within the last hundred years, because God is speeding up the pace of the creation. You, see, God will be introducing new life forms on Earth and the disappearance of the magnetic shield or ozone layer will allow more radiation on earth and it will change the genetic structure of some species as we now know them. They will become altered, changed in some way according to their striving here on Earth. The physical form is a mirror of the being's survival efforts and accomplishments. And weather is also changing. Global warming is a weather sign that we are making strides or improving in the love and fun areas of our development. Not all of us, but in general, we are improving in that aspect of our development."

"How do you know that?"

"I just told you, I ask God lots and lots of questions and God answers each and every one. Weather tells us how we are progressing and the state of our spiritual development. Cold and snowy places are places where people are not as hospitable, welcoming and softhearted and fun centered as, perhaps, a person from a tropical island. Rain means God is sad. Hurricanes and floods mean God is very angry with the people in the region, which is affected. It's all about our behavior and lifestyles. We follow man's patterns for success and happiness. God's rules usually have nothing to do with man's rules and customs, except to make God angry with us for following them. Have you ever wondered about major disasters which take many lives?"

"Yes."

"Well, many people lose faith when things like that happen and they wonder why God allowed such a huge tragedy to happen. When something like this happens, there is a great harvest of many souls who all have something in common. There are no coincidences that they all lust happened to perish together. Tragedies like the sinking of the Titanic, major plane crashes and such were in God's plans for those people. All of those people had reached a point in their lives where they needed to grow and develop in ways that staying in their present lives could not afford. It's about moving on and spiritual development."

"I see. Major tragedies are always devastating to those left behind."

"Yes, they are. This is one more reason why we need to listen to God. We miss essential guidance for our lives when we follow our authorities who may be passing on ancient lies and misconceptions, however well-intentioned they may be."

"How does God talk to you? Do you hear a booming voice from the sky talking to you?"

"No. Not at all."

"So, how does God communicate with you?"

"How did I ask God to communicate with me initially? I asked for signs, remember? God communicates with me through signs and through sleeping visions or dreams and sometimes through waking visions? My first prophecy that I was really aware of came through a dream. Some other people who are channels for God's healing do hear their angels or spirit assistants, but I prefer signs, dreams, visions and other ways of communicating with God."

"But science and psychology tell us that our dreams are our repressed wishes and unfulfilled fantasies and possibly eating too much before going to bed. Do you dispute that theory?"

"My dreams guide me and if others would examine the symbolism in their dreams, even the nightmares, they would find some guidance from their Creator. Why is it that people believe that the dreams of kings and pharaohs in the scriptures were divine revelations, but theirs don't mean anything. Why, even dogs, cats and other animals dream. It's a personal one-on-one way that God has of talking to each and every one of His creations, individually. We are taught through dreams. There's a lot we can learn from them about our lives and our very purpose on Earth."

"Rev. Clarence, do you believe we have a purpose here?"

"Yes. I know what I was sent back here to do. We can all find out our purpose just by praying and asking God and waiting for the answers to come. But, most people are not taught to do that; and, in fact, are warned against it. That's why we have a world full of *believers* and not *knowers*. There are no mysteries of life. God will tell anyone what life is all about, if they ask. Let me tell you about one of my church members who prayed to God to reveal to him his mission on this earth. This young man had a dream that he was a warrior in another life and that his country and religion taught him that it was honorable to deliberately give up his life in battle."

"Do you mean he was a suicide warrior?"

"Yes, he was. He was returned to earth plane after his death to learn how to love and protect his life above all else. We ask everyone except God what life is all about...philosophers, preachers, and teachers...anybody who claims to be an authority on life or at least some important aspect of it. Our so-called authorities know very little of the real purpose of life. They speak of love as the answer to all things, but love is not the only purpose for our lives...struggle and survival are paramount to our existence on Earth. God put us here to fight for our survival and to love. We are human, but we still have to abide by the laws of nature, which are God's laws, and the first law is that of survival. Food is first! The second law is preserving the species...mating and procreating. Procreate if you can, but no one is exempted from mating, even if your religion forbids it. Celibacy is man's way, not God's. God did not intend for sex to be solely for procreation; it is also for the expression of love between man and woman. We are supposed to mate until we leave this earth, even if we're 100 or so years old...if we're still capable. The game's not over 'til it's over. Normal sex between a man and a woman is not a 'dirty act'. It's a loving act that God intended to be enjoyable for us. If we can accomplish these two basics of survival without being subservient to any person or group, then we are on a good road to our heavenly goal of graduating from Earth and not having to return. Some people will have a hard time with that because many cultures teach subservience to a boss, commander, husband and so forth, but that kind behavior will earn you a round trip ticket back to Earth after you transition or die. Mates are supposed to be loving equal partners. We are supposed to be our own bosses, also. The only being we are supposed to be subservient to is God."

"When you said, we have to return, are you talking about reincarnation? Do you believe that?"

"I don't believe anything anymore. I am a seeker of truth and I ask God whatever I want to know. Yes, reincarnation is in the scriptures, also. They just don't interpret rebirth in that way, but that's exactly what it means. When we transition this life, many of us have not completed what God sent us to Earth to do, so we get another chance to try. We have had so many lives on this Earth, that we are about as old as dirt. Many of us cannot get into Heaven with the weaknesses that we have. God is not going to mess up Heaven by putting some of us in it. We have to come back and clean up our acts. I have a channeled sermon, which I delivered on that topic. I'll let you listen to it if you have a chance."

"I'd like that. Let's go back to what you said about survival. If we are not supposed to have bosses, how can we survive? All our economies are built upon the corporate structure or hierarchies. All military establishments are based upon chains of command. Are we to tear all that down and live in anarchy?"

"No. We are developing beings, my dear. We are still becoming. God does not expect us to develop overnight and become finished creations before it's time to be a finished product of The Living Creator. God wants us to work on our weaknesses, strengthen our weaknesses and become better and better with each incarnation. We are developing beings. We did not get this far overnight. We will reach our completion date at different times, depending upon when God made you and how fast you are trying to complete your mission. Some of us are newer creations and some of us are very, very old beings who have lived many lives here. We call some of our newer humans retarded but they are just younger than many of us, by many thousands of years. Some of them have just received higher body forms, up from lower primates. Like it or not, it's a fact of creation. We didn't spring up as the intelligent beings that we are overnight. Science bears witness to that fact. But, many people, blinded by their religious authorities, believe otherwise."

"Okay. Rev. Clarence, suppose we are evolving on Earth, just how many lives are we supposed to go through before we can enter Heaven and not return to Earth?"

"It's different with each person. That all depends on whether or not you have completed your mission. If you die before you have completed it, then you must come back. Your level of spiritual development, courageousness to stand up for what's right, mating, financial independence, love development...all of these things and more are what God judges us on when we cross over. If we are found wanting, then we must return . We get another chance to get it right. God has given us many chances to get it right, but we continue to listen to other authorities."

"I see. I guess each time a soul journeys back to Earth, he or she gets wiser and stronger. Is that right?"

"That's the general idea but some people don't make much progress because they choose pathways which take them backward instead of forward. One very important fact is that each time we have to come back, the world becomes more and more complex *and our lives become harder in many ways. I call it the 'tighten up'.* Think about it...God continues to make new life, but the old ones keep having to come back to Earth for following man's laws instead of God's laws...so, what do you have...a population problem. Earth is getting more crowded with each generation. Americans don't have this problem yet, but many countries struggle just to feed their people...food resources, energy resources...straight men...everything we all need to keep the species going will be in very short supply for the coming generations if we don't make some changes in our lives now."

"Whoa! I understand all of what you said except for 'straight men' . What do they have to do with the 'tighten up' and why do you call it that?"

"I call it the 'tighten up' because it's the most descriptive way I can convey the messages which God has given me about how God strengthens us. Imagine a body whose muscles are week and flaccid. If you are on an exercise machine, then the more weights you add to your load, the stronger, bigger and tighter your muscles will become. Well, life is kind of like that; the more challenging and difficult your journey, the stronger you will become. Ever heard the saying 'if it doesn't kill me it'll make me stronger'?"

"Yes, I have. But, what about straight men? What's that all about?"

"Two things ...men go to war and many are killed. That's one thing that diminishes the straight male population. Secondly, many women follow the weak customs of their societies or religions and they are subservient to men. Like I said before, subservience to anyone other than God is *not* God's way. It's man's way...one of those teachings that just got 'slipped' into some scriptures by only God knows who. Anyway, God returns these subservient women back to Earth to learn better ways...to become stronger human beings, self-assertive and independent. The way that God does this is to return them in the body type, which will help them to develop the strengths of character, which they need,...a male body. Remember, all reincarnations are correctional in nature. Each new life situation is designed to help the soul achieve strength and graduate from Earth, never to return. Men are treated and taught differently in most of our societies. So, these female souls in male bodies learn the strong behaviors taught to males. Does that make sense to you...do you understand that?"

"I understand, but why would God make them into men when they're women?"

"I just said, to help them grow...to strengthen them. Men learn different behaviors than women. And, on the other foot, men who are domineering and either verbally or physically abusive to women must return to Earth in the opposite body...a female form. Again, they must learn what it is to be in the other soul's 'shoes', so to speak."

"Rev. Clarence, are you saying that the dominator becomes dominated and the subservient become less subservient?"

"Yes. It's their karma. Some people call it retribution or payback but it's the same thing. I performed a past life retrieval, or past life regression, as some call it, for a young man once. We discovered that he had been a woman in a previous life and God returned him to Earth as a male to unlearn negative female behavior...subservient behavior. I tape record most of those sessions...I think I still have his. Would you like to listen to it?" (Please see Byron's story in Chapter 12.)

"Yes, I would... perhaps when we finish talking. While we're on the topic of homosexuality...we haven't called it that...but that's what you're describing...have you received any messages about the gay lifestyle? Does God approve of it or not?"

"Glad you asked. I wondered about that myself... so, I put that question down on one of my prayer sheets. The answer came to me in the form of a dream. In the dream, there were men and women in what looked like a gay bar, because the men were embracing other men and women were embracing other women. The bartenders... two of them...had on high-heeled shoes, but they were hairy-legged men. Three waitresses at the bar wore male attire, including pocket watches. At the stroke of twelve midnight, someone hollered 'change...change now!' and everyone got up and ran out of the bar as it went up in flames. I awakened from this dream, but it was still going on because while I was fully conscious, but with my eyes closed, I heard people screaming and crying and a chorus of voices singing a song I'd never herd before. It went something like this. (He sings) 'Sam Whisky, Sam whisky, is poison for your soul Sam Whiskey is a problem for your new life to behold. My men are like women, my women , like men. Sam Whiskey, Sam Whiskey, you know that's a sin.' I knew it was an angel chorus sent by God, because I have received messages from them before."

"Oh, my goodness. Your message will certainly not be well received by the gay community. They will think that you are homophobic and gay bashing!"

"I would hope not. I certainly don't fear them and I do not hate them. Their karmic load is difficult: they will long for what they cannot physically have. It's a spanking for their past life weaknesses related to learned gender behaviors. God does want them to interact physically and emotionally with the opposite body type. In other words, if they can't procreate doing what they do, then they are not supposed to do it. It's their debt to God and nobody's debt payment is fun. They certainly don't have to answer to me, but they will have to answer to God for their behavior if they are living the gay lifestyle. Like I said, God doesn't adhere to our politically correct rules."

"Whew! I cannot speak to that! Rev. Clarence, tell me about some of your other revelations."

"I would love to, my dear, but I'm running overtime now. I have some things to attend to. Can you come back another day?"

"Yes, I can. Thank you very much for your interview and for sharing your many spiritual experiences. I'll call you soon for another appointment."

[I returned to talk to Rev. Clarence on one more occasion . He allowed me to listen to and transcribe several tapes of past life regressions and I copied a tape of his sermon on the nature of the universe. The sermon follows this chapter. The past life regressions are in the section of this book on "ordinary people". In Chapter 11, are summations of more of Rev. Clarence's revelations.]

Chapter 10

Reverend Clarence's Channeled Messages

[Some psychics or mediums channel messages through a spirit guide or angel. Reverend Clarence explained that he does not channel through another entity because he is uncomfortable receiving messages through an intermediary with the knowledge that he has about spirit scam artist and their game of possession. He channels intuitively through God, directly. This is not to imply in any way that mediums who do channel through their spirit guides or angels are any less gifted or valid.]

"Today is Sunday, June 18, 1995 and I am channeling a message from God. Mankind has been evolving over hundreds of past centuries; and mankind will continue to evolve in the future. There are steps that we need to go through in order to evolve to the state of being that Our Creator intended. In other words, we are a model in the making and we are constantly undergoing changes, additions ... new additions to our minds and to our bodies to increase our abilities, to increase our stature and to increase our strengths; all of these strengths and abilities, when newly acquired by some people, often make them appear to others as geniuses or anomalies of some sort. Let it be known by all who hear these words that God is not about making geniuses just to stand out in societies or in the world. Geniuses are made because geniuses have earned their brainpower through efforts... efforts that have been going on for centuries. When we were all at the starting line, they (geniuses) shot out of the gates and they have been shooting out ever since. We are all reincarnated beings. We have not always been human beings. We have been other beings and if you want to know what your genealogical tree is like, you have to pray and ask God to take you way, way back... all the way back to the very beginning if you want to know all the beings you have been. You are a soul in transition. You are a soul, a creation of a mighty, creative, loving, kind, worrying, parental being who gave birth to us who created us, not as we are now but in a lower state initially. We have been evolving ever since: God has been working on us since the day we were created. We get new stuff (abilities and physical attributes) according to our deeds or efforts. New brain power according to our thought processes and our striving for excellence. If we do not strive for excellence we get some stuff (intelligence and physical attributes) taken back from us. Our mental abilities are decreased if we do not use our brains much; this should tell all of us that we should always use our mental abilities because we don't want any mental abilities taken away from us.

The way that we look represents the outcome of our past strivings... our past evolutionary histories. We are truly historical beings. God is still making us. We are still plotting our own course because we still have free will and we can do with our free will whatever we choose. If you choose to work hard, then those efforts will be rewarded. If you choose not to work at all, then those efforts will be punished. That's positive karma and negative karma. Now, if we choose to do just a little bit, that will also show up in our development. It will show up in the way that we look, in the way that we appear in the physical world. Shortness, tallness, blondness, darkness, lightness, colors of eyes... all these things and more show what our past efforts have been...what we have earned.

Now, let's go on to look at specific accomplishments. Worldliness.... people who are very knowledgeable about many racial groups and many ethnic groups are people who look at the world in its totality because we are a part of a larger whole. We are not just a slice off by itself. We are part of a big pie, so to speak and we shouldn't ignore or belittle any group because of their markings. We are all on a journey. We are all on a road. Some of us are ten miles down the road and some of us are one mile down the road but we're all going to end up at the same place so we should never ridicule or look at another person who is three or four miles down the road because we are fifteen or twenty miles down the road. We should never look at another person and laugh or ridicule or feel superior to them because they're going to get there and we're moving on. We're all moving on down the same road, down the same evolutionary road. Some are faster than others because of their strivings... because of their efforts; but, we're all going to get there at different times but we're all going to get there.

Heaven has a place for us. God has prepared a place for all of us in Heaven. Heaven is up, not down. God has prepared a place for us and there are many levels of Heaven. You get rewarded with a level of Heaven according to what you have done with your life. If you haven't done enough to get into any level of Heaven, then you must do what? You have to come back and be born again... go through another lifetime and learn some more, strive some more. The levels of heaven are where we go directly after we die and we are judged by God at that time. You receive a review of your life, the good, the bad and the ugly. There are many levels of heaven and you will be rewarded the grandest, highest level of Heaven if you are a revolutionary. If you have changed Earth from bad to good, if you have done something bold brave wonderful, if you have changed things for the better on this earth then you will go to the highest level of Heaven. Just remember that Heaven is a place where we do go. Whether you believe it or not, it is there. You don't have to believe it for it to be true. It's there... surprise, surprise! After you come out of your body...looky, looky, what's all this? The white light that many people see after so-called near death experiences is the light coming from the first astral plane of Heaven. They've got to go to the first astral plane first to get debriefed. After that, when they get debriefed, they get taught, they go to school. They learn what life is really all about, not some of the garbage they learn in some of the institutions on Earth that really don't know the whole truth. They learn ; they get debriefed on some of our societies' garbage they have been taught such as sex roles, such as what you're supposed to act like, such as what your life' s supposed to be like. Garbage! Lots of it! They have to be retaught. Some go into an area that is taught by some religions is purgatory which means it is sort of a holding area. They're not in jail. They can do work and have fun and converse and stuff like that, but they learn; they are also told that they have to come back. So, they are there for a while until they have to come back. When it's time for them to be reborn, God takes them and puts them in a new baby's body and they are reborn to new parents, maybe a new country and maybe a new sex depending upon their strivings in their other life or lives.

Now, as to the matter of race, races are different because they are our markings. In the lower animal kingdom, you have zebras, lions, tigers, elephants and other animals with various markings. They have stripes, spots and they are different colors. Birds are probably the most diverse when it comes to colors. We, humans, are different colors; we range in color from very dark brown skin tones to very pale pink skin tones. We all have markings and our markings tell about our past incarnations. We have different shades of natural hair color. Most brown shades of people have black to brown shades of hair. Most pink shade of people have blond, red and lighter shades of brown hair. Between the brown and pink shades of people are all the in-between shades of people and various textures of hair. All of these things tell us about our past development and our many incarnations. Our markings tell of our striving in our struggle to survive, how we have lived, how we have loved how we have tried, how hard we have tried and how much we have accomplished. Your accomplishments show up in the physical form of your body .All races have very intelligent people as well as mentally challenged people. Our markings are not about intelligence per se, but rather, about our survival habits and patterns.

Never, ever, ever let it be said that one race is above another. We all have our faults and our strong points. Every race has faults and every race has their strong points. There has never been, nor will there ever be perfect people on earth. Let me say it again: no one who has ever walked this Earth has been perfect and no one who will ever walk this Earth will be perfect. They wouldn't be on earth. Any being in a physical form is imperfect, has faults, needs work, and is under construction and rehabilitation by The Creator. Never let it be said that one race is greater than or better than another. It is just not so. We have our faults and we have our weaknesses. Our markings tell about our faults and our weaknesses. We are a walking talking story-book of our past, of our strengths and of our weaknesses. All we need do is look at somebody to tell what their history has been, if you know God's body language.* Some of those traits are still present; some of them have been improved upon. It's up to be individual as to whether or not he or she has improved on those weak points and kept those strong points. That is the end of this spiritual channeling. Thank you God for your loving guidance."

Chapter 11

Reverend Clarence's Revelations

[The following revelations are from conversations with Reverend Clarence and from the prayer lists that he used. As he explained in his chapter, he asks questions of God in prayer - any question about which he wants knowledge or guidance. Reverend Clarence recorded the dates on which he asked God questions, the dates God answered him and the types of answers God gave him. These prayer lists extended over a period of approximately twenty years. God gave him some answers the same day he asked them; other response times took from a week to several years. God did not always give him all aspects of an answer to a question at once; but, sometimes God did answer all aspects of a question at once.

God answered Reverend Clarence in various ways that included: dreams, wide-awake visions, open and guided meditation messages, and signs of various kinds. The God Force gave two of these revelations through a student participant during guided meditation. Reverend Clarence teaches that anyone can receive answers from God by simply asking God questions about life through prayer.]

The Creation

Our Creator has always existed. No one created God. In the beginning, God desired a world, so God created the universe and the life within it. All life was in spirit form and in heaven; we were all young angels who were very obedient to God. Then, there came a time when God's creations began to follow each other and listen to the stronger ones of their kind. We began to make our leaders our gods and God became angry. Our Creator punished those who followed their fellow beings instead of God by putting them inside flesh. This was our *original sin*. There are no innocents on earth. Even a newborn comes into this plane with negative karma to work on.

The Master Plan & the Struggle for Survival

God enclosed our spirit forms into flesh bodies and put us into a physical environment. Having a physical form means that we require food to stay alive. The covenant that God made with us was that every living being must follow God *only* in their struggle for survival. So that we can return to a unity with God, we must depend upon The Creator to guide us to what we need to stay alive. The two basic tasks of survival by God's rules are: (1) being independent in our quest for food (money in man's case); that is, having no master or boss to depend upon for your survival and (2) mating with the opposite sex (and propagating your species, if able). No one is exempted from these rules. In order to return to our heavenly home and not be returned (reincarnated), each person or creature must abide by these rules. Food is the priority; staying alive is the most important imperative.

Life on earth is a constant, never-ending contest or struggle for survival. All life, plants and animals, must seek food. Our Maker talks to every life form created. God gave each life the freedom to make choices, which I will call our *free will.* God grants your talents, abilities or punishments based upon how you exercise your free will. Our physical forms mirror our achievements or lack of them. (See section on *God's Languages*, this chapter.)

Humankind is an integral part of the food chain. While we no longer hunt food for our survival, we, nevertheless eat meats and plants bred and cultivated for our consumption. We must eat God's other creations . . . other life forms to survive. While we consider ourselves at the top of the food chain, we also are prey for other life forms that eat us. Microorganisms and other parasites feed upon our bodies just as we feed upon plants and other animal species. We are the meal of choice for many invasive life forms, some of which kill us when we cannot withstand their onslaught. They feed on our muscles, our blood cells and any other parts of our bodies that they choose to use for their food.

Nature vs. God

The laws of nature are God's laws. God combined the same chemical elements in different ways and in different proportions to create the universe. God made everything from the same building units: whether in spirit form or flesh form, the same basic components are found in every aspect of the universe. The same physical principles hold true from the smallest entity to the largest; e.g., electrons revolve around the center of the atom just as the planets revolve around the Sun. Scientists have long pondered the differences between magnetism and gravity. Messages from God to me have indicated that they are varying aspects of the same phenomenon. The same cohesive force throughout the universe operates at both micro (magnetism) and macro (gravity) levels. There are no unchanging or immutable laws of the universe. In fact, God is still creating the universe, gradually. This is not an unplanned universe; there is order and God is always in control.

God is still creating the universe, gradually, creating newer models and eliminating older, less efficient and less intelligent models of many species. The evolution of species is a reality.

We must grow and develop with each lifetime to reach our ultimate goal, which is to return to our heavenly home and never have to live in an earthly environment again. However, we must gain strength of character and spiritual fortitude on earth. (See "God's Moral Laws", this chapter.)   To grow and develop according to God's specifications, we must return to earth as often as it takes to achieve our goals. Reincarnation, then, is a necessary part of our existence. (See "Death and Immortality", this chapter.) Our spiritual and intellectual growth is mirrored by our physical appearance. Look at early humans and modern humans: we are more attractive. (See "God's Languages", this chapter.) The facts that there are child prodigies and super smart babies who are born knowing how to play complex instruments such as the piano at an early age or who can solve high level mathematical problems attests to the intellectual growth of our species. It also confirms that souls are reincarnated with some of the same talents and abilities, which they possessed in a previous life. Other manifestations of our growth confirm the fact that we are evolving or gradually being created on this planet: modern humans can now draw in perspective, whereas the cave dweller could not; also, the age of puberty is getting younger. God has increased the pace of our development. In other words, God has sped up the clock on our development.

In God's master plan, if we have not achieved certain developmental goals by a specific time, through exercising our free will, then God's will supersedes our will. Our Creator, then, makes us reach certain goals at specific times, according to The Master Plan.

Black Holes

God created many galaxies like earth's galaxy. God created some of them early, in the beginning of the universe. Some are newer than others. God is orderly and God neatly cleans up the God old debris from burned out stellar bodies and space "junk" by depositing them in trash cans. These are the black holes of the universe. The Master Builder created them for waste materials.

About God

Who is God and What is God Like?

God is the Creator of all life and the universe. God is good. No one created God. As hard as this may be for some to fathom, God is the one constant in the universe . . . perfect, eternal and infinite. God has always existed. There was no beginning of God and there will be no end of God. The circle is the closest figure that I can use to describe the existence of God, no beginning and no ending.

Our Creator is our loving parent. We would be correct to think of God as both father *and* mother although God is sexless, neither male nor female. Our Maker loves us all, unconditionally: the good and the bad children. But, like any parent who is both tough and loving, God does punish us to correct our behavior. God is the "Great Spanker" who runs an orderly universe, although, at times, humankind disrupts things so terribly that everything seems chaotic.

God is all-powerful, all-seeing and all-knowing. Our Maker is the Omnipotent Protector of all creatures. We are always under God's protective, ever vigilant eyes. Protection by God is what God promised us in the beginning of our existence. We all have it. It may seem that when we are undergoing severe karmic punishment that God has forsaken us, but God has not done that. Our protection is everlasting and eternal. You would be correct to compare this with a parent who loves and protects a child, and also spanks her for bad behavior. How are we to learn our lessons in life if there are no consequences for our behavior?

God is our judge and our jury. Many of us judge the behavior of others by standards and rules set my man. These rules or laws are not always following divine law. When we choose to obey the laws of our society, we must always ask God if the laws and customs are in keeping with Divine Laws. To avoid negative karma or punishment, we should always obey Divine Laws, even if they are in conflict with human laws and cultural traditions. Some religious teachings may not be in accord with true Divine Law. It is up to us, individually, to seek answers by asking God questions in prayer.

God instilled all of the personality characteristics in us that Our Creator possesses. God is playful, funny, happy, sad, angry, thoughtful, decisive and loving. God laughs at us when we are silly or humorous. God gets angry and upset with us for following wrong or harmful beliefs and pathways. It saddens God when we take a downward course with our lives and when we choose to do evil or harmful things to others. God cries. God loves. God spanks.

Where is God?

God is here on earth with us always. God is *everywhere* on earth, simultaneously. Our Maker is in heaven and throughout the vast, infinite universe, when God is here with us.   The God Force knows what is going on in the universe, everywhere, at all times. As we continue to evolve on this planet, so too, will our concept of God evolve . . . from looking like a man (or human) to a greater all-encompassing concept of a single supreme being: one who is not confined to place or time and exists beyond our little planet, Earth. God, The Great Spirit, is present in every place that God made.

Is There an Evil Power or Devil?

There is only *one* supreme being. Whether you call God Allah, Jehovah, Yahweh, or another name, there is only one supreme being. The Creator does not share power with anyone, past or present. There is no other God. No Satan or devil has power over God's children or God's universe. This, then, begs the question, "Why does evil exist?" Evil exists in many forms, but never in a god of evil. Evil exists because God gave all life free will, freedom to choose their course. Some chose lazy, slovenly ways. Some chose short cuts to survival or very bad, evil ways to survive. Life as we know it is infinitely better than it has been in our past epochs on this planet. God constantly revises and improves us according to our survival habits. (See section on "Heaven, Hell and Evil , and Reincarnation", this chapter.)

Evil will one day not exist because we are getting better and we will continue to improve according to God's master plan. Spiritually blind or evil ways will no longer be an attractive choice when our eyes are opened to the truth of life and God.

God Does Not Make Mistakes

Everyone on earth has a disability, seen or unseen. We are here because of our weaknesses and character flaws that we must correct before entering permanently into heaven's gates. Some of us are born with obvious physical afflictions that tell about our past deeds and how we need to develop in this lifetime. God does not make mistakes. A child born with defects is not a mistake; it is a negative karmic debt that the child must work on in earth's environment. Physical and mental flaws are never mistakes. They are God's tools for redemption. They correct our past behavior. Accidents and illnesses that maim are also negative karma for some behavior. Following laws that you *believe* are God's laws, but, in fact, are socially sanctioned laws created by man or by a religious institution may harm you.

Miracles

God still performs miracles, large and small. *Divine Magic* are the words that describe a miracle. When the odds are against you, and the world just seems to loom dark and ugly, a prayer in time may be your saving grace. Our Creator performs miracles to let us know that God is Lord, all-powerful and in charge of everyone and everything. Anything is possible and *nothing* is impossible for God. God maintains order and uniformity in the universe to let us know that there is a grand design and that there is continuity; but, the miracles that God performs let us know that God is real. So-called scientific truths are within God's domain to change at will; we are, after all, creations of The Divine Spirit who rules over all things and always has the last word on everything. A miracle is God's way of telling us, "I Love you".

God's Moral Laws

Self-Sacrifice and Self-Denial

The greatest sin is self-sacrifice. Self-denial is second. God created life for pleasure and joy as well as for work and love. We must seek our joy and pleasure and do good works. Many of earth's religions teach that self-sacrifice is a virtue and seeking pleasure is a sin. They also teach that God wishes us to deny ourselves for others and punish ourselves for a cause. Nothing could be further from the *truth*. God's first law is *survival by God's rules*. Self-sacrifice negates God's first law for us: a self-sacrificer is not trying to survive by God's rules, but instead, he or she is following the teachings of his or her society or religion. Celibacy, self-imposed starvation and denying yourself the pleasures and joys of life are all forms of self-sacrifice. Self-imposed denial of our basic drives and needs is not God's way. Humankind suffers because of our original sin of turning from God and following our fellow beings. Our belief that self-sacrifice is a virtue is just one more instance of us following each other.

Some religions in the form of killing animals and drinking their blood require sacrifice and eating their flesh as a part of their ceremonies. Other religions require sacrifice as a symbolic part of their ceremonies, substituting more acceptable, innocuous food and drink rather than actual blood and flesh. Either way, sacrificial ceremonies are not God's way. God never requires us to sacrifice anything to worship or be cleansed.

Suicide

One aspect of self-sacrifice is suicide. People who commit suicide receive the same sentence after death as those who have committed heinous, sinful acts toward others. God confines them to earth's plane for a time before they have to be reincarnated. God judges, in a negative light, those who aid others in committing suicide under the guise of medical beneficence. Suffering is a part of our earthly existence. Only God can set aside a sentence, lift a penalty or forgive a debt. God is Our Judge.

Following Others

The original sin of following our fellow beings and not following God was what caused us to inherit the earth and get kicked out of heaven. Our societies mirror this behavior in our social and governmental structures. Leaders of every type tell us how to live, love, feel, dress and how to do just about everything. God wants us to march to the beat of our own drummer. However, most of us conform to whatever we are taught and do not question those teachings. Following leaders blindly is a human weakness that will continue to earn us a place on earth instead of a place in heaven.

Gambling

Gambling is a waste of time, energy and hard-earned money. God's *law of survival* means that we must *earn* what we get by using our wits; this does not include outwitting our poker partners. Gambling destroys your creative efforts to fend for yourself. The lure of "something for nothing" is enticing for millions of people. However, even if you win money at gambling, The Great Score Keeper (God) will take it back from you, in some way, inevitably. There are, however, special times when God repays people for kindnesses or deeds done from the heart. The lucky people who seem to always win are the "givers", always doing for others, donating time, money, and whatever they have to share with their fellow man. Big lottery winners should know that when they cease to be on their mission of survival because of big ticket winnings, they stand a serious chance of dying because they will have aborted their earthly mission. Others win some and lose some; but, they always remain in square one, financially. So, what have they gained besides a thrilling time at the slot machines, blackjack table or whatever form of gambling they prefer? Gambling is a weakness that destroys human initiative, thrift and work ethics. Societies that depend on gambling for their economic support are destined to destroy the moral fabric that weaves together their communities. Organized crime, prostitution, loan sharks, suicides, and other undesirable people, conditions and acts follow in the wake of legalized and illegal gambling.

There is no such thing as chance or odds. Man has tried to make the occurrence of certain events conform to scientific laws and even created mathematical models that are supposed to say how many times in a certain number of times something will happen. If God wants something to happen, the chances are 1:1. If God does not want it to happen, the chances are 0:0. Chance is a fallacy.

Stealing

God's rules for getting what you need for survival do not include theft or stealing. Stealing is a sin and God will punish those who do. However, if someone needs to steal to stay alive, then that person should do whatever is necessary for his survival, even if it means stealing food, clothing or occupying a shelter. God is the judge of whether the person *needed* to steal. Although God will punish that person for doing the deed, theft is the lesser of the two evils: stealing or sacrificing one's life. Stealing, however, should never become a lifestyle.

Killing

Killing for food consumption is good. Killing to protect yourself and your family is good. Killing for revenge, lust, jealousy, and for any reasons other than food and protection are sins.

Judging

Those who judge need to know that God holds them responsible for their judgments of others. Every society has some system of punishing those who offend the laws of that society. Judges, juries and elders, in some societies, are always called upon to dispense justice to the alleged offenders of man's laws. Case by case, those who judge should confer with their maker on the laws and justice that they dispense. Man's justice or punishment cannot begin to compare with the punishment that God metes out to individuals; often, man's laws and God's laws are in direct opposition to each other. If you are a judge or even a jury member, stay as close as you possibly can to God's guiding hand because you will be held responsible by God for those whom you judge and punish. Divine law still rules. God is our Judge.

Honesty and Respect

We owe honesty and respect to God, Our Creator. God knows what is in our hearts and minds, and God knows our every deed. We cannot deceive or fool Our Maker. If you respect your fellow man and your leaders more than God, you are in trouble. If you respect the wealthy, the famous and the affluent more than God, you are in trouble. People who give respect and worshipful admiration to expensive, desirable material possessions are in trouble. You cannot deceive God with tithing and donations and still live a divided life: on one hand pandering to sinful worldly desires and on the other hand paying lip service to God. Do not even *try* to play God for a fool.

Those who deliver God's word to others should know that all the rituals and ornate raiment and magnificent edifices in the world cannot deceive The Creator from knowing whether you are an honest person whose desire is truly to serve God. There are those in the pulpit who mislead people and are dishonest in God's judgment. Rest assured that no one but The Almighty can dispense *real penance* to those who offend.

Social Security and Retirement

Many employment systems around the world are based on many years of service that, when fulfilled, lead to a blissful retirement and a permanent pension or financial support of some kind. In the eyes of God, the entire employment system is humankind's way of surviving and gaining dominance over the other animal species, which we had to fight and conquer. The group survival which humans have developed has kept us in this dominant status for many thousands of centuries. The human system of survival is interdependent and more efficient than any other species' systems or means of survival. Interdependence or division of tasks that gained us dominance will be the same interdependence that will spell out our doom, if we do not make some immediate changes.

God's first survival law tells us that we must fight to live. Fighting could be catching your food, hunting for it, or in modern humans, working for it. The way that we choose to earn determines many things about our present lives, and our future lives if we must return to earth. Earth life is a battleground and we must struggle for survival, whether we like it or not. Retirement means that we are stopping our work, leaving the battle, so to speak. Unless you are ill or otherwise incapacitated, this is a big "no-no" in God's judgment. So often, after people retire, they die soon after that. I once read an article about big lottery winners who stopped working and growing who died. The author cited a pattern of such deaths among these winners. Well, the truth about the matter is this: if you stop working on your primary mission here, then God will assume that you are through. Rather than let you stay here and waste your time doing nothing, God will call you back home to heaven and then send you back to earth to a new life that will help you reach your spiritual goals.

Social Security in the United States and other similar systems elsewhere in the world do not meet God's approval. Social Security is a form of man protecting man. The system is like an illegal pyramid money scam in many ways: those who come into the system at the bottom (younger workers) support those who have reached the top (retirees). When it first began, it seemed like a good idea to most people. There were more young people than old people and the system worked. However, people are living much longer lives than when Social Security started after the Great Depression. Now, the pyramid is becoming inverted, with fewer young workers putting money into the system to support the many older workers or retirees who are pulling money out of the system. Social Security will not last, no matter how government tries to patch it. We may not see its end in our lifetime, but other means of helping retirees survive need to be put into place for the future. People need to return to the days when they thought they could take care of themselves and they did! Social Security and the system of doling out money to people weaken a society; dependency makes many people stagnate and it destroys their creative, pioneering spirit and their ability to do for self. If you must depend on Social Security to live, then do so. Try to use your free time to establish a business or some enterprise that uses your talents and abilities to the fullest. Do as much as you can whenever you can. Self-reliance is a good thing.

Marriage and Adultery

Many centuries before churches were established, people chose mates and had families without marrying. God's spiritual laws of mating existed long before the tribal elders sanctioned monogamy or polygamy as a God-given law. Marriage laws were made by men to keep order in the group, to decide proper lines of inheritance, and to have a guaranteed sexual partner. It is anyone's guess as to when churches got into the mating game. Mating exerts a powerful control over peoples lives; sometimes, even more so than the food struggle for survival. God's messages to me regarding marriage are that God wants us to mate and love our mate(s). God has neither sanctioned nor condemned marriage as a way of life. God does condemn prescribed sex roles, which stunt our development because of our marriage vows. Marriage is man's law, not God's law. Adultery is a manmade condition of breaking the marriage law by having sex with another partner. Some religions that allow polygamous marriages allow multiple sex partners within marriage. Other religions do not; one man, one woman is all that they will allow and these religious sanctions are usually supported by civil law. God frowns upon female subservience and male dominance; subjugation of one sex's God - given rights are punished by Our Maker. We belong to Our Creator, and *no other*. Adultery is not a sin. God wants us to love whom we want, without being promiscuous. We do not belong to each other.

If you are in a marriage that is good for the spiritual and intellectual development of both partners and where both partners have equal rights in the marriage, that is good. If, however, you are putting pressure on your mate to be subservient to you, then, that is wrong and punishable by Our Maker.

Contrary to what some religions might teach you, divorce is an option out of a bad marriage that has God's approval. God certainly does not expect you to sacrifice your life to miserable, harmful conditions for the rest of your life. *God does not even want us to consider entering into irreversible situations.* Suppose you married young and made a bad choice. Do you really think that God would condemn you to that mistake for the rest of your life? Our Maker wants happiness for her children, not long-term misery. Marriage is a civil contract: nothing more, nothing less. If you decide to marry, make sure you have an escape clause in your contract in case you need it.

Pets and House Plants

All life forms have a mission. Each life must support itself according to God's survival laws. Pets that do not have a job and house plants that we must constantly tend are, in fact, surviving by the good will of their caretakers. Their survival skills become weakened by becoming dependent upon us for their care. Although we love them, we harm them by keeping them on our welfare system. God recycles or reincarnates them to help them overcome weaknesses fostered by human kindness.

Believe it or not, pets can fend for themselves if we allow them to do so. If they were free to live their lives among their species instead of with humans, the natural laws of God would balance the overpopulation of these pets. Neutering them would no longer be an option. We do great harm to them when we take away their God-given right to reproduce. Find your pet a job if you can: let them visit nursing homes; teach them to guard your home or do any useful thing that they can do to earn their keep. Please do not abandon your pets if you cannot find a job for them. Just love and care for them as you have always done. Always let love guide you concerning caring for your pets and house plants.

Truth vs. Philosophy

Yes, there are absolutes. There are absolute truths that anyone can know simply by asking God. Our philosophers and great thinkers have never fathomed the breadth and depth of God's divine mission for us on Earth. A philosophy of life is no more than a serious thinker's best guess about a problem, issue or some aspect of life, based on some logic and insight. However, our most cherished philosophies are not worth the paper on which they are printed if they are *contrary to the absolute truths.* Some philosophers have come close to the truth and some have missed it by a mile. But, why guess about life when you can *know* about it, simply by asking God?

Life-Giving Technologies

The modern technologies of cloning, in-vitro fertilization, embryo implants, stem-cell research and other current and future means of producing and preserving life do have God's approval. Infertility will continue to be a problem for humans as we alter our ways of farming, producing meat, fish and poultry due to increases in population. Agribusiness and the mass production of animals for food go hand-in hand with pollution of the environment; chemical cocktails added to the soil to grow crops and animal waste that runs off in our waterways harm us. Human overpopulation will continue to erode the quality of life on Earth for all species. Food sources that contain unnatural biotins affect reproduction and other health issues. Polluted air in most of our cities and highly chemically processed water that many of us drink will, eventually, affect our health, including our reproductive systems. So, alternate means of reproduction, in God's judgment are justified. However, God would like us to take better care of earth and our environment so that these technologies will not be needed.

Prayer

Is Prayer Necessary?

God is always helping and guiding us whether we pray or not. Prayer to God is you asking your parent for special favors, healing, guidance or whatever you want to talk about with God. Our Creator wants us to open a talk with God. Although God knows what we need and want,

God wants us to ask for what we want. I have asked for
money, special abilities, and even love. I have received all
that I have asked from The God Force. God wants us to be
supplicants and ask for knowledge about life, our purpose
here, and any other areas of life with which we need help.
We should not demand that God do anything as I have seen
some do. Disrespect for God and taking God's name in vain
is rampant throughout the world. How many of you swear
by God's name or exclaim,"Oh, my God!" for whatever reason? Prayer is necessary to lift us up and move us on when
we are in a bad place. Intervention is God's specialty.

Right and Wrong Prayers

There is no special way to pray. You may kneel, sit,
stand or lie prostrate in prayer. You may even walk, drive,
run or swim while praying. God will always hear you no
matter what you are doing. There is no special time of the
day or week when we should pray. God is a "24/7" Universal Creative Power: Our Maker will listen to you twenty-four
hours a day, seven days a week. God neither sleeps nor
goes off duty.
It is important to those of little faith to know that
you do not need faith for God to answer your prayers. Even
if you have no faith at all, God will answer you. Your faith
will blossom as your prayers are answered and your knowledge of God increases.
Right prayers are those during which you ask God to
help you accomplish your goals, teach you, guide you, tell
you why you are here, help you with a problem, heal you or
whatever you want to talk to God about. Your Creator is
your best friend, chief advocate and doting parent.
Wrong prayers are those that ask God to make
someone else do something or stop doing something. Although what we may wish for this person is very good, it
would be a mistake on our part to ask God to make them do
what we want them to do. Why? Because, to do so would
be taking away the free will of that individual. God gave everyone and everything free will. God will not take it away, no
matter what our choices are and where they will lead us.
We should always pray for spiritual understanding. Our religions are many and varied; their teachings, while well in-

tentioned, may just lead us in a direction other than the direction that God wants us to go. God always answers prayer, even if the answer is "No!" If you just accept everything, which your religion teaches you, without asking God the truth of matters, you put yourself in a spiritually precarious position. Misinformation and outright lies are contained within most of the world's religions and holy literature. They were written my man and humans are prone to make mistakes. Also, from what we know about clairaudience and possession, some messengers were tricked by spirit con artists. You must ask your Creator for truth to stay on the safe side. *God will answer everyone. You do not need a mediator between you and God.*

Spiritual Meditation vs. Prayer

Prayer is you talking to God. Spiritual meditation is one way that God answers you back. One should never be substituted for the other. Both prayer and spiritual meditation serve separate purposes. Hand-in hand, they provide for the enlightenment and uplifting of individuals who regularly use them as tools for living. People can progress to heights undreamed of if they follow the messages of God contained in meditative states. These messages, when combined with your prayers, complete the conversational circle with The God Force.

Karma

Pay Back, Luck and Destiny

Simply explained, karma is just pay back for your deeds. Karma is like a boomerang: when you throw it out, it will return to you. Karma is either good or bad. Can you imagine a world where there is no karma? I cannot. It would be incredibly boring. *Nothing* would happen, good or bad. It would be a plain, humdrum, existence. God gave us free will and told us to choose well; because, whatever we choose will have a consequence. *Your luck is truly what you make it. All in life is fair.*

Your destiny is yours to choose, so it behooves all of us to make wise and good choices, or we will suffer the consequences. Now, many would dispute the validity of that statement, because they think that they have made good choices and they are still suffering. Ask yourself and ask God this question: "Did I follow your laws and rules, God, or did I follow the sanctions of the world and my society?" In all cases of this nature, the person has followed some authority other than God in planning and making decisions for his life. God's laws do not always agree with human values and teachings. *Your choices always decide your good luck or bad luck.* Your individual destiny operates within the greater destiny of God's plans. God sets the boundaries within which you must live. Within those boundaries, you may choose whatever you like, but you must move forward with your life and in your development. God's will always supersedes your will. If, by a certain time, we have not progressed to the next stage of God's blueprint, for the universe, then God's will takes over and the pace of our progress is stepped up to a faster level. No one will take over God's world and destroy it. God will not allow it. However, God will continue to build certain places in the universe when they are needed for the Master Plan to move forward and trash them when they are no longer needed. What, exactly does that mean? It means that life has existed in other places besides Earth. It means that there are, indeed, rounds or stages of creation and each stage advances you in your overall development; i.e., you are improved with each round.

Beating the Odds

We are not all born at the same starting line: some are born rich; some are born poor; and some are born somewhere in between. Your individual accumulated karma earns you your lot in life. If you have not been given a perfect body, a functional, nurturing family, or if you simply lack much of what most people have, then your challenges for growth in your life are great. Your *attitude* regarding your lot in life can make you or break you. Looking at what others have and comparing yourself to them is a sure way to fail. Wallowing in self-pity will not help you achieve your goals. You can succeed by facing and overcoming your disabilities or challenges. Your struggle for survival may be harder than the struggles of those who have a different birthright, but you were given a set of circumstances that can mold you in ways that The Creator intended. If you must cross the proverbial "burning sands" before you reach the "cool oasis", then that is what you must do; any actions counter to that would take you on a downward course, possibly more dire than your original set of circumstances. To beat the odds of a hard or dreadful life, you must maintain a positive attitude and listen to the little voice inside you that says, "Yes, I can."

Diseases

Many microorganisms use us for their survival and some of them make us sick. We are their food. They are also evolving: they mate and borrow strains of DNA from each other to create new hybrid diseases, which are stronger than the parents. Some of them are so strong that our medicines cannot kill them. The struggle between humans and diseases is long and dreadful. Diseases have wiped out whole populations of humans and other species throughout history. There have been plagues throughout history: the black plague, measles, scarlet fever, tuberculosis, and AIDS, to name a few. We should fight diseases when they emerge and keep them in check. It will be difficult because there will always be new diseases that will replace those we have conquered. Why? It is because God will always correct our negative behavior through diseases, accidents and other special ways. The part of the body that the illness affects is one of God's ways of telling us what we need to correct (See section on *body language* in this chapter.)

Children who are born with diseases and birth defects have to overcome a negative karma from their past life or lives. No one is new on earth. We are all old souls; some of us are further along in our development than others.

Group Disasters

Disasters that affect several people or many people simultaneously mean that all of those people have the same karma. Disasters such as the sinking of the Titanic, hurricanes that kill or injure many have a common denominator. They all have similar lifestyles and values that are in some ways displeasing to God. A "group harvest" of souls or a "group spanking" of the injured is God's way of correcting many at once.

Plants also have group karma. When there are wildfires and many acres of forest are devastated, those plants that God destroyed all had similar karma. (See the section on plants, this chapter.)

Death and Immortality

The Astral Body

Your soul or spirit is encased in flesh. It is the real you and it never dies. The physical form to which we are chemically and electromagnetically bonded is destructible. The astral body, which is sometimes called the soul, spirit or ghost is immortal. We are all immortal beings, from the lowest life form to the highest.

In humans, we are attached to the physical body by an electromagnetic elongated mass of light-type particles called the *silver cord* It is like the umbilical cord that attaches a baby to its mother. When the astral body leaves the physical body, it leaves at a point at the back of the head where the hindbrain is located. For those of you who have traveled outside your physical body, you always remain attached to it by the silver cord.

A phenomenon known as the *phantom limb* or *ghost limb* is experienced by those who have lost their legs or arms, but who still feel their presence although they are missing. The astral body is always intact. Those who experience the phantom limb feel the limbs of their immortal astral body extended past where their physical limb would be.

Astral Physics

Astral physics is that particular branch of future physics that no one has explored. It explains a lot about our parallel spirit world and the various levels of heaven. Let me explain, that we do not need to know complex physics formulas, nor do we need to be rocket scientists to understand astral physics. Simply put, astral physics is the future branch of physics that explains the unseen spirit world that interacts with the visible, dense matter of our earthly existence. The Law of Ascending Vibrations explains it all. All matter is in constant motion at the atomic level, even a rock that is lying seemingly immobile is in constant motion. The Law of Ascending Vibrations states that everything in our world has a certain color, smell, taste, sound and temperature because of the rate at which the atoms that comprise it are moving. In other words, white light is broken into the colors of the rainbow; each color has a corresponding frequency of atomic movement. The same principle applies to sounds, odors, tastes, textures and temperatures. Matter that vibrates or moves at a high velocity cannot always be detected by our senses.

One analogy that I like to use is that of a fan that is turning at a very high rate of speed. If you look at it, as it increases in velocity, its blades seem to disappear to our eyes; we can see through the fan. This principle explains why we cannot see those in the spirit world. Their astral bodies are made of atomic particles that are moving at a higher rate of speed than our eyes can detect. Their voices are at a higher frequency than our ears can register. We can neither hear nor see them, except in special circumstances, which only God controls, when we are allowed a door into their world. These special circumstances include: the death of a loved one, when someone has a brief encounter with them after their death, and upon seeking help from the spirit world. Seeking spirit help may or may not be a brief encounter and it can be either positive or extremely negative and brutal. (See Rev. Clarence's interview that includes an explanation of spirit possession.)

The astral body or soul body vibrates at a higher rate of speed when it is outside our flesh. Much like x-rays, it can pass through denser materials like doors and brick walls. The Law of Ascending Vibrations also extends up through the planes of heaven. There are many levels or planes of heaven that correspond to a specific vibration. Lower planes have low vibrations and higher planes increase in vibrations as they go up. Going from one plane to another is easy for those who live on the highest plane; it is impossible for those who live on earth plane except for special emissaries or some mediums. People who live on the planes between the lowest and the highest can travel only to the planes that are beneath their plane. God does not allow them to travel to the planes above them. They, in fact, cannot get up to them because the layers of air as you go up form strong barriers of electromagnetic energy. This electromagnetic energy vibrates at increasingly higher rates of speed, too impenetrable for them to pass through. The atmosphere at each astral plane forms an electromagnetically charged belt at the upper limits. The atoms of air at each level move at increasingly faster rates of speed the higher up you go; these belts become increasingly stronger as you go up to the higher planes. No one on an astral plane can penetrate a belt that divides her plane from a higher one, but she can penetrate or travel down to a lower plane. God attunes our astral bodies to whichever plane we inhabit.

The lifestyle on each plane is better the higher up you go. God assigns you to a plane according to your deeds and accomplishments on earth. God assigns you to the highest plane if you have been a revolutionary and by changed earth for the better in some way. Earth is the lowest plane and it is also hell for those in spirit form who have done evil deeds or committed suicide. They must serve a sentence of earth confinement for a time that God designates before God makes them return to earth. They will be reincarnated because they cannot go onto an astral plane having the weaknesses and evil ways that they have. The God Force will not allow them to destroy the harmony of any level of heaven. Their behavior must be corrected on earth plane.

Mash-Ons

If you have ever wondered how we look after death, God gave me the answer. You look like yourself. Your flesh form is an outward copy of your astral form. You look just like the body that you have vacated. You may also wonder how you stay together since your flesh form is no longer present to hold your soul or astral body. God has provided us with a clear see-through outer covering, which God gives us upon death that keeps us in the same physical appearance as our last body. It is called a *mash-on*. The mash-on is a wrap or shroud for the astral body. Your loved ones who have already crossed over to the astral side will know you and you will know them. If you must return to earth or be reincarnated, God takes off your mash-on and gives you a new flesh body that looks different from your old one. How it looks depends on your particular karma. (See the section, "Body Language", this chapter.)

Reincarnation vs. Transmigration

Reincarnation is the rebirth of a person into another human body. The person must go through the womb and make another entry onto earth plane to work on specific karmic debts or faults and to enjoy life on this plane. How much you enjoy life depends on your accumulated negative and positive karma. Hopefully, your positives will outweigh your negatives.

The generally accepted definition of transmigration of the soul is that it passes at death from one body or being into another. The belief is that the being, which it passes into, could be a lower animal or another human. Transmigration simply *does not happen, ever.* God does not allow a being at death to continue in that manner. More important, God does not allow a being at death to snatch the body of any of God's other children (lower animals). The only time that another being can inhabit another person's body is during a case of "possession". (See Rev. Clarence's interview.)

Premature Deaths

People often wonder why babies, young children, teenagers and others who seem too young to die often are taken from their friends and families at such an early age. We must remember that each soul is sent here on a specific mission. When that person has completed his mission, then God takes them back to their heavenly home. Some examples of missions are: learning how to love; learning tolerance; learning generosity; learning how to love self first and foremost; learning how to fight for life; learning how to have fun; learning to enjoy sex the way that God intended (between men and women) and improving our performance in that area; and various other missions. Baby deaths may be the hardest to understand because they have not had much of a chance to do anything. The baby's karma is tied to her previous life in a way such that she enters and exits life, perhaps on the same day. "Why?"' you may ask. "A baby has not lived yet. She has not done anything!" That statement is nowhere near the truth. The truth is that we are all reborn souls on earth. No one in a human body is new to earth. The trauma of reentry and immediate exit from life is known and felt on an emotional level by the baby. The baby may have the karma of taking a life before birth or aiding in that event, so his or her karma is painful; but, the pain of doing that to another soul must be atoned for. What about the parents? On some level, their feelings about losing a newborn are deep and troubling. The parents have similar karma. Perhaps they aborted a child when they were younger. When they really wanted a child, God repaid them by taking that new life, just as they denied life to the aborted child. Some pregnancies come to early termination; the reason is specific to those involved. Generally, the reason is for repayment of a negative karmic debt for something done at another time, perhaps during another lifetime. It should behoove us to ask The Creator about our karma. God will certainly let us know.

Out-of-Body Experiences

Out-of-body experiences (OBEs) may be described as the soul or astral body leaving the physical body and traveling or hovering nearby while the person is still living. OBEs happen for various reasons. God takes a person out of the body to teach that person that there is a higher life awaiting them and to show them some aspect of that life. The individuals who experience OBEs, however, are usually at a spiritual level where they are either seeking a oneness with God or trying to search for truth and meaning in life. Other circumstances include that person acting in a healing capacity or being in danger of losing his life or freedom.

Not only do people who are highly spiritually developed experience OBEs, but those who have near-death experiences often report on their experiences of seeing a white light, going through a tunnel and seeing loved ones who have passed on before them.

Out-of -body experiences are proof to those who have experienced them that we are, indeed, immortal beings. God promised us everlasting life and God has given it to us. No one is dead and gone. We absolutely survive death.

Heaven, Hell and Reincarnation

Heaven

As I mentioned previously, there are levels of heaven called the astral planes. They are like the floors in a high rise building with the penthouse being the top level. There is a heavy side of our world and a light side. We, on earth, are on the heavy side: the side of dense, slow matter. The astral planes are the light, ethereal side where we go after death. God decides which level we graduate to after death, based on our deeds on earth. You might want to think of your deeds, survival efforts and spiritual growth on earth as money banked in heaven, because you will be repaid for everything, measure for measure.

If you have not grown enough or survived by God's laws, then you will go to the first astral plane of heaven that is known by some religions as purgatory. It is a holding place for those who must return to earth to grow and develop further before going onto the higher astral planes. Much of what goes on at the first astral plane level is educational. On astral plane number one, people go to school to learn about God's laws and to unlearn lies that they have been taught about God. People must be reeducated because many religions have taught them harmful, erroneous ways. Blind faith in a religion gets many good people sent back to earth. We must ask God for knowledge to make certain we are receiving the correct spiritual guidance. The Universal Creative Power will answer anyone who seeks God directly.

People do not readily remember their past lives when they return because some aspects of those lives might prevent them from functioning well in their new lives. Suppose, for instance you were the victim of torture and murder. All

178 The Unknown Connection

those memories would have a negative impact upon your present life and might stifle your development in your present life. God will tell us much relevant and helpful information about our past lives through dreams, meditation messages and also hypnosis. All we need do is pray and ask for that information. Ask God why you were returned to earth and what is your mission.

Some people retain memories of some parts of their past lives, especially if they possess a talent or special ability. God allows them to keep those qualities and ,hopefully, they will add to them in a future life. Child prodigies who play the piano at a very early age or who can perform complex mathematical computations are just two examples of this.

The highest astral plane is where revolutionaries go. They have earned the highest plane for their bravery and courage in changing negative things about earth, enlightening the world, moving mountains that could not be moved before and for being ground breakers for good causes and affecting the lives of many people in a good way.

People who live on the astral planes carry on lives that include music, games and lots of fun, love and many other aspects of spirit life that the angels would call "superb living". Of course, the lifestyle gets better and better as you go up to the higher astral planes.

We sometimes call people who live on the astral planes "angels" or "spirit guides". They are people like us who have not had to return to earth. They have banked enough good deeds, lived by God's survival rules and grown to an adequate spiritual level, thus earning a level of heaven.

Hell and Evil

Evil is the turning away from things godly and the adoption of things, which are against the fulfillment of God's grand design for us and the universe. Evil acts are sinful, diabolical, heinous and wicked and are usually planned with selfish, power-hungry motives in mind. Evil acts can also be unplanned deeds committed by those whose spiritual development is horribly flawed. Evil beings are those who deliberately harm others for pleasure, lust, hatred, anger, jealousy or for any negative reason. Evil exists because God gave all life free will. Some of us chose the righteous pathway and some of us chose the path of least resistance. God made laws for us to follow and those who know the laws, yet turn against them, are evil, not just disobedient.

Earth is hell. It is more hellish for some than for others. It is the bottom plane where we come to earn our places in heaven. Being on the heavy side means that you must eat, reproduce, and generally support a flesh body that requires much upkeep to stay alive. How you choose to do this determines everything about your next place in the universe and your karma in the present. Those in spirit form who inhabit earth in an invisible world that is parallel to ours are in the worst trouble with God. The punishment of having to inhabit earth without a body is a punishment of deprivation. They are either evil or they have committed suicide. They must serve a sentence for a time decided by God. The evil discarnates want the physical pleasures of eating, drinking, sex and other pleasures, which require a body. They long for things that they cannot have. The evil spirits can see old friends and relatives but they cannot talk to them. Some of them choose to enter a game of possession for another person's body while they serve their time. Only under special circumstances is this allowed. (See Rev. Clarence's interview.) These spirit beings, while *knowing* about God and life, because *God has already judged and sentenced them,* consciously choose to disobey God's will. They curse God and try to thwart God's plans for the universe. They try to mislead those in the spirit world who might repent and do good works; and they lie to those in the carnate world who can hear them. They can choose to work off their bad karma in good ways if they want. Those who choose to do good works can improve their lot in life for their next incarnation. Those who continue to do evil have a heavy karmic debt to pay in their next lives: some will be born into horrible circumstances; some will be born with multiple disabilities, but not everyone with a disability has been evil.

Those who play around with Ouija boards, séances and summoning spirit guides should beware. Evil spirits come to those who summon spirits. The harm that can come from those dangerous pursuits is sometimes irre-versible. If knowledge is what you are after, then, ask God for it.

There is no such thing as *privacy* in the universe. God knows and sees everything. The evil beings roaming earth see us and can read our thought forms (visible projec-tions of our thoughts) because their bodies are like x-rays and they can penetrate brick walls. They can enter any place they want. Even our angels whom God has assigned to us regularly come down to earth plane to visit with us and perform various missions of God for us.

Reincarnation

There is no such thing as *eternal damnation.* God forgives us our sins, corrects our behavior through tough love punishment and gives us as many chances as we need to get it right. God is about growth and development, not sadistic, perpetual suffering. Upon death, God judges us immediately so that we can continue to progress on the other side and not have to wait or stagnate.   Reincarnation is a tool that God uses to help us improve from one lifetime to another.   We *absolutely cannot choose what happens to us after death.* We *must* return to earth if God judges us de-ficient in areas that require earth plane to work on the weaknesses. I have often heard some spiritually gifted peo-ple say that they chose to come here to help others. Well, let me tell you, no one on earth is perfect and everybody here is here to work on one or more deficiencies. What angel would choose to suffer in hell rather than enjoy heaven? To do so would be a violation of one of God's survival laws: self-sacrifice. No angel or spirit helper would do it.

Earth is like a hospital or school. All are healing and learning here and we should pray to know our mission on earth. We must strive to use our minds as much as we pos-sibly can because God's law of "Use and Disuse" operates to improve or decrease our thinking abilities. What people do with their minds, even after death determines their fu-ture I.Q. Even if you have a job which requires physical la-bor, try to use your mind outside of work. Read, write, work puzzles, or play chess; do anything that challenges your mind and will make you grow in intellect. Not using your mind much will make your intellect reverse itself. *God may even punish you with a brain disease because of regressing in your mental development.*

God reincarnates some men as women and some women as men. Their karmic debt to God is that they have followed the societal sex roles dutifully, to a fault. When following rigid sex roles stunts spiritual growth, God will repay and correct that person's behavior by returning them in the body of the opposite sex. Although God made homosexuals, they are not supposed to make love to the same sex; it is a heavy, negative karma or punishment that they must work on. To do so will earn them much more negative karma and, perhaps, another *worse* reincarnation back to earth plane after death.

Some of us return as a person of a different race and/or gender. Racial karmas are similar to the karmas of our fellow animals in the wild, which have distinctive markings. They are related to our survival patterns and lifestyle. (See the section on "God's Languages", this chapter.) God places us in the body that will help us to grow in the manner that God knows we need to grow.

If you want enlightenment about your mission on Earth, pray and ask God who you were in your previous life and what God sent you back here to work on. Several people whom I know have done so and have had dreams about past lives. (See Rev. Clarence's interview.) Our names tell us a lot about our past lives. Names have meanings and are tied to occupations, places or some aspect of our earthly existence.

God also reincarnates lower animals. Reincarnation is always in one direction: humans do not regress to lower animal forms and lower animal forms are steadily progressing to more intelligent forms. Souls always move upward on the tree of life, not backward. When species become extinct, it is time for them to disappear and time for those souls to move up higher in the hierarchy of intelligent life forms. Their old model is no longer needed for their growth and God advances them to a higher level in the game of life, much like increasingly harder levels of a video game. Some of us are several millions of years old and some of us are just a few million years old, new to the human species. Retarded people are newer than most other humans. We must care for them, teach them and help them to grow to their full potential in their lifetime. God increases their abilities and intellect according to how well they use their minds for survival. Extinction is a positive thing. It means we are moving onward and upward according to God's blueprint for the universe.

We must each clean up our act, so to speak, before we can reach heaven and *stay;* we must correct our faults and follow only God's guidance. If we have gigantic ears that listen to every so-called authority on life and God, we always run the risk of being misguided by a kind, well-intentioned soul. God, ultimately, holds *you* responsible for what you learn and believe about life and God. Pray and ask God questions.

Lifestyles and Values

When You Have a Boss, You are Violating God's First Law: Survival

All modern, technologically advanced cultures encourage people to work in the corporate structure, whether it is in a physical labor job or a high-level executive position. The "system" as it is informally termed trains us from early childhood to get a good education so that we may become employable. Most of us go through life with this goal in mind for our work life. Some go on to higher education after high school and become proficient in some field so that they may become employed by a corporation or other employer. Rarely are we told or even encouraged to become entrepreneurs, because the "system" needs certain groups of workers in certain numbers to survive. So, the "hot ticket" jobs of today become what many people strive for. Some fields quickly become glutted with an overabundance of people in the field who cannot get jobs because they are filled. When this happens, people either become discouraged and accept lower- level, lesser paying positions or they go back to school and retool for other types of jobs to fit some employer's definition of a necessary worker. Hopefully, they will still be needed by the time their education is finished.

God's first law of survival requires that we become self-supporting, without the "boss" figure being a part of our employment; in other words, the way of the entrepreneur is God's way. Anytime you have a boss over you, you have a "master". The only master in your life should be The Creator, no one else. We should all strive for independence, even while working for the "system". If you do not, there will be karmic penalties to pay *and* you will have to return to earth plane instead of living on one of the astral planes after death.

The professional gambler is not considered an entrepreneur by God. All they do is play games of chance, which is not an entrepreneurial enterprise, but a folly of gigantic proportions. Living on undeserved profit is one sure ticket back to earth plane after death. God always repays whether it is with rewards or punishments. When we lose things or when valuables are stolen from us, Our Creator is balancing the scales of justice for our past deeds and profits which were in violation of God's rules for our survival. **We will be punished for ill-gotten gain, whether in this life or another.**

Male and Female Roles

Of all the lies told in *most holy books,* the stories of man's righteous domination of women have been most damaging and damning to females. It, truly, has harmed both sexes in ways that get them repeatedly sent back to earth plane. God intended for men and women to be lovers, best friends, helpmates to each other, parents and equal partners. The God Force did not tell women to be subservient to men. That lie, alone, has caused many women to return to earth in the opposite sex's body to unlearn weak ways of behavior sanctioned for females to follow. Conversely, many men who have developed into domineering, controlling persons in the lives of women are sent back in female bodies to help them unlearn those negative behaviors. Many men cling tenaciously to these stories or myths in their religions that they use as justification for abusing and mistreating females who do not obey them. In India women may be killed if they dishonor the husband; it is permitted, without punishment. In most Islamic countries, women cannot show their bodies or faces; they must be under the protection of a male at all times.

As the sexual behavior between men and women deviates from the behavior approved by The Creator, there will be increases in sexually transmitted diseases, some of which have yet to be created by God. Sexually transmitted diseases are one of the Universal Creative Power's ways of correcting our sexual behavior. AIDS, one of the most devastating STD's to come along in many years first started in the homosexual community, then spread to the heterosexual community in almost every country on the globe. God is "spanking" those who deviate from the sexual rules of conduct that God intended for us to live by. Females "giving in" to males just to please them is also not God's way. The subservience factor should never come into play in a sexual encounter. Positive, healthy factors in lovemaking include: mutual respect, love or liking and passion. Negative, sick factors in lovemaking include: domination, subservience, hurting, sinful lusts and unnatural acts.

Marriage and Adultery

One of my revelations that will probably surprise most people is that of marriage. Marriage is man's law. Before there were churches way back at the dawn of our history, there were men and women who mated, took care of families and survived. As the societies of humans proliferated and worship ceremonies evolved into formal churches, the community's elders sanctioned marriage as a way of deciding which males were responsible for which offspring. It was also a means of passing inheritances from one generation to another. Since most marriages were performed in churches the next logical segue was for the elders to indicate that God sanctioned marriage as a lifestyle and next, that it was God's law. Nothing could be further from the truth. Civil laws became intertwined with church laws and no one questioned the keepers of the faith, for fear of social ostracism.

Our Maker gave us all free will and God wants us to love our mate (or mates if we live in a polygamous society). However, God will not punish someone if she has more than one love partner whom she sincerely cares about. Loving more than one is not a sin. Insecurity, fear of competition and genuine affection for one's mate are what keep the institution of marriage alive. Sometimes marriages of the heart are more valid than some legal marriage in which couples stay together for all the wrong reasons that include: financial security, prestige, children and guaranteed sex.

Since marriage is not God's law, where does that leave the notion of adultery? Adultery is a manmade fabrication, as well. We each have the God-given free will to love whomever we please. We belong to God, not to each other. God did not give us to our partners and say that we will be punished if we ever leave that person or love another. That whole ludicrous concept is what has gotten many men and women sent back to earth plane. It is a form of self-sacrifice to stay with someone whom you do not wish to be with. Societal and religious sanctions against this type of behavior keep many men and women in marriages, which retard their spiritual development.

The Family

Western culture, during the last century or more, has seen the end of the extended family that included parents, grandparents, aunts, uncles and other assorted relatives. The family that most of us consider a family today is the nuclear family, which consists of the husband, wife and their child(ren).

God's will is that we live together in groups larger than the nuclear family. Tribal cultures are more advanced, socially, than cultures that isolate people and where the norm is the nuclear family. While Western culture has the technological edge over most of the other worlds, the West has a sicker social climate. In large cities, it is common for there to be an average of one and one half persons per household. The problems of loneliness, depression, latchkey children, teenage pregnancies, parental abuse, child abuse, and other ills are as a direct result of a disconnection between individuals and their social group. *Anomie* is the term that social scientists use to describe individuals who feel that they do not belong, fit in or have any vested interest in the society in which they live. Anomie produces people whose character is warped and twisted. Pedophiles, rapists, thrill killers and others of that ilk grew up in homes where there was a schism between them and their primary caregiver(s), or where there was outright abuse by them. In large family groupings, there is more help available for those troubled ones who might respond to the love of another family member; also, the watchful eyes of others would serve as a protective presence from some abuses.

In the West, people can live in a neighborhood for years and not know their next door neighbor. Many neighborhoods have ceased to be neighborhoods, they are just collections of houses with people in them who do not know each other. Many of our elderly live alone and die alone. Many of us have material wealth, but we are spiritually and socially needy.

God would like for the family to become the *superfamily* . The superfamily consists of large groups of people living together which include parents, grandparents, children, other relatives and even friends. The commune of the sixties and seventies was a good start. Responsibilities for parenting would not be solely on the shoulders of one or two parents, although they are the only ones legally and spiritually responsible for their offspring. Ideally, this new tribal community could better nurture people to become the best people they can be. Groups of about fifty people that I will call a *community pod* could interact with other community pods to form a network of people caring for people. They could live together in condominiums or cooperatives, with each pod having a community dining area, play area, study area and any other community areas that they want. People who feel pressured to work two and three jobs to support the lifestyle of the "Joneses" might take a second look at their stressful, heart attack and stroke-prone lives if they changed their lifestyle to include more people.

Children and Abortion

Of all the debates about children in the twentieth and twenty-first centuries, none has infuriated so many as the issue of abortion. Underlying the debate are religious views on when a fetus becomes a viable life as opposed to the medical views. The medical view does not consider a fetus a person, but a mass of stem cells and blood vessels.

How does God judge abortion?   God advocates a woman's right to choose abortion or birthing a child. Although this position may seem contradictory to most religious views, you must remember that God detests anyone taking away another's free will or right to choose. God judges abortion as a wrong choice and God will punish a woman for making that choice. However, God wants her to be free to decide in all areas of her life, including giving birth. Negative karma for abortion may take many forms: some women may not be able to bear another child; some may be aborted themselves when they need to return to earth; some may have to wait a long time before another reincarnation; or, she may have still births. There are any number of ways that God can repay women who make the wrong choice.

Messages from God to me have informed me that any life begun in the womb is a viable life from the onset. The spirit or soul, which God assigns to inhabit that body regularly visits the mother and goes into the womb readying himself for reentry. After the third month, the person assigned to that mother stays in the baby's body until birth. During this time, God cleanses some memories from the last life that might interfere with his functioning in the next lifetime. God shows him dreams about his past life and his future life to inform him about where he will go and how he is to interact in his world. It is a teaching mechanism, which God affords every human life. Babies sometimes see angels after they are born because the "other side" is still working with them and they will have these spirit helpers or angels throughout their journey on Earth.

Leaders and Followers

Our original sin that got us sent to earth plane was following leaders who told us what God wants us to do, instead of listening to God. (See section on "The Creation", this chapter.) We are a planet of conformists. Conformity to established norms permeates every society on earth. Those who challenge the norm run the risk of being ostracized, or worse. Humans, like many other species are herd animals. And, we *are* animals in the truest sense of the word. We are highest on the food chain, but we still belong to the animal kingdom. Leaders such as Adolf Hitler, Mussolini and others throughout history could not have come to power if the herd instinct to blindly follow the strong ones in the pack were not present in us. We need to assess our leaders more thoroughly and try to see through their political rhetoric. Past performance and their current agendas are always some good starts when choosing leaders. More important, their ties to various corporate and political groups should be examined. This should be a good indicator of where they will lead us.

What does God want for our leaders? God wants us to spread the power, so that we do not place so much power in the hands of one individual. God favors either dual heads of state, where two people have equal power or a triumvirate, a leadership of three equal individuals. The Eternal One favors any political system that allows people to use their God-given freedoms such as freedom of speech, freedom of religion and other freedoms. Repressive governments that deny people their freedoms will engender God's wrath and they will pay a heavy debt to Our Maker for their spiritual offenses. God favors democracy over dictatorships, and socialism or capitalism over communism.

Education

Any educational system that allows children to progress at their own rates of speed and intelligence levels is good in God's judgment. However, most educational systems retard fast learners by keeping them back in grades until their peers have caught up or finished the grade. Teachers should consider the individual learning styles of children, because everyone does not learn in the same way. However, this is not done in most school systems, to the detriment of many children who are sometimes labeled "learning disabled" if they learn differently. A total revamping of many educational systems is needed just to make the curriculum relevant to today's world. Basic, useful, life skills courses are needed to teach people two of the most important jobs they will have: parenting and managing money. Some systems do teach for today's world, but many are still stuck in the past. Colleges and Universities are advised to devise a system by which fast-track learners can follow an accelerated curriculum and finish early instead of the traditional four or five years.

Heroes and Role Models

Sports are for fun; life is for real. Some of the highest paid people in the world are sports and entertainment figures. Many people hold sports figures and entertainers to a higher standard than ordinary people because they look up to them as leaders and role models. Most cultures elevate these stars to the level of icons and some people worship at their altars.   Some entertainers and sports figures do much to uplift our spirits and inspire us and we do admire and even love them; but, our values are misplaced when it comes to whom we call heroes or role models. Real heroes are those who place their lives on the line every day such as police officers, firefighters and soldiers. Real role models are people who get paid very little for, perhaps, the most important job in the world: passing knowledge on to the next generation. These heroes are our teachers, professors, mothers, fathers, brothers, sisters and other mentors who teach and care for those young people. Other real heroes are the leaders who have fought for our freedoms and martyred themselves in the process. God wants us to get our values straight about who and what are important in life. Our priorities are upside down and backward.

Old Art and Stuff

We overvalue our old art, artists, objects and furnishings? Why? The older an object is, the more money it will bring at an auction or estate sale. People with the means to do so spend millions on old art of so-called masters, who, though deceased still live on through their works. How misplaced are our values when an old painting, sculpture or ancient artifact can fetch the price of a college education for three or four hundred people? Many people of means are philanthropic, but many are not. Some would rather flaunt a Flaubert than find an altruistic cause to support.

Living with a Blueprint

God wants each of us to know why we are here and what we must accomplish before we can go back to our heavenly home and stay. Living without a plan for your life is like trying to build a house without a blueprint. Your windows may be where your door should be and your ceiling where your floor should be. People who live recklessly or aimlessly have no plan. Even if you do have a plan, make sure that your plan is correct for your particular karma. Pray and ask God about your mission here. Ask God to give you the courage you need to live your life as you should, not as others think you should.

Religions

Beliefs vs. Knowledge

Religious indoctrination sets limits on our spiritual knowledge. Religious information is passed on from century to century without questioning the validity of it, no matter how much of it has to be interpreted by scholars on religion. There are many religions in the world, each telling us that they have the answers and other religions are wrong. God is the only one who can tell us which religions have the truth and which religions do not. The truth of the matter is that most religions have some truth; some have more of it than others; and some have it upside down and backward. There is a gap between religious dogmas and God's real truth, for all religions. People must pray to The Creator, individually and collectively for truth. Our Creator will tell you anything you wish to know about yourself, life, God, nature, science, love, sex...anything, except snooping into someone's business.

Sadly, we on Earth are followers and we have been misled, spiritually. God has let me know that some writers of holy literature, who are called prophets or disciples, were misled and lied to by those in the spirit world who were evil. They were scammed by some of the most evil, relentless and cunning confidence artists in the spirit world. What we have in many of our holy books is a mixture of lies with truth. Intermingling fiction with fact is sometimes more palatable that the harsh truth of our existence. Some writers were clairaudient, but for reasons known to God, their spiritual intentions became diverted and God allowed the evil ones to speak to them. What they brought upon themselves was a pack of lying pretenders who said they were messengers of God, sent to teach and guide them. Some stories are actual historical facts, but some teachings are not from God. We must pray and ask God which stories and teachings are true and which are not. I have done so. One story I can tell you actually happened is the story of Noah's Ark.

Sexual Misconceptions

God created the sex drive and a way to reproduce in all living things. Sex and sex role behavior is tainted in most religious literature, partly because of cultural customs and traditions and partly because of a weakness of many males, the desire to dominate the female. The larger part of the misconception was put into place by the evil spirit confidence artists. They wanted to stop God's universe from actualizing, so they plotted to get people to stop reproducing. If people stopped reproducing, then there would be no world for God to rule, they surmised. They taught the religious leaders who talked with them that sex was dirty and bestial; they told these religious leaders that sex was a base instinct of lower animals.

The first shackles on human sexuality came from religions. Purity was interpreted as virginity, not for men, but for women. Female virginity was considered a holy state for a female. Mary, the mother of Jesus, was said to be a virgin, as were most other females in history on spiritual missions. Women in service to God were either celibate or virginal. Even the Roman Empire had its vestal virgins. God has told me that things did not happen with Mary in that manner; in other words, she conceived and gave birth in the way that every other woman on earth does, by having sex. God does not impregnate women like the Greek and Roman gods, Zeus and Jupiter, in mythological accounts of their frolicking with beautiful maidens and producing half-human, half-god offspring. This notion of "purity" and "impurity" as it relates to our sexuality is a retardant to our complete development on Earth. Some religious orders are forbidden to do the "dirty deed" because of these early religious lies and misconceptions about sexuality. Celibacy is a form of self-denial, denial of a God-given drive. God does not like for us to deny the instincts and drives that God created in us.

When sexuality is allowed its normal outlet, a sexually healthy person thrives and perhaps reproduces with a loving mate. When the normal channels for sexual expression are cut off, cultures where this happens produce individuals who prey upon others in twisted, sexually sick ways. Suppression of the normal sexual drive causes it to resurface in deviant ways. The suppression of a wonderful, natural drive will reap the punishment of God, not the praise. After all, God created sex for us to enjoy and also reproduce. Promiscuity, of course, is not a good thing. Sexual freedom is what God wants for all adults who can perform, sexually. However, sexually transmitted diseases (STDs) and other medical conditions which affect the sex organs are one of God's ways of punishing us for our negative sexual (or asexual) behavior. You should always pray and ask God what you need to correct if you have an STD or other sex- related medical condition. Sex is abused, misused and grossly misunderstood by many on earth. If you have problems in this area, seek spiritual as well as psychological help.

Religious Institutions and Politics

Religious institutions are political and economic entities; sometimes they are more political and economic than religious. A hierarchy of power exists in most religions, which like most corporate structures, have governing boards and rules to follow in carrying out their duties. They, like any corporation, must thrive to stay alive. Money is the ultimate goal for any organization, religious or other, which seeks to stay afloat, economically. Power struggles in churches are as common as power struggles in the corporate world. There are winners and losers, as well.

Many churches allow the political issues of the day to influence their religious teachings. More specifically, throughout history, the practice of homosexuality was interpreted by most religions as a sin. When it comes to politics and money, some churches have decided to ignore their own gospels and sanction the practice, and also perform same-sex marriages. Heavy lobbying by the gay rights community has succeeded in changing religious doctrine in some churches. Formerly, they could not change hundreds of years of religious doctrine, so why not take it out of the religious arena and make it a human rights issue? If they can bend hundreds of years of church doctrine to fit their agenda, will other disparaged groups try this tactic? It seems to have worked. Politics, money and religion are strange bedfellows, but they seem to forge a symbiotic relationship when economically advantageous for all concerned parties.

Should You Go to Church or Not?

Going to church is a matter of choice for each person. If you prefer to worship with a group, then, that is what you may do. If, however, you prefer a quieter, intimate time with God, then prayer and meditation may be your best form of worship. Whether you are a member of an orthodox church or an earth religion that brings worship back to a natural setting, you should have the highest, spiritual intentions and desires. Whatever your form of worship, God will see and hear you and know what is in your heart.

You should always question religious authority. Take your questions to a higher authority than the church and your holy books: take them to God in prayer.

The Biggest Lies Ever Told on God

There are many caveats for the pupil who is learning *any* religion. Some teachings may be true; some may be half-truths and some are outright lies. Eleven of the worst lies taught by major religions, which will not be specified, are as follows:

1) **You should love your enemies and turn the other cheek**. God wants no such alliance between you and your enemies. In a world of survival, you cannot adopt this attitude unless you want to lose or perish. Suppose soldiers took this attitude; what would happen to them? God wants us to fight in this struggle for survival.

2) **God sends people to earth to save us.** God's angels or emissaries are the only ones whom God sends to Earth to help us; they are in spirit form and they go back to their astral plane when they are finished with their assignment; we may never actually *see* them. Anyone in a physical body who says God sent him to save us is misguided. He is here for his own karmic journey. He has his own debts to pay. The notion of us needing to be *saved* from eternal damnation is a fallacy. God promised us everlasting life. No one is going to suffer *forever.* We have debts to pay and we must suffer through conditions that will help us reach the state where we can return to our heavenly home for good. We have nothing to be *saved from, except ourselves and making unwise choices in life.*

3) **God *needs* us to help with Our Creator's divine plans for the universe**. God wants us to help *ourselves. God does not need to enlist our aid for anything.* God does, however, allow and appreciate our help. There are due dates on God's calendar for changes to occur in the universe, but God does not need us to improve earth. God does allow us to help speed up these changes by working for God as a *revolutionary volunteer.* In other words, if certain changes have not happened by a certain date, God's will supersedes our will. Then, God causes events to happen that changes in our lives, in keeping with the *Divine Blueprint.* As with many board games that we play, there are always exceptions to the rule: there are usually spoilers or catalysts. *There are no spoilers to overpower God's will, but a revolutionary volunteer may act as a catalyst and move God's Divine Blueprint forward sooner than the deadline.* Anyone with a sincere desire to serve God can be a revolutionary volunteer. God loves for us to help. Some people claim to be "called" by God. God does, indeed, call some to serve; but, all have the right of refusal. Remember, God gave us all free will. If you have not been "called" and you want to volunteer to serve God in any way you can, just pray and ask God if you may help. I already know what the answer will be. *Then, let God guide you in your service. Turn off the voices of the naysayers and so-called authorities and listen to God.*

4) **You must go to church to be saved**. You do not have to join a congregation to worship God. Everyone is already *saved* because God promised everyone immortality and we have it, no matter what. Put God in your heart and your head and pray for guidance. Ask God questions. Who would you rather get *the word* from: God or a secondhand source? God will talk to anyone who asks for knowledge. God is The Boss. The Boss has an open door policy: God will communicate with you anytime. If you let a mediator tell you that you *have to come through him*, then who's the fool? You do not *need* to go through others to speak to Our Creator, but if you do, you may risk being misguided. Do not be afraid to speak directly to God. God is your loving parent and wants with all His Heart to bring you back home.

5) **God made woman to be man's helpmate**. Our Creator made man and woman to be coequals and loving partners. During our early prehistorical evolution on earth, in exercising our free will and adapting to our environment, women and men divided their labor. Women agreed to the role of the nurturer/hearth keeper. Men agreed to other forms of labor and hunting and to also support the woman and children if there were any. Naturally, the person who provides the food holds the upper hand over the other person. Female subservience had its early roots in prehistory when the role of hunter/gatherer was agreed to by men and nurturer/homemaker was agreed to by women. God is our master and God does not want us to be subservient to *anyone else*.

6) **We were made in God's image**. If we were made in God's image, we would be spread out like jam, all over the universe. God is both formless and present everywhere in the universe at the same instant of time. What we do not fully comprehend, we bring down to our level of understanding. So, we anthropomorphogized God. God is no more like a man , than God is like a lion or any of God's other creations. This statement is also born of the *hubris in man. We are probably the most arrogant species God ever created.*

7) **God gave us dominion over other animals**. In the struggle for survival, God's rule states that the fittest will survive. During the time of prehistory when humans did not populate earth, the dinosaurs and other reptiles had

dominion over earth. The dawn of our birth found us not quite in charge of things the way we are now. It took humankind's collective struggles to gain dominion over other life forms. We *earned dominion through our survival efforts*.

8) **Marriage is God's law**. There are no marriages made in heaven. Part of our struggle for survival involves competing for a mate. Marriage is not God's law; it is man's law. People mated before churches even existed. You are compatible with more than one person. God gave us free will to choose for ourselves. God does not arrange marriages; but, God may introduce you to someone who may be a good mate for you. The God Force does act as "Cupid" sometimes, but you are not obligated to stay with that person for life if you do not wish to do so.

9) **God has *chosen* people whom God favors above all others**. Our Creator loves all of us, unconditionally. God loves the sick, the poor, the tired, the downtrodden, the rich and famous, and even the evil beings because we are all God's children. *God does not approve of all of our behaviors and God will correct us with accidents, illnesses and other negative situational karmas, but God loves us all, without favoring one race, ethnicity or gender more than another*. God never, ever gave one group the right to rule over another, enslave another, or have any sort of dominance over another group of people. Our flagrant, evil, power-mongering ways lead us to these false conclusions.

10) **God wants us to avenge his honor and harm people who offend God**. Vengeance and retribution should always be God's domain, exclusively. Man has no right to seek revenge and punish those whom they consider wrongful in God's eyes. They will be judged harshly for trying to usurp the power that belongs to only God.

11) **Only the Good Die Young.** God brings people back home whenever there is a need or when they have completed their missions. On an individual basis only, young people, old people or a person of any age dies because of their developmental status, which could be very good or very bad. God is our judge. Some young people who are sinful and incorrigible die every day. The good and the not so good die young. The good news is that everyone gets another "shot" at returning to Earth if God judges that is what they need.

Mystic Places

There are places around the world known as *mystic places*. These places have an atmosphere of spirituality about them. People who go to them often come back with a renewed sense of their spiritual mission and they are empowered to move in different self-affirming directions in their lives. You may or may not visit one of these places. However, you may create a mystic place right in your own home or apartment. Just designate an area, a closet, space under a stairway or any place where you can sit, kneel or stand to pray and meditate. Bring to this space whatever is sacred to you, such as: scriptures, candles or religious objects. Arrange them in your sacred place. Plan to go to your mystic place at least once a day. I guarantee you, your life will change and you will see things in a different and more enlightened way.

In today's world many people are lost in a spiritual sense and they are tired of being dictated to by religious authorities. These people often leave the church and turn to promiscuous sex, drugs and alcohol for solace, or become atheists. These people need more from religions than religions can give them. They are usually highly intelligent and refuse to believe the conflicted stories in some holy books and the illogical conclusions drawn by some religious scholars. To those people, those who need more than *beliefs,* I challenge you to pray and ask The Creator questions about your life and your mission. Get on your pathway back to your heavenly home. Seek truth and you will be given it; but, seek it directly from God.

God's Languages

God Speaks Directly to Everyone

God not only speaks through prophets and chosen ones; God also speaks directly to each being that God created. Parents and others in charge of us as children teach us from the cradle to believe in our religions. So, we are pretty much in the dark about the many intimate ways that God speaks and reaches out to us, individually. Most of us go through life with vague notions of what God wants from us and what life is all about on this planet. Since most people follow others who teach them about God, their spiritual knowledge is limited and sometimes, erroneous.

You may ask, "How do you know that it is truly God speaking to you?" The best answer I can give you is that the proof is in the results. In other words, when you receive a message that is a prophecy and what has been prophesied actually happens, then you should know that it is from God. No one else has power in the universe to say what will happen in the future, except God. When you receive messages that are not prophecies, but messages of guidance, you should look at these universal signs and apply them to your life. (See "God's Languages", abridged signs listings in the Index.) If you are truthful to yourself and are not in denial about the circumstances in your life, you will apply the signs to your situation and both learn and benefit from God's guidance. You will see the truth if you are truly seeking it. If you do not understand your signs, then you should pray and ask God for explanations, as often as it takes for you to understand. God is a very patient teacher.

God's Sign Languages

God speaks to all living things through a language that each being can understand. Even plants talk with The Creator. The messages that we receive from God are usually messages to guide us in all aspects of our lives. Some may be prophecies; some may be warnings; others may be indicators of health and well-being; and, some may be God's command to stop a behavior. A person who knows how to read her own signs can stay far ahead in the game of life by using God's direct messages to self-actualize and stay on her mission. Not only will The Creator guide her to financial necessities, but God will also tell her things she needs to know for her own good about her mate, children, family members and friends. Messages about others are usually to either help the person whom the message concerns or to enlighten the receiver about the impact of that person in her life. If events in another person's life do not concern you, then God will not give you a message about them.

Dream signs are also one of God's ways of talking directly to us. The dreams of prophets for the masses were

God's messages to that prophet for the people. Your dreams are God's messages to you for yourself. Some dreams are symbolic and some dreams are given to you "straight", telling it like it is. Symbolic dreams are the ones most people call "weird" or "crazy" because they do not know the language of the dream.

God speaks to us through the languages of color, numbers, weather, body parts and functions, directions, astrology, extrasensory perception, hunches, deja vu, instincts, psychic voyages, divinations, animal signs and many more ways. How can you educate yourself in the knowledge of these languages? First, get a notebook. Second, make up a prayer list. Third, pray and ask God, "How do you speak directly to me?" Pray every day until you get all the signs written down in your notebook. If you ask God, "God, let me know for a certainty that it is your message.", God will give you verification that it is, indeed, God speaking. God speaks to each person at his own level of understanding. So, a child might get a message through a cartoon character, while an adult might get the essence of the same message through other means.

In spiritual numerology, the numbers 9, 12 and 13 are indications of God's degrees of anger; thirteen is God's highest degree of anger. Some old so-called superstitions do have a ring of truth. Number 1 means commerce or buying and selling; getting a mate; getting what you need to survive. Number 3 means God's will. It is, essentially, God's signature.

Weather signs indicate how we are growing; they indicate how we, as a group, in a particular region are developing. Some regions experience harsher weather than others. In some places, there are endless halcyon days and nights; in other places, there are endless cold, harsh days and nights. All weather signs, including floods, hurricanes, snowstorms and even sunny weather are ways in which God both punishes and rewards us. Group karma is a part of this because weather affects more than one person at a time.

Just as God controls nature, God also controls the planets, stars and moon. Astrology is based on the movements and positions of these heavenly bodies. They are God's clocks. The timelines that God has drawn on the blueprint for the universe correspond to the *great timepiece* of heavenly body configurations. There is a set time for our development to move forward and astrology lets us know when it is time for us, as a species, to reach greater heights.

Around twenty-five years ago, God let me know that the calendar year is getting shorter by very small increments, because God has increased the pace of the creation. Planets are reaching points in their orbits sooner than in the past. Our Creator is changing our world. Astrologers should consider this fact when making charts; otherwise, they may be slightly off or behind in their forecasts. **One caveat: beware of the charlatans in this field. Only deal with an astrologer who has a known good reputation.**

The ancients used divinations to guide them in their daily lives. Divinations are still one of God's ways of communicating with those who want to use these ancient spiritual readings for guidance. Tarot cards are a popular means of divining today. Crystal readings are also very popular. Runes, tea leaf readings, stones, bones and many other divination methods represent some of the infinite ways that God talks to us. These divinations are usually interpreted by a person who is experienced in whichever method(s) he uses.

I discovered a modern divination method that I came upon quite serendipitously. While thumbing through a dictionary for a word, I noticed that certain other words that caught my eye fit together to form a word puzzle. That word puzzle gave me a message about something I had been pondering. I tried it several times after that, just thumbing through the dictionary, looking at the first word or phrase on a page that caught my eye and writing it down. I did this until I reached a word that meant the same thing as *stop*. My message was always there! It was always about either something going on in my life or the life of a loved one. I got others to try it and the same thing happened to them. Sometimes two or more words fit together; sometimes one word was a message standing alone. You have to look carefully at your dictionary messages to get the meanings. If the meanings are not clear at first, pray and ask God to explain, further. You will receive answers.

Directions such as north, south, east, west, up, down, high and low also have meanings. In dreams and other divine signs, moving upward always means improvement in some life condition; moving on a downward path always indicates a lessening of your progress or regressing in some area of life. North and south have implications for economic prosperity; east means systemic conformity and west means innovation and pioneering.

Your conscience is also a sign. You should always pay attention to that nagging little voice inside you. It is God telling you something for your own good. We all have psychic gifts to a greater or lesser degree. If you have ever had strong thoughts about someone and then they either called or you saw them shortly after that, you were experiencing God's thoughts to you telling you about that person. Also, if you have ever seen someone who looked like someone you know, then you either saw that person or received news of him shortly afterwards, that was also one of God's ways of telling you something about that person. People who use their psychic gifts regularly have stronger abilities than someone, who either does not pay attention to their psychic perceptions or who only pays minimal attention to them. Some psychic gifts include the ability to move things with the mind (psychokinesis), super strength, prophesying, healing, giving divine messages to others and much more. There are charlatans in every field and, of course, there are psychics who claim to have these abilities but they do not. How do you tell the fake psychics from the real ones? Never let them ask you questions about your life. If they are truly gifted, they will *tell you* about yourself.

God's Body Language

Everything about your physical appearance tells a story about you, from your hair texture and color to the shape and size of your feet. You are a mirror image of your cumulative developmental progress on earth. *Every part and function of your body has a meaning based on the following:* your survival habits, sexual striving, thriftiness, love for others, work accomplishments, understanding of God (or who to worship), use of speech (to build up or tear down), repentance for past deeds, conformity on nonconformity, and other aspects of your character development throughout your prior lives on Earth. Our looks are our "markings" just as a tiger's stripes and a leopard's spots are their markings.

God made us, not in God's image, but according to a standard model that includes appendages, sense organs and internal structures with specific functions. Each of our senses and bodily functions represents developmental milestones of various kinds. Height, hair or lack of hair on a body part represents thoughts about a certain aspect of survival. Various aspects of our sexual growth and development are represented by the size and shape of the sex organs, breasts and buttocks (sans fat). Birthmarks tell a story of our past life, also. The size, shape and location of a birthmark tell about past deeds in the immediately preceding life.

Beauty is not really in the eyes of the beholder: God established standards of good behavior that correspond to set standards of beauty. Beauty is as beauty has done. These standards transcend racial boundaries.

Illnesses that affect a body part or function are a clear indicator of the type of behavior that the ill person needs to change. If you know what the body part means, then you can act accordingly. If you do not, pray and ask The God Force what it means. Even the fact that we return to earth through the pain and suffering of birthing means something. The pain of getting sent back to earth plane (hell) is painful for all involved, especially Our Creator. It is tragic that we continue to listen to others guiding us, instead of Our Creator. God hurts and cries about us.

Serendipity

People usually think of serendipitous events as coincidences. There is no such thing as a coincidence. What we call luck, chance, or coincidence is God's intervention in our lives. Some so-called serendipitous events such as the apple falling on Sir Isaac Newton's head and the displacement of water in Archimedes' bath were on God's schedule to occur. It was at those moments that God stepped in and gave us *the law of gravity* and *the physics laws of displacement and volume*. It is that "aha!" factor which suddenly enlightens us and moves us on to greater knowledge. God always gives the same message to more than one person whenever it is time for us to move forward according to the *divine blueprint.* **God does this to assure that the message will reach us and that someone will act upon it. Whenever there is a global raising of consciousness on issues such as the rights of women or human rights, God is at the center of it all. The God Force moves us on to become better, more compassionate, freedom-loving, and more enlightened beings.**

Intuition

Each living being possesses intuition. It is one of our senses that is underused and underdeveloped in most people. Why? The age of science and technology takes a dim view of knowledge that is not of a purely scientific nature. Many people frown upon individuals say that they know *something that they saw in a dream or vision or that they feel something is going to occur.* All animals, including humans have intuitive faculties that God built in us as another tool for staying alive. It is also present in plants. Electrical impulse studies done on plants have shown that plants react to people who have intentions of hurting them.

If you have ever had a hunch or strong feeling about something that came to pass, you have experienced intuition. The intuitive sense becomes stronger the more you pay attention to it and use it.

Clairaudience and Clairvoyance

Clairaudient people can hear sounds above the normal range of sound for most humans. Clairvoyant people have visionary insight or can see into the future. Some people are born with these gifts. They *are* gifts as are the gifts of exceptional musical or mathematical abilities, or any other talent. God gives some people these gifts for the same reasons that God gives others different gifts: their past striving and accomplishments in a specific area or interest. Clairaudient people may sometimes hear astral music from the heavens, hear their angels or spirit helpers or hear other sounds which others cannot hear. This type of hearing is distinguished from the voices heard by schizophrenics and the sounds heard by people who have the disease, tinnitus. A clairaudient person experiences sounds and voices of a spiritual nature and they are usually momentary and spiritually uplifting . The clairaudient person may turn off this faculty at will if she so desires. The schizophrenic and the tinnitus patient cannot control the voices and sounds and they are not having a spiritual experience. What they are experiencing is negative karma.

Deja Vu

Deja vu means a view of the past. If you have ever been somewhere that you know you have never been or seemed to know someone with whom you had no previous contact, you have experienced deja vu. Also, if you have ex-perienced feelings about places that you visited for the first time, in terms of where certain buildings and cultural sites are located, you have experienced deja vu. Deja vu is not limited to either places or people; it also includes a certain knowing about various things that you have neither seen nor experienced in your current life.

Deja vu is always about your past life or lives. It could be the smell of a foreign food that captivates you and you know how it is going to taste before you get it in your mouth. It could be the sight of a local flower or plant whose smell you know without having smelled it before. God is try-ing to get you to pray and ask about your past: to ask about your lives on earth and why you are back here, again. Our Maker wants us to *know* why we are here and to be on our *mission*.

God as Therapist

Who has not had problems of a personal nature at least once their lives? God is always available for personal counseling. God can help you solve problems with your family, your love and sex life, work problems and any other problems that you may have. You do not need to make an appointment; just call God on the "hotline" and ask for help. Just pray and you *will* receive answers; they may not be what you want to hear or what you expect, but God *will* answer you, even if the answer is "NO!" Continue to ask God for clarification if, at first, you do not understand the answers. God is a patient teacher and will give you the answers as often and in as many ways as it takes for you to "get it".

Justice

Divine Justice

God's justice is perfect. It fits the offense like a perfectly tailored garment. Divine law is always superior to man's law. We, on earth have devised our own set of laws that are, often, in direct opposition to God's laws. God is our judge; God is our jury; and God is our executioner. God is our *all: beginning and ending; yin and yang.* The justice that we, humans, mete out to individuals cannot compare to God's forms of justice or retribution. Humans only have the power to jail or kill offenders. God has unique plans for each soul to make the punishment fit the crime. The problem with man is that man does not think that God will even the score; man does not think that God is paying people back for their wrong deeds. If we did, there would be no need for our systems of justice, because we would *know for a certainty* that God was taking care of things. Because we cannot see every divine punishment and we are uncertain that the guilty will be punished, we dispense justice for ourselves. We are not *sure* that God is watching and doing the job. Little do we know, God always dispenses *perfect justice: the punishment always fits the sin.*

Man Judges Man

Humankind has devised a justice system that evolved into what we have today: judges who decide punishment, juries that decide guilt or innocence, lawyers who argue guilt or innocence, expert witnesses and eyewitness testimonies. Our jails and penitentiaries are bursting at the seams from overcrowding. We have a problem of gigantic proportions with our justice system in the USA: we must free some felons before they complete their sentences to make room for new ones, thereby releasing potential dangers to already dangerous communities.

As science has advanced, we now know that many people whom we have jailed never belonged there in the first place. Eyewitness accounts that placed the accused at a certain place doing a certain deed at a certain time and date have been found seriously flawed. Science now knows that two people can witness the same event and report entirely different versions of it. New DNA testing results have freed many men whom society unjustly jailed for many years. Innocent people have suffered along with the guilty in man's system of justice.

The Salem witch trials were some horrendous examples of man's justice. Ignorant, frenzied hordes executed many people because they were suspected of being witches. Now, there is some evidence today that a fungus on the rye bread that people ate during that time (ergot) has the same effects as LSD on both animals and humans. People who acted oddly might have been on a bad "trip" from eating the stale rye bread.

People who work in the justice system and who decide the fate of others should ask God in prayer about their decisions or judgments. God will guide them in a timely manner; sometimes God answers you instantaneously.

Capital Punishment

"Judge not lest ye also be judged" is a quotation which many religious people say regularly. Make no mistake about it; God understands why we jail certain criminals. We need to get them out of circulation so that our societies will be safer. God understands and God does applaud our efforts when we protect the weaker members of society from evil predators. However, taking away a life that God created does not meet with God's approval. *We have no right to kill any of God's creations, except in self-defense or for food.* Those who do so for any other reasons must answer to The God Force.

Freedom vs. Anarchy

God created us to live free; but, we have legislated ourselves into a box called "conformity". We have agreed to sameness in our collective lives. We have allowed the majority's values and opinions to rule our lives. Being a member of a society means that we have given up certain God-given freedoms for the right to live within the confines and laws of the human box called "conformity". Society labels anyone who steps outside that box as: a weirdo, kooky, eccentric, malcontent, or any number of negative terms. Freedom is a hard commodity to keep on earth these days. We constrict our lives and even our thinking to fit the norms of the "box". Fear grips most of us with just the thought of going outside the "box".

Living freely means living according to God's laws, not man's laws. In living freely, a person must be strong and able to withstand negative public opinion for going outside the "box". Public opinion can be a cruel, "beat-down" tool of the conformist majority to keep individualists in line. Happiness eludes many who live inside the conformity box, but they are afraid to venture out and taste what life has to offer outside those confines.

Living totally free is a dream for some people. Inside the "box", this dream is sometimes called *anarchy*. Anarchy in this sense means living with no laws. There is no such thing or state of being. We are always living under *divine law* whether we know it and trust it or not.

Plants and Karma

Plants on a Mission

All life forms, including plant life, have a mission: survival by God's rules. They must get food and reproduce their kind, the same as life in the animal kingdom. Some get food by growing roots into the ground; some get food by living in a water system such as oceans or rivers; still others get food by absorbing nutrients from the air or from other plants. Some carnivorous plants get their food from the animal kingdom by trapping insects in their sticky juices. Still, other microscopic plant life gains food from animal hosts, including humans. Plants reproduce in various ways: some are pollinated by insects; some spread their seeds when the wind blows them around; still others spread their seeds through the feces of animals that eat their flowers. The microscopic plants divide themselves to reproduce. The ways that plants reproduce are varied.

Every living thing has a *mind*, including plants. They have some sort of intelligence and language system that only God knows and through which God speaks with them. This includes your bacteria, fungi, and all plant life. *Mind* is not always housed within a brain; the locus of the mind is different for different life forms. Plants feel and they think. They also talk with each other. Some scientific studies on plants have shown that they react to people who wish to harm them; there is an electrochemical response much like the responses recorded by a lie detector. Their electromagnetic impulses go up when danger threatens. Other studies have shown that some trees communicate insect invasions to each other by releasing a substance into the air, which travels from tree to tree; then, their leaves become coated with a substance that repels the insects. Both plants and animals have survival mechanisms that they use to stay alive. We are not much different in that respect.

Plant Life and Free-Will

In the beginning, when God was creating the universe, life was not as we know it today. Life that God created, which evolved through millions of years, began in a more simple form. Those rudimentary life forms were given a mind and a will by The Creator. Again, the mind is not always housed in a brain as we know life today. Those early life forms had an intelligence that they used to become the living beings that we see on earth today.

God gave us choices then, just as God gives us choices now. Free will has always been a part of God's *divine blueprint*. God gave these early life forms a choice in how they wanted to get their food: by standing still or by moving and getting it for themselves. Early plant forms chose to be immobile in their struggle for survival. Early animal forms chose to move about for their food. What we see today, in all their variegated forms are the evolved progeny of those early life forms. Most life is either plant or animal, except for the euglena and fungi. Euglena have the characteristics of both plants and animals. The euglena took other directions that both transcend the strict guidelines of both kingdoms and incorporate the best in survival mechanisms of both.

Most plants are green except some that do not make chlorophyll. The many colors of plant flowers and the sizes and shapes of them tell about their spiritual development on earth. The colors in the plant kingdom mean the same thing as colors in our world. Colors show their survival habits, how hard they are trying to stay alive, and how well they are accomplishing the task. Size, fragrance, leaf formations, growth schedules and all botanical features of plants relate directly to their struggle for survival.

Plants that have chlorophyll can make their own food. They must have sunlight to do so. Plants that do not contain chlorophyll are plants that have not chosen positive survival means. They are usually shade-loving plants that respond to moist, dark places. Some of them are even parasitic: they live on the energy of other harder working plants. There are scavengers in the plant kingdom and the animal kingdom that are not doing God's will.

The Plants We Love

Humans and other animal life are in a symbiotic relationship with the plant kingdom. We breathe oxygen and give off carbon dioxide; they breathe carbon dioxide and give off oxygen. We need some of them for the medicines that we extract from them. Others, we love for their beauty and decorative qualities. We eat many of them. They sustain us in our survival just as the animals that we eat nourish our physical bodies.

House plants have more negative karma than most other plants because they are kept by us. They do not have to struggle for survival because we feed and protect them from the elements and also from insects and other dangers to their lives. House plants and outside plants will undergo corrective reincarnations, just as we must do.

Many people love to decorate trees for the end of year holidays. Cutting down or killing fir trees by the millions is a ritual that happens every year. We celebrate and approve this ritual, while we condemn killing animals for fur. There is not much difference between the two practices. We decorate our bodies with the skins of animals that we have killed; we decorate our homes with the trees that we have killed. What makes one practice more acceptable than the other? Is it because we do not think plants feel, think or fear? They do. Humans just do not know their language. If we did, we could hear them scream at the raising of the axe, saw, tractor blades or scissors to kill them. Killing either plants or animals is violent, but necessary for food.

Vegetarians vs. Meat Eaters

The only meat that we are not supposed to eat is human flesh. No life form is supposed to devour its own kind. This is God's rule. We are supposed to eat whatever is available to us in our environment that does not harm us.

During the early days of our evolution on Earth, there were both meat- eating and plant-eating dinosaurs. They chose their food according to how hard they wanted to struggle for it. If you were a flesh eater, you had to catch your food, possibly run after it or find it in the seas. If you were a plant eater, food was in abundance and all you had to do was eat it. It did not run from you. The problem with the latter choice is that you sometimes had to eat around the clock to get enough food energy in your body. The meat-eaters did not have to constantly eat for food energy. So, the line of least resistance is not always the best choice. The meat-eaters dominated during those days.

Vegetarians would like nothing better than to have the whole world convert to a diet of only vegetables. They say it is cruel to kill animals for food; they deserve to live, also. Plants deserve to live also, but we kill them when we harvest our food. They had ambitions of staying alive and reaching a ripe old age like our giant redwood trees. Again, plants feel and have minds. When we kill them, we just cannot hear them scream and die. But, if we had the correct scientific equipment to place on their stems and leaves, we would see the needle jump to the high anxiety category. So, the next time a vegetarian looks down his nose at you meat-eaters, ask him if he heard the screams of the juicy tomato or ear of corn he just ate. They were killed to feed him. Plants have feelings, too. God's law of survival says that we must kill or be killed. It's nature; it's life; it's God's law. Eat what you like.

Miscellaneous Revelations

A Planet Based on Two

Earth is a planet based on the number two. Two means conformity and group membership. Almost everything about life on Earth is based on two. For instance, there are two sexes; we have two legs, two arms, two eyes, two lips, two ears, two nostrils and two feet. We cannot perpetuate our species without the participation of the two sexes. Even in the plant kingdom, there are both male and female parts of plants needed for reproduction.

A planet of two-oriented life forms means that we and other life forms like to group or bunch for our survival. It also means that as conformists, we do not like change much, nor do we like *differentness*. We love *sameness*. Many of our problems center on our differences in ethnicity, race, gender and other characteristics. It is a basic insecurity within us that needs development and that causes us to fear and hate people who look and act differently. The story of *Jonathan Livingston Seagull* by Richard Bach is a good example of two-type behavior. Jonathan did not want to conform to the standards of his flock. He wanted to test his mettle. So, he tried to fly higher, dip lower, swoop fancier than any seagull had ever done before. His valiant efforts angered his flock and they ostracized him. So it is with us. Many who take the road not traveled do not conform; they are the trend setters, standard breakers, the originators and pioneers of the world. We all are here to be pioneers of our own destiny, but we must work on our two-type behavior that makes many stagnate and some turn outlaw. The problem is that when conformists look at nonconformists and compare themselves, they find themselves lacking in some ways. So, instead of working on whatever they perceive those deficits to be, they turn on the nonconformist to denigrate that person for whatever reasons they concoct. This makes the conformist feel better about himself. If he can make the nonconformist out to be a "wacky or crazy" person, then all the better for conformity. Those examples are the negative side of our number two-based world.

On the positive side, our grouping and joining together in loving relationships is a very good thing. God loves for us to be together in groups for our personalities to develop properly and for our love relationships with our peers to develop.   Social isolation is a problem in some countries, especially in the Western World, spawning social ills that range from latchkey children to elderly citizens living alone. Cultures like these breed asocial individuals, perverted predators and murderers. It really does take a village to raise a child.

Are We Alone in the Universe?

No. We are not alone in the universe. There are many galaxies in the universe like ours. There are many suns, moons and stars that are not a part of Earth's galaxy. God created life in many other places besides Earth. These other planets have life forms that may be compatible with our environment. Many people claim to have been abducted and experimented upon by alien life forms. Many people have experienced the "missing time" phenomenon: they have been gone for a period and have no memory of what happened to them during that time, unless it is recalled under hypnosis. Some people, however, do remember without the aid of hypnotherapy.   Some people have scars and other telltale physical indicators to show that someone has cut them and implanted devices in their bodies or that something else, experimental, has been done to them. When these victims report these experiences, scientists and doctors usually dismiss their claims as hallucinations or hoaxes.

God has informed me and one of my spiritual meditation group members that there is, indeed, life on other planets. There are visitors who come to earth to experiment with our bodies and they are doing so because they like our physical strength. Their bodies are frail compared to ours. They are experimenting with a hybrid species that would be part human and part them. Mentally, they are superior to us;   they are further along in their development than humans. They do not intend to harm, but they do intend to harness whatever resources that they can use from our planet for their own existence elsewhere in the universe. God created them and they, too, are our kin. We are all God's children. Heaven holds a place for them and also for us; except, their heaven is in a galaxy that is adjacent to their physical planets. We need to know that God did not stop creating life with us. We need to stop hiding the truth just because most religions do not know it and therefore, it is not included in most religious dogma.

Twins

Identical twins have a special karma on earth. Their karma involves being so close to another individual in a previous life that they limited that person's growth and development. Possessiveness is another way to describe it. We are individuals who need the freedom and space in our lives to grow without the constant attachment or presence of another individual in our lives making decisions and thinking for us. Fraternal twins have karma similar to that of identical twins, except the severity of the offense is not as great. Siamese twins have the most punishing karma of the twin sets: in a previous life, they were possessive of another person to an enormous degree. We belong to God, not to each other. God does not like it when we covet the life of another to the degree that they have difficulties being free of us when they need to be independent. We should give as much love and medical help as is available to Siamese twins who want independence.

The Lost

Nothing in the Universe is ever lost. God knows where everything and everyone is found. We lose articles for a reason. Each reason is different for each person who loses something. Pray and ask God why you lost an article or person and God will let you know.

If you lost an article, ask God to help you find it. If God is willing, your article will be returned to you. I have done this often and each time, my message is different. Sometimes God gives the article back to me after I have understood the reason God took it from me. Sometimes, God does not give it back. You must ask *why* because there is always a negative karmic reason for it and you need to know it to correct your future behavior.

People who are lost to us are never lost either. The most painful of all losses is the loss of a child or other loved one. Clearly, no one wants to see this happen to anyone. If you have lost someone, ask God these questions: (1) Is my loved one safe or not? (2) Why did this happen? (3) Will you help in getting them back? and (4) Ask any other relevant questions. It is up to God about whether that person returns to you; but, you will receive answers if you are sincere in your prayers. One more consideration is: has that person finished his mission on earth and gone home to heaven to stay? The reasons for a tragedy differ with each loss, but God *will* let you know *why.*

Mind Over Matter

The mind controls the body to the extent that if the body feels certain sensations, the mind can will them away. People have reportedly walked on hot coals, stuck pins through their flesh and even lifted weight many times their own body weight. When these events occur, God suffuses that person's body with electromagnetic energy that causes them to feel no pain and gives them great strength. The mind interacts with the body in a way that directs it to do its bidding. The mind greatly affects whether or not a person speaks and feels. It can prevent an otherwise healthy organ from functioning. It can also augment the performance of certain functions and abilities. God knows our will and whatever good growth efforts we are attempting. God will help us do it. In suppressed functions, such as the sudden loss of your voice, usually a traumatic event has occurred and the mind overcompensates by suppressing a function to deal with the trauma.

Memory

There is a scientific explanation for everything that is part of the universe, and a spiritual explanation. The locus of long term memory is outside our bodies. Memories of our past lives and memories of events in our current lives are stored by God on electromagnetic storage waves. When we want to recall some long past event, God induces messages to the brain and we recall the memory. God is very active in our day to day actions. People who have a negative karma regarding memory, however, do not experience this. God does punish us with loss of memory and worse. All of the karma related to the mind deals directly with use and disuse or misuse of the mind. Short term memory is stored in the brain for a brief period before God stores it in our long term memory bank.

People who have experienced a past life regression session know that memories of past lives come flooding back into their minds, as if they are watching a movie of another person's life. You can pray and ask God for a past life regression during spiritual meditation, in a dream or however God wants to give it to you. You *will receive the memories.*

The Future

Cheating in the Game of Survival

Since humans are cheating at the game of survival by pooling resources and using the might of the group to forge ahead of other species on Earth, there will be cheater penalties to pay. The first penalty will be that our population will be so great that we will outnumber any other warm-blooded species in our world. Every country has experienced increases in population. Our great success at this game of life has increased our numbers to the point where we are so numerous in some countries that governments limit the number of children couples may have.

Malthus' law of population and economics states that population increases geometrically while food grows at an arithmetic rate. In other words, there will not be enough food to feed all the people on earth. He also believed that populations are kept in check by famine, disease, pestilence and catastrophes. If world populations continue to increase in this manner, the competition for food will be much greater.

Priorities, Priorities, Priorities!

We are visiting outer space regularly, gathering scientific data about other stellar bodies and other scientific studies related to space exploration. We spend millions of dollars on these projects to increase our knowledge and to compete with other nations for dominance in space related matters. Meanwhile, on earth, we can hardly breathe the air in some cities for the pollution of the fossil fuels that we still use. Our power sources on earth are archaic. We still depend on oil drilling for oil-based resources. Drilling for oil and just transporting it has killed various life forms in areas where there are major spills. Our electric power source is still strung up on poles across thousands of miles of our countries. Sudden storms, hurricanes and tornadoes regularly plunge un into darkness because of our archaic wires in the air. They all fall down!

Too many of our waterways are polluted and killing the fish and other sea creatures within them. Because of our proliferation as a species, we have encroached upon the living spaces of other animals and driven them into near extinction. We think very little of preserving green space (plants). But, guess what? We need what green space and *only* green space can give us: oxygen! What will we do when oxygen levels in the air drop to very low levels, so low that some of us die of it?

Our priorities are in the wrong places. Space exploration has its place in our world, but not at the expense of neglecting our number one priority: a safe, healthy earth environment. We are too technologically advanced to still depend upon wires in the air for electricity. We can do better. Oil is something that we must give up as populations grow and more cars are on the roads. Cleaning up air and water pollution is not as high on our list of priorities as it should be.

God punishes us when our priorities are detrimental to our development on earth. God does not set us down gently from outer space when our primary needs go wanting. Sadly, too many brave astronauts have died because of our out-of-order priorities on earth. Earth is home, and taking care of home should come first on our list.

Male/Female Relationships

The rigid sex roles which men and women still insist on playing will cost them, dearly. As God sends more women back to earth in male bodies (male homosexuals) to correct their weak behavior, there will be fewer men in male bodies for women to choose from. Vice-versa, domineering males will be returned in female bodies. There will be new and more terrible sexually transmitted diseases that will kill many more people than AIDS *and in a shorter time.* Male dominance and female subservience is *not* God's way. We have been lied to, conned and tricked.

Section Two

Ordinary People

Chapter 12

Past Life Regressions

[I was present when a group of people interested in reincarnation conducted some informal "past retrieval" (past life regression) sessions to take people back into their past lives. Some people who were regressed were hypnotized and others were not. After opening their eyes, some people remembered everything which they had said and seen; and some people remembered nothing! Those people who were not hypnotized went back into their past lives while they were fully conscious! This simply means that they were receiving messages and seeing visions while they were wide awake rather than while they were in an altered state of consciousness.]

The purpose of the past life retrievals was to help the individuals understand why they were sent back to Earth and what their mission should be in their current lives. Although some psychotherapists use past life regression (or retrieval) to treat phobias and other psychological problems, the sole purpose of these regressions was to find out what the person should be working on to correct their past life mistakes, violations and shortcomings so that they could move on to a higher plane of existence after death instead of returning to Earth.

Many physicians and psychiatrists use hypnosis as a form of therapy. Many physicians use it to eliminate pain or other sensations and to suggest away symptoms of diseases and also to relieve anxiety. Some psychiatrists use hypnosis in the treatment of neuroses and psychoses. Some psychiatrists have even reported that their patients have recalled past lives but psychiatrists, generally, reject reincarnation as an explanation for recalling past lives. They call these reported past lives of their patient's fantasies, and most psychiatrists try to manufacture explanations to do away with the facts the patients report.

Each participant and the hypnotist sat at a table facing each other. Each participant was asked to stare into the flame of a candle until he felt drowsy. The candle was used just as an object for the participant to fix his eyes and attention upon. Two people were taken back into their past using the candle and one person was taken back using a swinging key which was swung slowly, like a pendulum, about three inches from his nose in his field of vision. Any other object could have been used such as a small water fountain, flowing water from a tap, a colored light, or anything upon which a person could fixate his attention. These accounts focus on several people who participated in the sessions.

Michael's Regression

The first participant was a 26 year-old Caucasian man named Michael. He was told to stare at the candle until he felt drowsy. He stared at the candle until he felt drowsy. He stared at the candle for about three minutes and then he said "Well, I don't feel like closing my eyes." So, the hypnotist replied, "Would you mind just closing them anyway? Let's see what happens. O.K.?" He closed his eyes and the hypnotist continued:

Q.   Can you recall anything which happened to you when you were a child?

A.   No.

HYPNOTIST: Just relax and try to clear your mind so that thoughts can come through. Michael was then asked about different ages during his childhood and he could recall nothing. He was told to relax and no questions were asked for about 45 seconds.

HYPNOTIST: Now, just close your eyes and tell me whatever you see about your past.

A.   I see when I was a kid. I had a truck and it had one wheel off of it. I never could find the right wheel to put on that truck, so we threw it away.

Q.   How old were you?

A.   I was about 2 years old.

Q.   Do you see anything else?

A.   I can see the candle burning with my eyes closed.

Q.   Can you describe it?

A.   The bottom of the flame is blue and the tip is yellow. (The bottom of the flame was not blue. The candle was red and the actual flame was yellow throughout. He said that he wanted to stop there so he was told to open his eyes. Michael was clearly uncomfortable during the session, so he said that he would try it again at another time. He remembered everything which he had seen and all of the thoughts which had come into his mind.)

Rita's Regression: I Was Another Race

The next participant was a 26 year-old African American woman named Rita. Rita was given the same instructions as Michael. She stared into the candle and said that she felt sleepy after about three minutes. She was told to close her eyes and the session proceeded as follows:

Q.   Rita, do any thoughts come to you about your childhood?

A.   I was in school. This boy got sick. He was real sick and I remember the teacher. She always made me stay in because....I don't know why Miss West didn't like me. She used to make me stay in every day at lunch time.

Q.   How old were you then?

A.   I was seven.

Q.   Does anything come to your mind about what you were doing when you were five years old?

A.   My granddaddy use to keep me when I was five and my granddaddy used to feed me a lot of candy and a lot of cakes. He used to dress me wrong too. He used to put my clothes on backwards.

Q.   Do any thoughts come to you, Rita, about what you did when you were three years old?

A.   No.

Q.   Do any thoughts come to you about your life when you were two years old?

(about a 6 or 7-second pause)

A.   I had a red dress. It was a red check dress and it had lace on it. I just wore it to play in. It had ruffles and it was pleated at the bottom.

Q.   Do any thoughts come to you about your life before you were one year-old?

(about a 1 1/2-minute pause)

A.   I see a house.

Q.   What kind of house?

A.   A big yellow house.

Q.   Are there any people in the house?

A.   Yeah. They're strangers ...strange people. They're mixed...mixed Indians.

Q.   Can you describe everything you see and feel?

A.   I don't like that house. Everybody's mean. They act mean.

I'm in there but I'm gon' leave! (She seemed to be experiencing negative emotions about the scene and the people whom she described. Her facial expression even changed. Her facial muscles tightened and her mouth pursed as if she was very angry.)

Q.   Can you see yourself, Rita?

A.   I see myself.

Q.   Can you describe yourself? What do you look like?

A.   I've got a band around my head and I have on Indian clothes. I've got a feather in my head.

Q.   How old are you?

A.   I'm about 18.

Q.   Where are you?

A.   It's out West. It's hot! (brief pause)

Q.   What are you doing now?

A.   I don't like those people! I'm leaving!
[She had a very determined expression on her face.]
Q.   Who's with you?
A.   Nobody's with me. I'm just walking.
Q.   Where are you going?
A.   I haven't made up my mind where I'm going.
Q.   What do you see? Can you describe everything you see?
A.   I see dry land and a clear highway.
Q.   Are there any trees around?
A.   No trees. Pretty green grass is on the ground.
Q.   Are you leaving because of the people in the house?
A.   Yes. They didn't like me. They just didn't like me.
[The hypnotist was unable to get any specific details about Rita's relationship with the people in the house except that they were mean to her.]
Q.   What else do you see? Describe everything you see.
A.   I see the sun. It's just as bright and it's hot! It's so hot!
[No questions were asked for the following response. Rita continued talking without being asked a question.]
Rita: Oh, oh! here comes a car! I've got a ride!
Q.   Who are you riding with?
A.   A man.
Q.   Would you describe him, Rita?
A.   I don't like him! He's mean!   [Her tone of voice changed and she acted as though she was disgusted about something which the man had said or done.]
Q.   Where are you now and what are you doing?
A.   The sun is still bright and I'm still walking. I've made up my mind where I'm going now. I'm going to California.
[About a 2-minute pause elapsed while the hypnotist waited for unasked responses.]
Q.   Where are you now and what are you doing?
A.   Now I'm in California, I'm going to school. I'm going to college.
Q.   What's the name of the college?
A.   I don't know the name of it; but I'm enrolled in a teacher's college and I'm on the dean's list.
Q.   How are the people in the college?
A.   The people in the college are real nice. I'm just

studying hard and going to school. I'm working too...part time!

[She sounded excited and happy.]

Q.   What's your name? What do they call you?

A.   My name is Linda. They call me Linda.

[The hypnotist asked for a last name but got no answer about it.]

Q.   Did you graduate from the college?

A.   I graduated. I teach school and I enjoy my work. (brief pause)

Q.   What grade do you teach?

A.   I teach first grade.

Q.   What are you doing now?

A.   I'm still in California.

Q.   Do you have a husband or children?

A.   No. I don't have any social life. I just teach and go home. I stay to myself a lot. I'm sort of bashful.

Q.   You don't do anything else?

A.   No. I do the same thing every day; I teach school and I go home.

Q.   Are you getting any older?

A.   I'm about 30 now.

Q.   What are you doing?

A.   I'm still doing the same thing every day. I still teach the first grade and all I do is teach school and go home.

Q.   Are you getting any older? (There was about a 30-second pause.)

A.   I'm oooold....real old!

Q.   How old are you?

A.   I must be 75!

Q.   Are you still teaching school?

A.   I'm old! I can't see too well. I had to quit teaching. I retired.

Q.   What are you doing now?

A.   I'm just sitting in a rocking chair.

Q.   Where are you?

A.   I'm still in California because it's hot. I couldn't see too well.

Q.   How did you die?

A.   I just died a natural death.

Q.   How old were you when you died?

A.   I was 85.

[The hypnotist tried to take her back into another previous life but time did not permit.] Rita was told to open her eyes. She was asked if she remembered anything which she had seen. She did not remember anything at all about what she had said about her childhood in this incarnation or about her previous life as the Indian girl, Linda.

Rita, who was an Indian woman, Linda, in a previous life is now a member of another race. She is now African American. She received the message through her past retrieval session that she was sent back to Earth in order to learn how to love people and have fun. She did not grow and develop in this way when she was Linda because she had no social life or love life; so, this is what she must try to do in her present life as Rita.]

Bernard's Regression

The third participant was a 24 year-old Caucasian man named Bernard. He was told to stare at a swinging key rather than the candle flame. The hypnotist held the key about 3 inches from his nose. After he was relaxed, the hypnotist started questioning him:

Q.   Can you see yourself when you were 10 years old?

A.   No.

Q.   Can you see yourself when you were 9? Do you get any thoughts about what things were like then?

A.   I lived at... (He gave the address of the house where he used to live.)

Q.   Can you see yourself when you were seven?

A.   I live in a white house. I used to play a lot with my brother...the one after me.

Q.   Anything else?

A.   No.

Q.   What were things like when you were five years old? (About a 1-minute pause)

A.   I remember a big peach tree. It was right across the street from us. I remember we used to pick them and Miss Brown used to holler at us. We used to pick her peaches every day. I remember we used to go across the fence and there was a big oak tree with a swing on it and we used to go across the street and swing.

Q.   How old were you then?
A.   I was about four or five.
Q.   Can you see yourself when you were 2?
A.   I don't remember. I don't remember.
Q.   Do you recall anything which happened to you be-
fore you were one year-old?
A.   I don't remember.

*[At this time, the young man became rather tense. He was
told by the hypnotist to relax and to report anything which
came to mind or anything which he saw while his eyes were
closed. The hypnotist waited for about 2 minutes and then
proceeded.]*

Q.   Now, can you remember how things were before you
were one year-old?

*[At this point the man's facial expression and tone of voice
changed. He seemed to be squinting with his eyes closed as
he exclaimed, "I see a house! It looks like a shack!" He
seemed to be surprised and a little uneasy. His brow wrin-
kled as he still seemed to be squinting with his eyes closed.]*

Q.   Are there any people in the shack?
A.   I think so. [He replied slowly, shaking his head up
and down.]
Q.   Describe it for me.
A.   It's a shack!
Q.   Is it a one-story shack or a two-story shack?
A.   It's just a shack!
Q.   What color is the shack?
A.   It's unpainted. It's unpainted...no paint on it.

He was asked other questions and he responded by
saying that he did not remember. He was visibly tense so
the hypnotist told him to open his eyes. He remembered
everything that he had seen.
The hypnotist told the group afterwards, "Anyone
can recover his or her past life. A person can either recover
her past by herself or with the help of a friend. If you conduct a past retrieval session alone, it is a good idea to use a
tape recorder or have a pen and sheet of paper at hand so

that you can record or write down your ESP messages and visions. Say a prayer for understanding before you start. Next, close your eyes and relax. All you need is the desire to know!" *[Please refer to Self-Hypnosis for Past Life Regression in Appendix H.]*

Byron's Story: From Female to Gay Male

[The following account of a past life regression is from the audio taped files of Reverend Clarence. Reverend Clarence performed a past life regression on a young man, Byron J. when he was a teenager. Church members were encouraged to undergo a past life regression in order to understand and direct their lives. They believe that they are on a spiritual journey in each lifetime and that with each journey or reincarnation into Earth's plane, the person improves his life in ways that went lacking in the previous life or lifetimes. For instance, if a person did not learn to love, he or she is returned to Earth by God to learn how to love. The person is placed in the family, race, country and circumstances which will help her to develop in the ways she needs to grow. The ultimate goal is not to come back to Earth but to be so improved and to have passed God's Earth tests and graduate (die) to the next phase of life and live in Heaven. The session took place in the mid-nineteen eighties.]

Rev. Clarence (C): The subject is a fourteen year old Caucasian male whose name is Byron J. Byron is the third son in a family of five children and he lives with both parents. He is a good student in school, making mostly A's and B's. He enjoys helping his mother around the house and he likes to cook. He also enjoys playing baseball. Byron's mother is also here with us. Byron, are you ready for your past life regression?

Byron (B): Yes, Rev. Clarence, I'm ready.

C: Good, I want you to lie back on the couch and just relax. I'm going to play some very soothing music and I want you to lie back and just stare at this pendulum that I am going to swing before you. O.K.?

B: O.K.

C: Keep your eyes open for as long as you can. Just watch the pendulum swing and when your eyes get too heavy to stay open, close them.

B: O.K.

    (Soft music that sounds like the waves of the ocean and other soothing instruments play for about five minutes.)

C: I see that your eyes are closed, Byron. Can you still hear me?

B: Yes.

(The music has stopped at this point.)

C: Byron, do you like water and beaches or do you like the mountains and dry land better?

B: I like water and beaches.

C: What is your favorite color?

B: Purple.

C: I want you to see yourself on the shore of a beautiful sandy beach. The waves are lapping onto the shore. The sun is high in the sky and warming you. It is such a beautiful day. You see a little purple sailboat and you get into it. The waves are rocking you back and forth, back and forth and you feel so good. You feel so relaxed. The wind and the waves are carrying you out into the water. The little sailboat just rocks you gently from side to side as it goes further out to sea.

    I'm going to mention some parts of your body, and as I do I want you to relax that part of your body. Let all of the muscles in your forehead relax. Just let the tension go. Relax the muscles around your eyebrows, eyes and cheeks. Feel the tension leave your face. Feel the muscles in your neck and shoulders relax. Release the tension as you go deeper and deeper. Relax the muscles in your back as you go deeper and deeper, deeper relaxed. Let those muscles in the small of your back and your buttocks muscles relax. You feel more relaxed than you have ever felt before. Relax the back of your thigh muscles. Just feel them go loose and limp. Feel the tension gently fly away from your body. Relax your calves and then let the relaxation go on down to your heels; let it travel on to the bottom of your feet as you go deeper and deeper. Let the wave of relaxation travel to the toes and the topside of your feet. Just feel the tension fly away as you go deeper and deeper relaxed. Feel the topside of your thighs relax. Now, feel your stomach area relax as you go deeper and deeper. Feel your chest muscles relax. Just feel the tension and tightness leave, fly away from your body from head to toe. Let all the remaining tension gently lift away from your body and go out into the universe. I am going to let you rest for a little while and when you hear me again you will be even deeper relaxed. (Approximately one minute and 10 seconds of silence passes.)

You are warmed by the sun and you feel so relaxed. You see another shore in the distance and your sailboat is carrying you in that direction. You are coming closer to the shore and it looks so inviting. You are still relaxing on your sailboat. You have never felt so relaxed before. It is so peaceful and beautiful here on the sailboat. You are coming closer and closer to the other shore. You are still very relaxed. Your sailboat lands on the shore and you get out. In front of you is a beautiful purple staircase which is leading down into a lovely garden. Do you see the purple staircase?

B: Yes.

C: Good. Now, Byron, I am going to count backward from ten to zero. You are going to descend down the purple staircase into the beautiful garden with me. Nod your head if you are ready to go down the steps with me.

B: (Silence. Byron apparently has nodded his head.)

C. Very good. We are entering a beautiful, peaceful place of deep hypnosis. Is that O.K. with you, Byron? Nod your head if it's O.K.

B: (Silence. Again, it is apparent that he has nodded his head.)

C: Good. When we get to the bottom of the staircase, you will be more relaxed than you have ever been before. You will be so relaxed that you will feel wonderful and at peace. Ten. You are on the first step with me. It feels soft and warm under your feet. It is a beautiful carpet and it also smells wonderful. Nine. Step down one more time and let the sunshine warm you and relax you. Eight. Step down again. You are becoming more and more relaxed with each step down into this beautiful garden. You have never felt so good before. The birds are flying in the sky and you are feeling so very relaxed. Seven. Take another step down this beautiful purple staircase. You are just feeling more and more relaxed with each step downward. In fact, you feel better than you have ever felt before. Let the sun warm you and let yourself relax and enjoy the warm breezes. Six. Step down with me again and feel yourself relax even more. Your whole body feels calm and relaxed. You feel better and more relaxed with each step down into this beautiful garden. Five. Step down again. We are in the middle of the staircase and you can see even more of this beautiful garden. Look at the beautiful vines and trees and let their beauty relax you even more. Four. Step down once more. You are feeling so wonderful. Your body feels relaxed. Every muscle from your head to your toe is so very relaxed. Three. Step down again. We are almost there. The scenery and the sun are relaxing you so much that it feels wonderful. You have never been so relaxed in your life. You feel happy and relaxed here. Two. Step down on the beautiful purple carpet again. Enjoy the smell of the carpet and the feel of the warm sunshine on your face and arms. You are feeling so very relaxed. One. Step down again. You are so very, relaxed. Zero. Step down from the last step. We are now in this beautiful garden and you are totally relaxed from your head to your feet. You are taking in the scene here and feeling just so very, very relaxed. I now want you to talk to me and tell me what you see.

B: I see a beautiful garden with many flowers, trees and shrubs. I see a stream of water running through the center of the garden. It is very pretty here.

C: Wonderful. I want you to walk toward the center of the garden and find the golden door which is located there. Do you see the golden door?

B: Yes.

C: Good. Now, Byron, I want you to walk up to the golden door and open it. You will go on a journey through your past. My voice will go with you. Open the door, Byron. Walk in and tell me what you see.

B: I see myself when I was twelve years old. I'm at school in the gym playing basketball. It's a hot day and all of the guys have taken off their tops to play because the coach said we could. I didn't take mine off, though.

C: Why not, Byron? How were you feeling?

B: I just didn't want to show my chest. I felt embarrassed, like I was getting half naked and I didn't want to.

C: Anything else?

B: Now, I'm in my class at school and I'm nine years old. Ms. Greene is at the blackboard writing down some numbers and we are supposed to do our math problems from the board.

C: What are you thinking?

B: I don't really like math and I don't want to do the problems. I want to draw and paint. I can't wait for my next period class when I can finish my painting. I love art.

C: Anything else?

B: Yes. My friend, Charlie, is throwing a paper plane at me and I laugh out loud. Ms. Greene doesn't see what happened, but she turned around and glared at me when I laughed. She made me come up to the front of the room and sit in a seat beside her desk.

C: Where are you now and what are you doing?

B: Now, I'm at the store with my mom and we are shopping for groceries. I am putting some peanut butter in our basket. Mom takes it out and she tells me that we already have enough, but I'm arguing with her because I emptied the jar two days ago. She relents and lets me get it.

C: What else?

B: I'm at home now. I'm sitting in my bedroom watching TV and I'm seven years old.

C: Is anyone else there with you?

B: No. Not upstairs. My mom is downstairs fixing dinner. I was helping her fix the chicken but I dropped a couple of pieces on the floor and she said she was in a hurry so she told me to go and watch T.V. She didn't want me to help her today. (He begins to sob.)

C" What is wrong? What are you feeling?

B: I wanted to help her and she got mad with me. She hurt my feelings when she hollered at me for dropping the chicken. I like to cook. It's fun and I can get to eat what we fix. My little sister loves for me to cook stuff for her.

C: What else is going on?

B: I'm real little. I'm about three years old. I'm playing with a dolly and my dad is very mad about something. He snatches it away from me and I run to my mother and start crying. I don't know why Dad is mad with me. He and my mother are arguing and he says something about me not being a girl and he is using bad words. I grabbed my dolly and ran upstairs and hid her. I love my dolly. I asked Mom for it one day at the supermarket and she bought it for me.

C: How are you feeling?

B: I'm confused because I don't know what I did to make Dad mad with me. I'm crying and I'm afraid of Dad.

C: Anything else?

B: I'm a baby, now. I'm four months old. I see my mother breast feeding me in our living room and Dad is reading the newspaper. Mom is getting up to put me in a crib upstairs and I don't want to go. I start crying when she puts me down. I feel lonely. I want her to hold me. I want her to let me stay in her arms. I don't like the dark. I cry and cry and nobody comes. I see two bright and shiny people perched on the rails of my crib. They are singing to me and I stop crying. I love them. I was with them on the other side, before I came through the haze. They are my friends and my mentors. They live on a high level in Heaven. They helped me make my transition back to Earth. I love them.

C: What are they singing?

B: A song we used to sing while I was on the other side. It's called God is Up & Down & All Around. We all used to sing it before I came back. Harriet has her violin.

C: Who is Harriett?

B: My friend and mentor on the other side. She was like my mother over there. She loves me very much and she tells me that after she and Larry sing to me.

C: Who is Larry?

B: The other person who is with her. Larry lives in heaven, too. He used to play with me a lot. He taught me a lot, too. He loves me too. They both kiss me goodnight and go upward through the ceiling of my room and then they are gone. I feel better now and I am drifting off to sleep.

C: What else do you see? What is going on?

B: I'm back in the haze.

C: The haze? Where is that and what are you doing?

B: It's where I was right before I came back to Earth. It's where people become used to a heavier atmosphere than Heaven. It's how we get to try out our new physical forms...our new bodies. Our mentors take us there and they tell us about our new parents and the new life that we will be going back into. It's like a practice time before coming back. You should pray and ask God to help you in your new life. You get to actually see who you will be born to. You get to know a lot about your new life even before you are born again. You get to look back over your last life and see the mistakes which you made and you are told why you must return to Earth. You are warned to stop listening to everything you are taught by this world and you are warned of the pitfalls of following many cultural and religious traditions. We are taught a lot of wrong ways of behaving on Earth and we must stop listening to our authorities on everything like they are Gods. The Haze is where you may make trial trips into your new body to either turn it in your mother's womb or stay there for a while and enjoy the peacefulness of her womb.

C: You are allowed to go into your new body and leave it at will, while it is still developing in your mother's womb?

B: Yes. It is in various stages of development and when it is ready for the new life to reenter Earth, we have to stay there. We are then "glued" or bonded to the physical body and not allowed to get out.

C: What do you mean by glued?

B: It's an electromagnetic chemical process which bonds our electromagnetic astral body which some call the soul or the real person to the physical form which he will be in for the new lifetime.

C: What about timing? When do you have to be glued into your new physical body?

B: It depends on whether or not your birth will be on time or early. If it will be early you are bonded in around the time of the delivery. But if it is on time, you are bonded in around the time of the eighth or close to the ninth month period when delivery is due.

C: Why is that?

B: Because you have to get inside in order to be born again and you don't necessarily have to stay inside for the full time that the baby is being carried. You still have ways to grow even in the waiting period and that would be like wasted time if you just went in as soon as the mother conceived and stayed there for nine months or so.

C: Are you certain?

B: Yes, my angels are with me in the haze and they tell me about God's plan for my new life. They would not tell me anything that was not true. They would get demoted and maybe sent back to Earth and Earth is Hell. They would be breaking their promise to God. They don't do that.

C: I see. What else is happening? Are you still in the haze?

B: No, I'm in a Japanese city and I am at home preparing a meal for my husband and children.

C: Where are you?

B: I am in Japan. I am who I was before I came back to Earth.

C: You are a woman now?

B: Yes.

C: What are you experiencing or seeing?

B: I am walking in our garden. I seldom go outside because my husband does not allow it. I have to respect him and give in to his wishes and demands. I pretend that I am happy when he is around, but I am very unhappy.

C: Why don't you just leave?

B: No. I cannot do that. It is the custom of a Japanese woman to obey her husband. She will bring dishonor to everyone if she does otherwise. I do whatever he tells me to do. I do his bidding and I live to make his life comfortable and satisfactory.

C: Do you love him?

B: Not really. I must stay, though because I am a good Japanese wife. I will not dishonor our family. I was once a geisha in another city and he married me and brought me here.

C: What did you do as a geisha?

B: I was a companion to men of high breeding. I entertained them and kept them company.

C: Is your husband there with you now?

B: He is at work now, and I am doing my tasks around the house.

C: Who is there with you now?

B: I have a woman here who helps me with the chores. My husband pays her to help and keep me company.

C: What are you doing now?

B: I am now back in the haze.

C: What are you doing there?

B: I am with my angels and they want to know if I want to see my life before I was a Japanese woman?

C: What are you telling them?

B: I am telling them that I do want to see who I was before I was a Japanese woman. They said that I had to come back to earth as a white male this time to learn how to be my own person... to learn how not to be totally dependent and obedient to a man. They say that God's way is the way of strength, independence and obedience to God, not to man. They say I will be taught the strengths of men, like earning my own way, and not being a man's robot. I am a female in a male body because God wants me to unlearn the wrong ways which my culture taught women. My angels tell me that God does not want anyone to be subservient to anyone on this earth. They say we need to question what we are taught by our world... our cultures and our religions.

C: Are you saying that you are a gay or homosexual person?

B: Yes, I am.

C: As a female in a male body, what is your purpose?

B: To develop the strengths of men. I have to learn how to be my own person and not be subservient to anyone. My angels are also telling me that I cannot engage sexually with the same sex without penalties from God. They say my karmic debt to God will be worse if I live the gay lifestyle. It is my burden. It is my negative karmic load, they say. I must bear it like a cross, but I will grow stronger in the process. They say I am supposed to have sex with females since I have a male body. My angels say that God is both punisher and nurturing parent to all God's creations. My karma is for two purposes: to help me grow stronger and to punish me for my wrong and harmful behavior in my life as a Japanese woman.

C: I see. Are you still there in the haze with your angels?

B: No, we are going through a big brown wooden door. It's hinges are so heavy you can hear them creak when the door opens. We are going back to my life before I was a Japanese woman. We are entering a place which has a lot of plants. It looks like a forest or a jungle of some sort. I am walking through this place with my angels.

C: Can you see yourself?

B: I can see my body. I am very dark. I am very, very dark. I am an African woman. I have on a beautiful robe. It has gold threads and many colors in it. I am entering a city and going to my work. I have many friends at work. I work at an outdoor market. I am speaking to all of my friends and each person greets me with a smile and a warm hello in my native language.

C: What are you doing?

B: I am leaving work now and going home to my husband and children.

C: What are you doing now?

B: We are at a wedding. My cousin is getting married and we are having a big celebration. There are hundreds of people there. My cousin is a government official and he knows many people.

C: Do you know which country you are in?

B: I am not given the name of the country. My angels want me to know that I was returned to a life in Japan to help me learn to be thrifty and good with handling money. I have been through at least thirty lives as a human being, they say. They tell me that I was in other life forms also.

C: Are you still there in Africa?

B: Yes. I see a beautiful mountain and there are gorillas on the mountain.

C: That is wonderful. Byron, I am going to bring you away from that place in a very few minutes. I want you to come back through those doors with me. Wave goodbye to your angels and I will count from one to five. On each count, you will become wider and wider awake. Do you understand?

B: Yes.

C: Good. One, you are coming away from your past lives, passing back through the doors that you went through to get there. Two. Feeling wider awake. Three. Coming back. Four. Feeling wider awake. And Five. You are now fully awake, feeling very, very energized and wide awake. Open your eyes.

[Byron apparently opens his eyes. They discuss whether or not he remembered anything from the session. He did not. Rev. Clarence told him what he experienced under hypnosis and Byron expressed shock regarding his two prior incarnations. Additional information on reincarnation may be found in Chapter 11, Reverend Clarence's Revelations.]

Chapter 13

True Experiences of Ordinary People

I Saw My Doctors Save My Life When I Died

[This account of a hospital operation was told to me by a young woman who, at the time, was around 30 years old. She had scheduled her surgery and everything was proceeding normally, or so they thought, until she was declared dead due to an allergic reaction from her anesthesia. She was revived, and the following is an account of her experience. Her name and other identifying facts have been changed. The account of her story, however, is entirely intact.]

My operation was scheduled for a Tuesday morning in October of 1994. It would be a routine D & C (Dilation & Curettage). Many women have it after childbirth and for other gynecological reasons. It simply involves dilating the uterus and cleaning the inner lining of whatever should not be present. I was not at all concerned or worried because my physician had explained the entire procedure to me.

That morning, my husband dropped me off at the hospital on his way to work. My mother was babysitting our two children for us that day. We had a three year-old boy and a 2 months-old daughter. I insisted that he not stay because it was such a simple procedure. He really did not want to leave me there alone, but I insisted.

After he checked me in, he made sure that everything was on schedule before he left. He said he would return that evening to pick me up; we said our goodbyes and the nursing staff took over and prepped me for the operation. The staff was very friendly and there was a lot of camaraderie between them as they joked about various things. Everyone was lighthearted and one of the nurses jokingly said to me, "Christine, do you want a cowgirl hat to go with those stirrups?" We all laughed and were having a great time. My doctor and the anesthesiologist came in and I knew then, that it was time to get down to serious business.

The anesthesiologist asked me how much I weighed. I told him that I weighed one hundred thirty pounds and he looked at my chart and checked off something. Then he put a needle in my arm and started the IV. He said, "You're going to enjoy this, just a nice peaceful nap this morning. Start at one hundred and start counting backward." I started counting, "One hundred, ninety-nine, ninety-eight, ninety-seven..." I started to feel myself become very, very drowsy; my eyelids closed and I felt myself going into a peaceful oblivion. My ears started ringing and I could feel myself sinking further into a comfortable darkness. I didn't know what was wrong because I suddenly came out of it. I Heard cries of alarm! "Get the cart! Get the cart!" I heard someone scream. I opened my eyes and I was floating on the ceiling inside the operating room. I saw my doctor, the anesthesiologist, the nurse and two other people administering paddles to my chest. I thought, "Oh, my God, I must have died!" I was looking at my body on the operating table. They were working on me. I saw my doctor, the anesthesiologist, the nurse and two other people administering paddles to my chest. I thought, "Oh, my God! I must have died!" I was looking at my body on the operating table. My doctor shouted, "Clear!" I saw my body jerk as he administered the electrically charged paddles to the area around my heart. I thought, "My heart must have stopped beating! But, I'm not dead! I feel great!" As I hovered on the ceiling, I could see that they were feverishly, frantically working on me. My doctor shouted, "This is unheard of! Did you check to see if she had allergies or reactions to any anesthetics?" The anesthesiologist didn't answer; he just kept a stern face as my doctor worked on me. I felt good; I felt light and free. I didn't want to go back into my body. Then I thought about my children and my husband. They needed me. I prayed and asked God to let me live again and I started crying. I was both happy and sad. I loved how I felt. I could move about on the ceiling. I started to move outside the operating room, but something kept pulling me back. "I can't leave them. Please, God. Don't make me leave them now." I prayed. I was being drawn down the hallway by a force which was very strong and fast-moving. I was moving upward at a very rapid rate. I came out of the roof of the hospital and I was moving upward into the sky. I was suddenly aware that two beings of light were with me. We slowed down some and they told me, "You must go back. God is allowing you another chance to change your life. You must stop what you are doing. It will ruin your life and the lives of your family. You must earn whatever you get; nothing is free on Earth. Measure for measure you will be repaid, both good and bad." Suddenly, I felt a tug and I was being drawn back into my operating room. My body was still lying lifeless on the table. They were still working on me. I heard my doctor swear and then I felt another tug; the darkness came again.

I awakened in the recovery room. I told my nurse that I saw them working on me and her mouth opened but no words came out. I said, "I know I died and you guys brought me back, didn't you." She still said nothing. I said, "I heard my doctor and the anesthesiologist. I told her what my doctor had said and she was dumbfounded. She said, "Yes, everything happened just as you said, but how do you know this?" I told her that I had seen and heard everything from the ceiling. She said, "That's really hard to believe." I asked, "Why? Don't you believe in the hereafter?" She replied, "Yes, but ..."
I said, "I know what happened and I will not sue the anesthesiologist if that's what you're worried about. I just received confirmation from God that life is everlasting God let me stay here because I prayed to stay here and raise my children. I was leaving, but I prayed to stay and finish my work. Thank you, God!"

Afterwards, I told my doctor and the anesthesiologist that I was not angry. They, too, were dumbfounded when I repeated my experience to them. I am grateful to God for allowing me more time to be with my family. I know that I have work to do here and I will certainly change things in my life that I was doing wrong. Drinking to excess was one of them; I am a recovering alcoholic. The other problem was an addiction to gambling. I had squandered my husband's money and money from my part-time job on many occasions. We almost lost our house once. I have stopped doing both. I know that God showed me through that experience that I must change my life or lose it. I chose to change it.

Mama Came to Tell Me Goodbye After She Died

I had just come home from the office after working late on the evening of October 19, 1999. I was exhausted and had planned to do nothing more than eat something light, soak in a hot bubble bath and get into bed. My twenty-two year-old daughter who was attending law school and staying at home (not to her liking) greeted me at the door , took off my coat and asked me to sit down and rest myself... not her usual style unless she was about to play a prank on me or something was wrong. My first questions were, "What? What's wrong? What did you do?" She hesitated and she kept insisting that I sit down and she told me that she was going to get me a glass of water. I said, "Come back here Paduka (one of my many nicknames for her). What are you up to? Did you have an accident with the Jeep or lose something of mine? Why are you acting so weird?" She started wringing her hands and after a couple of seconds she responded, "Auntie Nibbles just called and she said that they took Grandma to the hospital. Ma, don't get upset." I was very upset. My eighty-plus mother had Alzheimer's disease and I thought that something had happened to her as a result of the progression of the disease. I cried and my sweet, loving daughter comforted me by hugging me and offering words of comfort.

I immediately made a long distance call to my sister, Nibbles, a nickname someone had given her when we were kids because she was a quick eater and she liked to eat with her hands then. When I talked to Nibbles, she said that our mother had a stroke that afternoon. My kind and nurturing sister had been caring for our mother, first in her home and then in my mother's home after mama decided that she did not want to live with anyone and that she wanted to go back to her house. Between Nibbles' full time job, caring for her husband and grandchildren, and caring for our mother, I knew that she must have been very tired. Nibbles would go to our mother's house every morning, give her medicine, feed her, leave her job at noon for lunch, go to our mother's house and have lunch with her, come back in the evening before going home, fix mama's dinner and make sure she was fine for the night. I tried to relieve her whenever I could come out to stay for awhile, but we lived over seven hundred miles apart and my help was not frequent. Our male cousin lived downstairs in the house with our mother and that was some comfort, but he did not have time to do all the things for her that she required. We were just grateful for his presence because he would look in on her periodically. It was Nibbles who found her around lunchtime that day, unable to move from her bed, still clothed in her bathrobe. She usually got up, bathed, ate breakfast and sat in bed in her robe and read the morning paper. When Nibbles found her, she was still able to communicate with her. Nibbles said that when she left the hospital, mama was sleeping. I told her that I would catch a plane out first thing in the morning.

I went alone because Paduka had a couple of midterm tests the next day and we thought that mama would recover soon and be able to go home. The plane left on time. I didn't like my seat, however. I was in one of those seats which faces the rear of the plane and you ride backwards. I hate riding backwards on subway trains, let alone, an airplane. I was reading a magazine, when for some reason I looked down the aisle and I saw that a woman who was facing me, approximately six rows away was a dead-ringer for my older sister who had passed from breast cancer a few years earlier. I couldn't take my eyes off her. I couldn't believe it. I thought that this must be some sort of message that God was giving me. My sister's look-alike was on this flight with me! The thought came to my mind that God always sends a comforter in times of trouble. I felt that God was telling me that my big sister was, indeed, by my side, in spirit. Then, I wondered if God had sent her to accompany mama. I believe that we are escorted on our journey to our heavenly home by those who have an attachment to us as well as by our angels. I wondered if I would get there in time to see mama. I was sick inside at the thought of losing her. Before her illness struck, she had been our right arm, our hub in the wheel of our lives, and our loving confidant...not only to her daughters, but to many who knew her. She gave to everyone, unselfishly...her church members, her friends, and her family. She was dearly loved by many people. I kept staring at the lady who looked like my deceased sister, but she never looked in my direction.

Nibbles picked me up at the airport and we drove directly to the hospital from there. The doctors had put mama on life support. When we went in to see her, she looked like she was sleeping peacefully. She was breathing with the aid of the life support system and she looked very peaceful. We went to the hospital twice that day, morning and evening. We thought that she would pull through; her doctors said that she had a fifty-fifty chance, however.   I told Nibbles that I would spend the night at mama's house since our cousin was out of town. She said, "O.K. I'll pick you up tomorrow morning to go to the hospital."

I retired around midnight after reading a couple of magazines to relax. I slept in the guest bedroom near the bathroom. I am a very sound sleeper, especially when I am tired. Normally, I require eight to nine hours of sleep in order to function adequately. I was suddenly pulled out of my sleep. It was still dark. Every cell in my brain and body had suddenly gone from sleepy to wide awake and alert as if an alarm had just gone off. I lay awake wondering what was going on. I am never, ever alert at night, and mornings are not much better. Suddenly, I heard, "I love you." It was mama's voice! She sounded happy and I sensed that she was with someone else; I sensed the presence of two others. I mentally responded, "I love you, too, and I want you to be happy." I waited for a response back, but there was none. I lay in the darkened room waiting for her to say something else, but I sensed that they had left. I turned on the lamp by the bed and looked at the clock. It was 6:00 A.M. She was gone. She had died. I knew it. God had allowed her to come to me and tell me goodbye before taking her to Heaven. I wondered who the other two beings were. I thought that maybe one was my sister who was already on the other side and the other one might have been her guardian angel. I believed that was who they were. My sister was sent by God to accompany her home. Maybe that's why she sounded so happy! I went back to sleep feeling comforted, but knowing that mama was gone.

Nibbles awakened me at ten o'clock that same morning. It was now October 21. She said, "I'll pick you up around noon; I already went out to the hospital early this morning, and she has had no change. I think she's gone, though. I'm glad I got to tell her I loved her the day she took sick. I asked mama to squeeze my hand if she understood me and she did."

I said, "Nibbles, she is gone. She left this morning. She came by here to tell me goodbye." I told Nibbles what I had experienced and we both agreed that mama had died and gone to Heaven.

Three more days elapsed before we decided to turn off mama's life support. It was well past the time to do so. She had left this earth and we were holding on to an empty shell. They cut it off at our request and she, indeed, was not breathing on her own. The doctors said that she died on October 24, but we know that she died on October 21. She began her journey to heaven on that date, but not before coming home to tell me goodbye. I thanked God for that moment with her before God took her home. She sounded so happy!

The Out-of-Body Traveler

[The following is an account of ten educators at a West Coast college who participated in a meditation workshop in the late 1970's. The workshop lasted approximately two hours. It was conducted in the early afternoon on a day when the college was in full session for the fall semester. Each participant volunteered to join the group because he or she wanted to learn the art of meditation for the purposes of relaxation, reflection, planning for the future, and other self-actualizing endeavors Actual names and other identifying information have been changed for legal reasons.]

The session began with a challenge from our convener, Dr. Greene, to stretch our minds and reach beyond
the known and accepted ways of thinking about our universe. He said, "Life is full of knowns and unknowns. We
are comfortable with the known, the tried and true, but very
uncomfortable with the unknown. Many times, in fact,
when we are confronted with unknowns, we deny the existence of the unknown simply because it does not fit into our
framework of known constructs or facts. How, then, are we
to learn if the unknown presents such a frightening, sometimes angering proposition for us? The question we must
ask ourselves is this: Are we brave enough to challenge the
accepted ways of thinking about our world or will we deny
the existence of those frightening unknowns, even when we
are staring them in the face? Many choose to deny that
things, which are a part of the subjective experiences of
others, really exist.

Science says that if we all cannot experience something, then one individual cannot experience it without others in his presence experiencing the same thing. We deny
the existence of extra-terrestrial beings even when we know
that there are perhaps millions of solar systems in other
galaxies like ours which may support life. We are foolish
beings, we humans. We are fearful beings. So, we ridicule
cutting edge ideas, pound the authors of new theories into
the dust with jealous rage, and subject free-thinkers to ostracism because they dared to think outside the proverbial
box. We don't like change very much, especially when it
shakes our beliefs and causes us to think in other ways,
think about the possibility of the scary unknown being a
real phenomenon or fact. Ladies and gentlemen, are you
brave enough to open up your minds to the exciting, inner
world of metaphysical truths? Are you bold enough to em-
bark on a journey into the unknown? If you are, you may
consider yourselves like the timeless traveler, Odysseus,
who traveled into lands unknown and experienced many
things. Your Odyssey, however, will be for your own self-
enlightenment and self-fulfillment. If you are ready for your
voyage into uncharted seas, let's begin. Are there any questions before we begin?"

Ms. Douglas asked, "Dr. Greene, How will we know
when to stop meditating. Suppose you want to stop and it's

not time to stop because the group is still meditating? Can I
stop whenever I want to or do I have to wait for you to tell
me to stop?"

Dr. Greene replied, "Ms. Douglas, you may stop
whenever you like. No one can force you to do anything in
here against your will. Let me make this perfectly clear,
group. Everyone is here because he wants to be here.
Right?"

"Right.", they all replied.

"O.K. Here's the deal, whatever you don't want to do,
don't do it. If you want to stop in the middle of your voyage,
just open your eyes and sit quietly until the group finishes.
Allow others to finish without disturbing them. Is that alright with everyone?"

"Yes.", the group replied.

"Alright, then, let's catch our starship. I want everyone to get comfortable and relax. If your shoes hurt, take
them off. If your belt is too tight, loosen it. You should relax
as much as possible." The group, which was seated around
a large oval table, was sitting in large plush leather chairs.
Some of the men loosened their ties. A couple of women removed their high-heeled shoes and a few people took their
last sips of water for awhile. Dr. Greene continued, "I will
not be meditating with you, today. I will be monitoring and
observing you. O.K? Before I begin to meditate, I always
pray to God for guidance and enlightenment or about specific matters. I don't know anyone's religion here, but let us
observe a moment of silence so that those who pray may do
so. (Approximately one minute passed.)   O.K. Everyone,
close your eyes."

All eyes closed and Dr. Greene continued, "I want
you to think of this day as the most magnificent day that
you have had in a long time. You are feeling great. Your
health is good. Your job is satisfying and you are one of the
happiest people on this planet. Oh, sure, there are some
problems, everyday ones which come with just living. But,
for today, there is nothing...absolutely nothing that is going
wrong in your life. God is in Heaven and Earth and every
little or big thing is going to be alright. Just relax and in
your mind's eye think of a blank movie screen. Imagine that
you are sitting in a movie theater waiting for the picture
show to start. The screen is blank and you are very relaxed

and comfortable in your seat. You don't know what movie will be playing today. It will be a surprise for you. You will enjoy it, however. Just look at that blank movie screen and throw all extraneous worrisome thoughts out of the side door of that movie theater. Whenever a bothersome thought comes to you, just mentally pitch it toward the door and it will go through it like an x-ray...over and out.   Relax and enjoy the calm and peace of the darkened theater. As soon as you are relaxed and ready to watch the movie, mentally push the on button located at the top of the screen to the left. It's a blue button. Just push it on and your movie will begin. When you are finished with your movie, your screen will go blank and you may open your eyes and sit quietly. You will remember everything about your movie after you open your eyes."

Dr. Greene said that the first person to open his eyes did so after twenty-five minutes of meditation and the others opened their eyes at various intervals after that. After one hour, only one gentleman, Dr. Cotton, had not opened his eyes. Dr. Cotton's head was resting on his chest as if he were in slumber. He was breathing normally, but the group only had approximately forty minutes for feedback. Dr. Greene decided to ask Dr. Cotton to come out of his meditative state and join the others for a feedback session.

"Dr. Cotton," he said. He got no response. Again he said, "Dr. Cotton, please open your eyes and join us. We are about to tell about our experiences." There was still no response from Dr. Cotton. Dr. Greene walked over to Dr. Cotton and shook his shoulders vigorously to bring him out of his meditative state. Dr. Cotton's head jerked up from his chest, his arms flailed the air and his legs went up and down in a quick motion as if he were trying to balance himself. Dr. Greene asked, "Are you O.K. Dr. Cotton?"

Dr. Cotton replied, "Yes. Yes, I'm fine. That is, I think I'm fine."

"Great," said Dr. Greene. "Now it's time for us to share our experiences. Who wants to be first?"

Ms. Douglas raised her hand and said, "I'd like to be first, Dr. Greene. My movie screen was so funny. I saw myself when I was a child. I had fallen into the mud playing on a rainy day with my friend, Becky, who lived next door to us. My mother had dressed me for a birthday party and I was supposed to be eating in the kitchen, but I sneaked out the back door. She was so angry when she found me, that she spanked me and made me change my clothes. Next, I saw several scenes from my high school days. My old boyfriend and some of my friends were at a bonfire on the beach. We were roasting wieners and having a good time when we heard screams from the lake. Two of our friends had gone to the edge of the lake to be alone in a canoe, but they paddled it out into the lake and tragedy struck. Both the boy and the girl drowned. Next, I saw her face in the clouds. She was waving to me and she said these exact words, 'We're not sleeping up here. We work and we have fun. I love it.' I saw a few other scenes from my first marriage, but the scenes were as they could have been, not as things actually were. In other words, I saw myself doing more positive things and speaking in a more conciliatory manner to my first husband instead of criticizing him for various things."

"That's all very revealing, Ms. Douglas. You were shown many things through your meditation visions. You got a look at Heaven; you saw how you could have saved your first marriage; and, you saw how rebellious you were as a child. Before we leave here today, I want everyone to write down as many things as they can remember about their "movie" today. If we do not get a chance to finish with everyone, I can meet with you individually to go over your experiences at a later date. "

Mr. Jones interjected, "Dr. Greene, may I be next? I really would like to share this with the entire group."

"Certainly, go right ahead," said Dr. Greene.

Mr. Jones said, "I saw a most frightening thing on my screen. That's why I opened my eyes early. I didn't want to see anymore of it. I saw myself in a war. The equipment was old, the artillery was old and it looked as if I was in another century...in another country. If I had to guess, I would say that it looked like I was a Roman soldier. I had on sandals and a leather tunic; I was carrying a sword and I wore a metal helmet. I was so tired from marching through the countryside that I had a youth that I met on the trail carry my weapons and other gear for me. My feet were sore and bleeding. I was hungry and half-sick. It smelled awful

where we were because there were bodies on the ground. I really didn't want to see anymore, so I opened my eyes."

Dr. Greene said, "Mr. Jones, I certainly understand your being uncomfortable with your movie, however, you missed the important part of it, the outcome. You see, meditation always supplies answers to our problems, issues, dilemmas or whatever is going on. The war is symbolic of a struggle going on in your life. You must deal with it like a warrior. If you had continued to watch your "movie", a solution to your real life problem would have been offered."

"Oh, maybe I will try it again, then... on my own. Thanks," said Mr. Jones.

Dr. Cotton raised his hand next and blurted out, "You all might have seen movies, but I think I saw some real life action. I was in Texas at my parents' house. Mom was sitting in the kitchen in a yellow flowered dress peeling potatoes and chopping onions to go in a beef stew she had simmering on the stove. My dad was in the living room reading a book and the old dog, Jeremy, was lying at his feet sleeping. I walked all over the house and outside, too. I walked all over the neighborhood and saw a lot of sights. The next thing I knew, I was back here in this chair. What was that all about?"

Dr. Greene said, "Dr. Cotton, what you are describing sounds very much like an out-of-body experience. Now, it doesn't happen often, but if God has something extremely important to show you about life and death, it may very well occur, even when you are not meditating... under other circumstances. That is what I have observed; and, I have been in this field about twenty years. The only way to find out if that is truly what you experienced is to call your parents and ask them what they were doing about a half hour ago. You can verify it with a simple phone call. Would you like to do that now or wait until our session is over?"

Dr. Cotton said, "Heck, let's get it on. I want to know now if I was out of my body!"

Dr. Greene said, "Please ask the person in charge of long distance dialing here to make the call to your parents' home. Just so the group and I will know exactly what your parents tell you, you should talk to them and just ask them to tell your 'friend' what they were doing half and hour ago.

Don't say why yet, just say you're involved in a little experiment for now. O.K.?"

"Sure. Fine," Dr. Cotton said. They drew lengths of paper to determine who would be the person to verify Dr. Cotton's experience. Dr. Lillian, as everyone called her drew the shortest piece and she was the verifier. The call was made from a phone in the room. Dr. Cotton handed the phone to Dr. Lillian after he asked his mother to describe what she was doing. Dr. Lillian asked, "What were you wearing while you were doing that and where was your husband and what was he doing?" Dr. Lillian's eyes opened very wide and her mouth formed an oval. She said softly, "Thank you very much. Here is your son, again."

After Dr. Cotton chatted with his parents for a couple of minutes, he promised to call them back later. He hung up the phone and looked at Dr. Lillian. "Well?" he asked.

She replied, "Your mother said she was cutting potatoes and onions for a beef stew which she was fixing for dinner. She said she was wearing a yellow flowered dress. She also said your father was reading in the living room and that he was in there with the dog."

Everyone was astounded. Dr. Cotton had experienced out-of-body travel during the session and had re-entered his body only when Dr. Greene shook him. The rest of the group related their experiences but no one really could forget the one very unusual experience of one in their midst.

Afterwards, Dr. Greene talked to Dr. Cotton and discovered that matters of life and death had always puzzled him. He was not certain that he even believed in life after death. His faith was on shaky ground and he needed that verification of life outside of the physical body. God showed him firsthand that he was inside of flesh and that he could exist separate from his physical form.

[The following accounts were written and submitted to me by people who wanted their stories included in a regional journal on E.S.P during the early nineteen seventies.]

Shana's Eye of Understanding

I had a personal experience that was both surprising and revealing. I was bathing in warm water in the middle of the day. The bathroom was full of steam. For some reason, I thought about meditating. Maybe it was because of the steam which reminded me of fine mist or maybe it was because of my constant search to uncover some of life's mysteries.

Anyway, I forced myself to be calm. I put a warm cloth to my face and I inhaled the warm soapy vapor from the washcloth. I closed my eyes and I started meditating. I tried to keep all problems and earthly cares from entering my mind. After batting these kinds of thoughts from my mind, I concentrated on God and a deep, warm feeling of love poured into my being. All of a sudden, I saw this eye! It was peering at me - one eye! It looked like it was really looking at me. The eye was like a vignette; at the outer edges, the eye seemed to blend into the blackness which surrounded it. I can't remember if the eye was blue or brown. Anyway, it jolted me. I snatched the washcloth from my face and started wondering about it. It stayed on my mind for a couple of days and I thought to myself, "Should I paint it?" But I felt too strongly involved with the eye then to paint it.

So, I wrote my friend who is sensitive and I related the whole experience to her. She wrote back that she saw an eye on a black telephone a few days before I wrote. The company which she works for had just moved into larger offices. She said that she picked up a black telephone in the new office and there, taped to the inside handle of the receiver was a blue eye! It seemed rather odd to her, she said. I couldn't quite figure out what it meant then and I sort of let it go. But, about two weeks later, I was at another friend's house and I saw another eye! It was in a painting which she had painted five years ago. It, too, was surrounded by black and staring at me. It was a brown eye!

Since then, I've learned through meditation and asking questions in prayer, that the eye means understanding about God and life. The color blue stands for good spiritual growth and development and brown means strength and power. My vision of the eye was a message from God telling me about my spiritual development.

Jacqueline's Spiritual Geometry

After arriving home from participating in a "past re-trieval session", I read a magazine; then, I meditated. About 9:00 P.M. during meditation, I saw a round circle of light; then it changed into a diamond shape. About two weeks ago during one of my meditation periods, I saw a pyramid shape with an eye near the top.

I know that thoughts are alive. One day not so long ago while working around the house, I was thinking about the different things I would like to have. After going to sleep during the night, I dreamed about these things. The mes-sage that I heard between sleeping and waking was, "Thoughts are alive!"   We must get rid of the negative thoughts and raise our consciousness to the positive as-pects of life. I have since learned that each geometric form has a meaning. God speaks to us through these forms and through many other ways. The circle means protection and the circle of light represented a message about safety and my protection. Usually, it means money or some type of safeguard. The diamond represents a message about rein-carnation. Seeing the two together is a sign that my means of support would cause me to come back to earth because there are weaknesses associated with it. God's first law for all the life on earth is "Survival of the Strongest." We must compete for everything in order to survive and develop courage and strength; each person must depend on God, only, to guide them in their activities.

Patrice Sees the Afterlife!

You know, I used to sit and read the Bible all the time when I was pregnant and I used to meditate quite fre-quently. Well, one day I was reading the Bible and I stopped reading for a while. I just sat there thinking about what I had read and a picture of what I had read came to my mind.

Next, I went over to the bed and I lay down because I wanted to relax for a moment after reading. I wasn't really tired, but I'm just saying this to let you know that I wasn't... you know...asleep! I lay there for a few minutes still thinking about what I had read when all of a sudden, I felt myself sort of lifted up! I had a sort of buoyant feeling - a floating feeling! All of a sudden, I heard the most beautiful music! There sat a group of unfamiliar people. There weren't any steps, but they were placed as if they were sitting on steps and they had instruments which they were playing! It was beautiful! I had a very happy feeling. And, the music - I don't know - it's so hard to explain because it was the most beautiful music that I had ever heard in my life! I wanted to stay when, all of a sudden, I happened to look down and saw my body lying on the bed! The first thing I thought was, "Oh, my goodness, don't tell me that I've died!" Then I thought about the baby I was going to have and I prayed, "Please, Lord, don't let me die now. Please let me go back and have my baby!" Then I started jerking myself and I kept jerking myself and...I don't know. It seemed like a long time but I don't really know how long the experience lasted; but after I jerked myself awhile, I finally found myself floating back down and I was back in my body again."

[Patrice experienced an astral projection (a separation of her spirit body or soul from her physical body). This phenomenon is also known as an out-of-body experience or OBE. These experiences are thought to be for the purposes of divine healing and spiritual enlightenment]

Frederick and the Unheard Caller

One afternoon as I was working around the apartment, the telephone rang. I picked it up and it was my mother who lives in another city. We scarcely had a chance to say hello when, suddenly, the phone connection went bad. I could hear her very well but she said that she could barely hear me. I had to almost scream through the phone to make myself heard but I could hear her voice clearly. I guess she got tired of trying to hear me so I told her that I would call her back in a couple of days.

I did call her back a few days afterward and she told me that someone had called my aunt who also lives in another city and whoever it was could not he heard on the telephone. My aunt thought that it was me calling her long distance. Then, I talked with my dad, he told me that he was visiting my uncle who lives in the same city as my parents and someone called long distance while he was there. The only sound which came through the telephone was the operator's voice because this caller could not be heard either! For some strange reason they all thought that it was me on the other end trying to get through.

Well, to top it off, the very next day after I had talked with them about the strange long distance telephone calls and the caller who could not be heard, something even more unnerving happened. I got up that morning and I was feeling fine, but as the day progressed, I started feeling very tired so I lay down to take a nap. I rested for about an hour or so and then I got up. After I had been up for about a half hour or so, the telephone rang. I picked up the phone and nothing came out of my mouth! I had lost my voice! I had laryngitis and the sounds which came from my throat were merely squeaks and low sounding growls.

My family thought that the voiceless caller was me: my mother could not hear me although I could hear her and my aunt and uncle both received calls from someone whom they could not hear.

I know now that it was a sign from God letting me and my family know in advance that I, indeed, would not be heard because I would lose my voice temporarily. I know also that when I lost my voice, I was getting a "spanking" from God about work because the throat area of the body deals with work. A new work venture of mine was floundering because of my bad judgment and procrastination! The three phone calls symbolized God's number or God's will! [Frederick was a student of divine signs and symbols at the time he related this story.]

Some Dreams and Visions Come True

Sally's Vision:

On this particular afternoon, a situation took place at the office where I work. I was sitting at my desk. There was another worker sitting across from me and there was a vacant desk in front of her. There suddenly appeared in pale-golden light the body of a female. I mentioned this to my co-worker. I asked her if she saw it and she said that she did. I, then, told her to speak to the female in the light because my co-worker "sees". She knows more about visions than I.

She spoke to this lady and the lady said that she was coming to work within 30 days. The woman in the light said that her name was Jean and my co-worker observed that she had blond hair. Within 30 days a lady with blond hair reported to work and sat at that desk.

Bill's Dream:

I was working on a construction job at the time this happened. I always have had true dreams and I've been able to foretell the future sometimes because I get feelings about things before they happen.

Well, one night I had a dream about my foreman. In this dream he was walking around just as healthy as you please and then the next thing you know, I saw this clock in the dream and this clock struck one o'clock and I heard a voice say, "Big John died at one o'clock." I thought it was real, but then I woke up and realized I had been dreaming.

The boys at work know I have true dreams and they get scared sometimes when I tell them things. I told one of the boys about the dream I had and he walked off shaking his head. He said, "Bill, don't tell me no more. I don't wan'na hear no more."

Everything went along O.K. for two or three days, then one day when I was working, my friend came over to me and he said, "Guess what, Bill?" I asked, "What?" He shook his head as he answered, 'Big John just dropped dead, man!" My mouth dropped wide open; then something told me to look at my watch. I did. It was one o'clock - just as it was in the dream.

[In both of these true accounts each person had a vision. In the first experience, two people had the same wide-awake vision (waking-vision) and in the second experience, the man had a sleeping-vision (dream). The only difference between the two types of visions was the person's state of consciousness or wakefulness.]

One Sign for Many People

Grace's Experience: Tadpole in the Sky

This incident happened about 6:30 A.M. one December day, I was going to work and it was dark. I looked up in the sky and there was an orange oval light. It was shaped like a polliwog or tadpole. I continued to watch the oval as it expanded into a larger oval. There was a man standing at the bus stop with me and I called it to his attention. He thought it might be the Army shooting rockets from Wallops Island, Virginia.

A woman pulled up in her car and got out of the car to mail a letter and I mentioned it to her. She saw it. She got back into her car and drove off. Then after a few moments, from the upper left-hand top corner of the polliwog-tailed oval there was a movement which proceeded out and away from the oval and in a straight line; and, then it just disappeared into nothing.

Polliwogs or tadpoles are baby frogs. Frogs are a symbol of evil and harm. The baby frog meant a growing evil or harmful condition on Earth. Orange, which is a combination of red and yellow, has a double meaning. Yellow=truth and purity and red=a weakness. Even the time which I saw it (6:30) is a message. Six is God's command to stop something and 3 (3 + 0 = 3) is God's will or wishes. The fact that the polliwog changed into a straight line was an admonition to follow the "straight and narrow" pathway in life. God was giving us all a sign about listening to some religious authorities and being misled. It was also a message about conforming to weak and harmful social customs or traditions.

[Grace was also a student of divine signs and symbols at the time she experienced this phenomenon.]

Chapter 14

Everyone Has Intuition

Anyone Can Channel

"Learning How to Channel the Safe Way" was the theme of this workshop which took place in the fall of 1991. Six doctoral candidates were present, including myself as the convener, two spiritually gifted ordained ministers, one of whom was Rev. Mother Mary Braganza (one of the seven shamans), two spiritually gifted laypersons and three guests. This day long workshop was in fulfillment of one of ten required peer days in our doctoral program. A peer day could be on any topic chosen by the convener and agreed upon by the participants. It could be a day long activity, a course of study, or any meaningful and worthwhile endeavor.

Our day began at 9:00 A.M. in my home with a continental breakfast, which I served. During this time guests and peers discussed their concepts of channeling as well as their individual interests and experiences with it. My role was a dual role: I was both the convener and one of the presenters.

I presented the portion of the workshop which explained how to channel and the various types of communications which are received during channeling. As a former student of the spiritual science religion, I had been trained in the development circle to both give and receive information during classes in spiritual development which trained people for spiritual or religious work. People who channel are sometimes called mediums or psychics; however, the term, which I prefer, is "spiritually gifted". In the development circle, I learned to interpret the information and symbols, which I received as a channel. Many of the symbols or signs such as colors, numbers, geometric forms and animals needed interpretation. Many times, the languages of God are given to us symbolically so that we may exercise our still developing minds and thereby increase their capacity and improve their function; also, symbols are given so that we will not be frightened by any "bad news".

What is channeling? For our purpose, we will use the dictionary's definition of a channel as being "a path along which data passes". Let's expand this definition to include a person as a "channel" The simplest way to describe a channeler, then, is one who is a conduit for information which is coming from a source outside of herself, through her neural pathways or senses. Everyone has the ability to channel in one or more states of awareness. What does that mean? We are in various states of awareness or consciousness during each twenty-four hour period...from the various stages of sleep to being wide awake and very active. Everyone is a channel for dreams during sleep. Much of the data which enters our minds during the dream stage of sleep are regarded as *making no sense, eroticism or wish fulfillment.* Why don't our dreams make more sense to us? It is mainly because of the symbols present in some of the dreams, which we receive. What I would like to do at this point is to stop calling them dreams and start calling them *sleeping visions.* Why? Because dreams are a type of vision which all of us receive during sleep. Dreams are for several purposes and they are all communications from our Supreme Being. They may be for the purposes of prophecy; guidance (even nightmares); wish fulfillment (but always with suggestions on how to make unfulfilled desires and dreams come true); and release of emotions (including erotic dreams and dreams of violence and humor)."

I began, "I have had dreams that led me to financial profits. I once had a day care center and had a dream of where to find free equipment and supplies. I followed through on the guidance in the dream and received almost four thousand dollars worth of free equipment, desks, chairs, lockers, tables and other items. A dear friend, Dick, once had a dream of a friend from his old neighborhood. In his dream, the neighbor was ill. Several days later when he was talking with his sister, she told him that the neighbor, indeed, had suddenly taken ill. His dream was a prophecy. I also foresaw the demise of both my sister and my father, several months before God took them back home."

I explained, "While everyone dreams, whether they remember the dreams or not, a few people also receive *waking visions*. Waking visions are communications, which are received in a state of wakefulness. Some of these people are called psychics or spiritually gifted."

I said that there are several types of communications, which almost all of us have received, at one time or another. The types of channeled messages that almost everyone receives are:

1) Hunches.Most people have experienced a hunch, which is a strong feeling or "gut feeling" about someone or something.

2) Dreams. Most people have also experienced dreams, which seemed strangely related to things which were going on in their lives.

3) Déjà vu. This is another experience, which many people have had when they went somewhere new, they felt that they had been there before or when they met someone for the first time, there was a feeling of having known them before.

4) Intuition. This is sometimes called "feminine intuition", has also been experienced by many people. It is simply, knowing something without having concrete proof of it.

I continued the session by explaining, "A channel is a person through which messages are transmitted. The source of the messages is from the Universal Mind of The Creator. Now, some channelers use a spirit guide or spirit assistant whom some call angels or healers. That's fine, if you know what you're doing. But, almost everyone here is a novice, so we will not use that method because there is always the possibility of being opened up to an undeveloped impostor which is not good."

One of the participants asked, "What do you mean by an undeveloped impostor?"

She explained, "Some people teach channelers to get a guide, but I have counseled too many people who have been victims of evil-doers of the spirit world and who dupe them. Guides are fine if you know for certain they are God's messengers, but as newcomers to channeling, I thought it best to warn you that if your intentions are not of the highest spiritual nature, there is always that danger. So, to avoid this problem, we will use only the intuitive method of channeling which does not involve an intermediary."

The group wanted to discuss the ramifications of both types of channeling. There is a safe way to channel as well as a dangerous way to channel. Table 1 shows both doorways for receiving channeled messages:

Table 1. Doorways To Channeling

Door A – Safe	Door B – Dangerous
Intuition	Ouija Boards
Dreams	Automatic writing/drawing
Inner visions	Seances
External visions	Escapist activities (e.g., drugs or alcohol)
Extrasensory perception	Spirit guides*
Remote sensing	Suicide attempts or death wishes
Hunches	Any spirit summoning ritual**

Note. *Some gifted spiritualists safely use spirit guides as a part of their religious rituals. Their intent is not to be led by the spirit, but by God through the intermediary. God is the judge of whether or not our intentions are good.

** Rituals which are God-seeking are a part of some earth religions which do call upon certain deities to intercede on their behalf. The spiritual leader is protected under these circumstances.

I continued, "During safe channeling (Door A), the source of the messages is from the Universal Mind of the Creator. Door B is the route you *do not* want to take. Let me tell you a story, which I was told by an associate who was acquainted first-hand with the real priest who performed the exorcism for the child who was portrayed in the movie, *The Exorcist.* First of all, the child was not a girl, but a boy. He lived in Riverdale Maryland at the time of the exorcism. My colleague, who is a highly respected, world-class medical professional, was an altar boy in the Catholic Church at the time. The boy had been playing with an Ouija Board trying to contact his dead aunt when he first came under siege by an evil discarnate being. My colleague said that the boy would go to school and objects in his classroom would fly around; for those of you who are not familiar with that type phenomenon, it is called 'psychokinesis'. Also, the boy would come to school with red welts on his body. The priest, who performed the exorcism was a very robust man, I was told. During the approximate six months or so that he was performing exorcism rituals on the boy, the priest lost so much weight that his frail physical condition was obvious to all. My colleague shared this story with me because he knew I was conducting research on paranormal phenomena. The boy moved to Texas after he got better. I don't know if he had a relapse or not, but, I believe in the movie version of this story, the child got worse   That's one of the reasons we will not use any dangerous doors to channeling. Okay?"

The group was silent for a few seconds, then two of the spiritually gifted people explained to them that they had guides or angels with whom they worked and that it was their particular way of channeling and that they had no negative incidents because they were *protected channels.*

I continued, "Most of the categories under Door A are self-explanatory, except for remote sensing. Remote sensing is a type of intuiting which sometimes involves guessing about cards or other objects which someone in another location is holding. It is also used by some military operations to gather information. Under Door B, most of the categories are self-explanatory, except for, perhaps, automatic writing and drawing which is a type of involuntary movement of a person's hand to write messages or draw pictures. Some people who do this say that a spirit guide is inside them when it happens. This method is always solicited by the person who does it. The category on escapist activities does not mean that you may not drink alcohol or take drugs without putting yourself in danger; but, rather, it means that if you do these things with the intention of escaping from life, there is always the danger of being opened up to discarnate beings who are evil."

Next, we discussed intuition vs. cognition, the two means of perceiving in this world. Table 2 compares the two ways of perceiving:

Table 2.   Comparisons of Cognition and Intuition

Cognition	Intuition
Informed through the five senses	Informed through extrasensory perception
Outward perceptions	Inner perceptions
Obvious	Subtle
Known source	Unknown source (for most people)
Tangible	Intangible
Acts are judged to be rational and acceptable	Acts are judged to be irrational and unacceptable
Objective (We *all* see or experience.)	Subjective (Only *you* see or experience.)
Judged scientific	Judged unscientific

I explained, "The categories under cognition and intuition are, for the most part, self-explanatory. Intuition is subjective: the message is perceived only by one person even though others may be present. Cognition is objective: the message is received by all who are within the sensory range of it. Cognition is relied upon as being a scientific means of perceiving the world, whereas, intuition is considered unscientific because it does not lend itself to the established steps in the scientific method of inquiry."

"Anyone can channel", She explained. "Channeling goes beyond the narrow confines of religions and dogmas. What you need most at this time is an open mind and a desire to learn. If you think that you know all that you need to know about God and this Universe, stop now. Don't go any further. Just sit back and observe. But, if you are willing to expand your consciousness and break the chains of cultural and religious programming and learn directly from The Creator, then come along. Channeling is done for both personal development as well as to help others. You may do both directed and undirected channeling. Directed channeling is used when you need answers to a specific problem or concern. Undirected channeling is for general information or whatever God wishes to communicate to you."

We discussed the **Law of Ascending Vibrations** that makes everything appear different in the universe. I explained that I had received many messages from The Creator regarding scientific matters through meditation as well as other means. One of these scientific messages was the Law of Ascending Vibrations. This law governs every living and non-living thing in God's universe. In essence, all matter is in constant motion, even the atoms of a hard piece of rock are in constant motion, although to our eyes it appears perfectly still. Everything in the universe looks different because the atoms, which make up the matter or energy are moving at different rates of speed. Stated another way, the many aspects or qualities of sound taste, smell, vision and touch correspond to an electromagnetic vibration whose speed is different from the speed of any other kind of energy or matter in the universe. Further, the higher the speed of the atoms in an energy source, the more unaware we are of its presence. In other words, we cannot see x-rays, ultraviolet rays or gamma rays; but we can see white light. The white light which our eyes can see has a limited, narrow range of vibrations. Electro-magnetic vibrations below the white light frequencies are called infrared rays. We cannot see these rays because they are not vibrating at a rate high enough for our eyes to see them. Simply put, our senses, while we are inside of bodies, can only respond to certain vibrations. These vibrations include sound, light, taste, smell and other aspects of our universe. We see and hear only a very limited amount of the many different qualities of our universe.

I explained that we cannot hear subsonic or ultrasonic sounds either. Some animals such as dogs and bats can hear outside the normal human range of hearing. Our ears can detect only a very limited range of frequencies or vibrations. Hearing the voices of people in spirit, then may be explained by the Law of Ascending Vibrations. It is similar to the difference between AM and FM radio waves. You cannot receive FM on an AM station and vice-versa. During our waking hours our ears are aware of sounds that we may consider are on an AM frequency. When paranormal events such as hearing an angel or a deceased loved one or a heavenly choir occur, our ears are aware of both an AM type frequency as well as a higher frequency, which she called our *astral frequency.* I said, "Everyone has an astral frequency. However, it is not always turned on. Why? It is because the sounds that you may hear at that frequency would not contribute in a positive way to the developmental karma which you and each person must work on. They would be too distracting. The Creator in all his/her wisdom knew this and so, we are limited to a range of hearing, seeing and perceiving that we need to function in our physical dimension. Now, there is also a down side to *astral hearing.* How many of you have ever watched the cartoon which was popular during the 1980's called *The Flip Side?* (One participant raised her hand.) Remember all the evil and awful things that happened to the characters when they went to the flip side? Well, the flip side of hearing angels and loved ones is hearing evil discarnate impersonators; that's the trouble side of the phenomenon. That's why I said, channeling has a safe door and a dangerous one. Are we all clear on that? Alright."

I explained colors to the group. I said, "Each color looks different to us because of the rate of vibration of the electromagnetic wavelengths of which light is composed. Sounds sound different because of the differences in the rate of vibration of the electromagnetic wavelengths of the sounds. This law also explains how man exists outside of a body. The astral body or soul is very light in weight. Just as we cannot see a radio wave or television wave floating through the air, we cannot see people in spirit under normal circumstances because the rate of speed of the atoms of which the astral body or soul body is composed are vibrating at such a high frequency that our eyes cannot see them. Let me give you an example of what I mean: If you have ever seen a fan sitting in a window and watched the blades spin, the blades seem to disappear because they are spinning around so fast. This is similar to why we cannot see people in the spirit form of life until we, too, come out of our bodies. Our physical bodies slow the astral body down when we are inside of flesh."

I continued, "There is another aspect of The *Law of Ascending Vibrations*, which we will not deal with at this time, but which may be of some interest to you. Scientists today are unable to explain the difference between magnetism and gravity. I have channeled messages about this, too. Many of my messages are science based because I pray for answers to scientific matters as well as personal matters. I do so through directed channeling or meditation. I have received information that there is a cohesive force which is throughout the universe. This same electromagnetic force, which holds the atoms of a molecule together is the same force which holds our solar system and the entire universe together. It keeps the Earth from flying into outer space. In other words, magnetism and gravity are varying aspects of the same phenomenon."

Next, we discussed the *aura* which is the protective electromagnetic shield around people. This shield prevents evil discarnate people from harming us. They are in a sort of "spiritual jail" serving a sentence here on earth as God's punishment for their wrongdoing before they died; they search for people whose auras are reversed or *open* so that they can begin the spirit confidence game of *possession*. Those whose auras are "open" can hear them, but they never say who they really are. God opens a person's aura only if the person is seeking spirits or doing other dangerous activities such as those we talked about when I explained about Channeling Door B. A person whose aura is open has his hearing turned up to the "astral frequency" and he can also hear the normal human range of sounds.

Figure 1 shows a person whose aura is closed. His shield is intact so that the only "astral frequencies he hears are good ones, from The Creator, an angel or a loved one during a special event during which God allows them to communicate with you. The sine waves which contain messages, like radio and TV waves penetrate the shield and are directed to the proper area of the brain which controls the sensory area which is receiving the message. Some channels actually see auras which may be different colors, indicating the emotional or spiritual state of the person . Some channels even smell odors, hear sounds such as music or words, some feel sensations such as coldness or heat and some see visions. Whatever you experience today, you will be protected because you are seeking God's guidance.

Figure 2 shows an aura with the electromagnetic field force reversed. It is an open aura. The person is not protected and his hearing has been raised to astral frequency, but he is not hearing angels. The impostors have entered his shield. You have not need to worry about that. We will channel safely.

We began channeling by using the undirected method, which meant that we would receive any messages, which God would stream through us. I instructed, "Please get into a comfortable position. You need to be relaxed and perfectly at ease. If some of you are too crowded on the couch, feel free to sit or lie on the floor. You may put your legs on the hassock or the coffee table. Just make yourselves comfortable." The group shifted positions in order to become more comfortable."

I continued, "This will be an undirected channeling session. First, let us pray. Dear God, we are

Figure 1

Figure 2.

gathered here today to receive your wisdom and guidance. We wish to be led directly by you or by your angels, if you so desire. We are here to learn as well as to praise your Holy Name. Please give us your guidance for our lives, collectively and individually. Please protect us from any unholy beings or negativity. Dear Mother-Father Creator, we thank you in advance for your guidance and love. Amen."

I instructed the group to keep their eyes closed and to imagine that they had a mental club to bat out any and all frivolous or fleeting thoughts that came into their heads. "Clear your mental circuits of all thoughts of what you will do later on, tomorrow or next week. Try not to think about what you will eat tonight, where you are going or anything like that. We will meditate like this for approximately fifteen to twenty minutes, quietly, with no sounds. Some of you will see various things such as colors, geometric forms, or pictures of people, animals, or scenes. Whatever you experience, please try to remember it in detail so that you can share it with the group. Any questions?"

One of the female doctoral students said, "Yes, I have one question. How hard do we have to concentrate on this to receive a message?"

"That's a good question. You do not need to concentrate on receiving a message. You are not pulling in a message. You are a receiver, like a radio or TV set. You are not doing the work; God or God's angel is doing the work. Please don't do anything but relax and clear your mind so that you may receive God's guidance."

Everyone relaxed in a meditative state for about twenty minutes. At the end of that period of time, I asked everyone to open his or her eyes and stand up and stretch. I said, "What we will do now is tell what we experienced. Let's start with the group on the couch and go around the room. Of the three doctoral students sitting on the couch, two women and a man, only the man saw something. The women said that they had no experiences at all, but that the meditation was relaxing. I replied, " Sometimes that happens, especially if it's your first try. It takes longer for some people to channel than it does for others. God knows when you are ready to receive and when you are not quite ready." The male doctoral student said that he received a message for one of the other doctoral candidates. He called her name said; "I am feeling that someone who does not have your best interests at heart will become ill in the near future." One of the other students said that they had seen colors and light. Another had seen geometric forms floating into and out of her inner visual field. Most of the doctoral students who were channeling beginners had seen some type of inner vision or had received an intuitive message.

The next phase of the channeling day included the spiritually gifted leaders who were present. The doctoral students did not participate in this phase except as observers and learners. The two ministers each told about their ministries and how they channeled. Rev. Mary Braganza told about her early gifted experiences and how she became a minister. Rev. Vickie, told us about her spirit guide or angel who assisted her in her spiritual readings. Two of the laypersons were affiliated with one of the local experiential churches. I had attended their services on several occasions. On one of those occasions, I was very impressed by three children channelers who delivered messages to others on that day. These children were trained to receive God's messages and minister to those in need. One was a teenager and the other two appeared to be preteens.

The laypersons channeled, one by one and gave a message to each person in the room. The messages consisted of readings on their health, love lives, work, and other matters which were personal to them. The recipients verified the facts of each reading that were verifiable. Each person received individual messages from people who had never seen them before. Most notable was the fact that two of the spiritually gifted channelers added on to the message which one of the doctoral students had given to the young lady about someone, who did not have her best interests at heart, becoming ill. One of the channelers said that this person was a man. She saw him standing in the rain and saw him becoming ill. The other channeler gave her a similar message with ominous warnings to beware of the man.

Our day ended with a prayer of thanks to God for our messages. Those who were able to spend more time went out for dinner together and the rest went home.

Approximately two weeks after our channeling day, a couple of the other doctoral students received word from the young lady who had received all of the ominous messages about the man in her life who meant her no good. She said that he had been attending a convention in a major metropolitan area when he was stricken with a heart ailment and had to be hospitalized. His prognosis was good, but he was very ill. The three channeled messages, which she had received about him several days before had come true.

Prior to our channeling day, several of the doctoral students, including myself, had a peer day at Folgers Library in Washington, D.C., a repository for Shakespearean artifacts as well as an arena for the production of his plays. We met in the lobby of the library the morning of September 9, 1991. The curator of the library was our tour guide for the day. She first took us into the reading room that is solely for the use of doctoral candidates (or by special permission if you are not working on a Ph.D.) The reading room is a beautiful room full of sixteenth and seventeenth century oil paintings and suffused with light streaming through stained glass mosaic windows. The curator took us to the stacks of rare books written before 1650. We entered these stacks trough an underground vault. Even though there were only three doctoral students and the curator, another museum worker was required to go into the vault

with us to assure the safety of these rare books, we assumed. One of the doctoral students who could channel
asked the curator if she could hold one of the books and
channel back to that age. Sometimes, holding an object
helps her to channel, but it is not always required. The curator acquiesced and she was allowed to hold a 1623 volume of Romeo and Juliet. What God channeled through
her was that Juliet was pregnant at the time of her death
and that her period was six weeks late. Many people would
have been hurt by the lovers' predicament and the teenagers saw suicide as their only way out. They made a suicide
pact and carried it out much like some teenagers today.
What a whole new slant on this tale!

Experiencing Waking Dreams

A series of experiments was conducted which helps
to explain what wide-awake visions look like. Six men and
four women participated in the experiment. The instructions to them were as follows:

"Close your eyes and rub them with the heel of your
palms. Rub them inward. Rub them as if they were itching.
Rub them about ten times. Stop! Keep your eyes shut and
tell me what you see."

*[The same instructions were repeated a second time except
the participants rubbed their eyes outward rather than inward. Before you read on, try it yourself and write down
what you see.]*

Each person said that they saw different objects and
colors. When she rubbed inward, one woman saw "a green
ball" ; while another woman said, " I see a chalice. It's all
different colors; the colors are all coming out of it - they're
radiating from it!"

When the men reported, one said, "I see the letter
"H" in white on a black background." Another man saw little spots of light with a reddish glare; there was darkness in
the background. A third man saw a four-sided geometric
form with its right side a little longer than the left. A fourth
man saw himself engaged in sports activities.

When they reported what they had seen after they had rubbed their eyes outward, one woman saw total darkness, after having seen a green ball previously. Another woman saw an outline of a human body. She said, "The body is the color white. It has a round head and there's green in the background!"

One man reported seeing two vertical lines on the outside in white; and another saw two pulsating dots. He said, The dots seem to be trying to come together ...to unite! There's a reddish light on the outside of them." Another man reported seeing a blue cross. Still, another man saw a vision of himself in his bank.

The group leader said, "This experiment is further proof that everyone receives visions from God. You really did not need to rub your eyes to receive the vision. This was done to relax you so that you would not be frightened by the experience. Each symbol and color had a special meaning for each of you. Each vision, which was received was a symbolic message about your life and the conditions in your life. Some were prophecies, some were guidance and some were warnings. Some people received less symbolic messages which were 'telling it like it is'. God talks to you at your own level of understanding."

She stated further, "Each color has a special meaning; for instance, red symbolizes a weakness, blue means improvement and even shades of colors have a meaning. The letter "H" is the 8th alphabet and the number 8 means a double weakness or fault is present in some condition in your life."

Our group leader explained, "There is no such thing as 'developing' psychic powers. The physical and spiritual mechanisms are already present. When you participated in this experiment, some of you just had a waking-vision, which some people practice 'developing' for years. It's just like our sleeping-visions or dreams, which are just as important in the messages they carry. We should pray and ask God what the symbols mean if we don't know."

Section Three

The Survey

Chapter 15

A Survey of Paranormal Experiences

Summary

Selected demographic variables were examined to determine if they have a relationship to experiencing psi. Two hundred two (202) adults between the ages of 18 and 65 completed the Sloan Paranormal Survey.

Similar larger studies by T.W. Smith (1992), J. McClenon (1994), Sheldrake (2003) and Palmer (1979) also examined some of the same demographics and their relationship to experiencing psi phenomena.

The Sloan study found that almost 54% of the group had experienced some type paranormal activity. Females reported having more paranormal experiences than males. African Americans reported more paranormal experiences than other racial or ethnic groups. People whose family origins are in the southern parts of the U.S. reported more paranormal experiences than those from other areas. The experiencing of one type paranormal event may either precipitate or be related to experiencing certain other paranormal events.

Some psi experiences of this group included seeing deceased loved ones, having dreams and hunches come true, foretelling events and déjà vu.

A large scale study conducted by T. W. Smith (1992) at the National Opinion Research Center of the University of Chicago surveyed the experiences of paranormal phenomena in the U.S. Smith found that a quarter to three fifths of his population reported ESP experiences. He also found that: (1) attending church frequently was actually associated with less paranormal experiences; (2) frequent prayer, feeling near to God, and belief in an afterlife were associated with more ESP experiences; (3) people in isolation had more psi experiences; (4) psi experiences are more common among Blacks, Native Americans and Latinate Europeans (Italian, French, and Spanish) and less common among Northern Europeans such as Scandinavians and Germans; (5) experiences were least frequent in the U.S. East South Central region and most in the U.S. West South Central region; and (6) paranormal experiences were more common among younger adults, women and people living in large cities.

Sociologist, James McClenon (1994) reviewed hundreds of accounts of psi events which he called "wondrous events". His accounts included many cultures: American, European and Asian. He included both modern and medieval accounts. He also surveyed well over 1000 university students from the U.S., Japan and China, and elite scientists of the American Association for the Advancement of Science (AAAS).

McClenon found that, at the University of Maryland, more older science students (69%) were "believers" when compared with younger science students (51%). He also found that the area of academic study, religious preference and scientific training did not affect the incidence of psi experiences.

The survey of Chinese, Japanese and American university students reported similar types of psi experiences which included out-of-body (OBE) experiences, spirit communication, déjà vu, ESP and sleep paralysis, suggesting to McClenon that some psi experiences occur independently of race and culture. He concluded that the experiencing of psi or "wondrous events" is universal. In a study by Palmer (1979), it was found that over 50% of the general adult population reported psychic experiences. These experiences were not related to the age of the experiencer. Mental telepathy experiences with telephones are very common. Sheldrake (2003) surveyed people in Europe, North America and South America over a five year period to quantify the number of people who know who is calling before they answer the phone without the help of caller I.D. or any other identifying information. He questioned over 6,000 people at lectures, seminars and conferences. On the basis of a show of hands, 80% - 90% claimed to have had this experience. In another follow-up survey, Sheldrake asked groups of people attending lectures and seminars in Britain, Germany, the U.S. and Argentina to fill out questionnaires about their experiences with telephones. A total of 1,691 people responded to the survey; 92% of that number (1,562) indicated that they had thought of someone just before the phone rang or just as it rang and it was that person on the telephone.   Sheldrake conducted more formal telephone surveys of randomly selected households in the U.S. and England, which yielded similar results. In London, 51% said they had known who was calling before they answered the phone; 49% knew in England and 47% knew in California. A higher percentage said they had telephoned someone who said they were just thinking about telephoning them (65% in England; 78% in California). Notable is the fact that more women than men claimed to have had these experiences.

Knowing that someone is staring at you has a strong body of research to support it (Sheldrake, 2003). The largest experiment of this nature has been going on since 1995 in Amsterdam, Holland. Over 18,700 looker-subject pairs have participated in this research. The looker in this experiment sits behind the subject and is instructed whether or not to look by a signal on the computer screen. The subject guesses verbally and the looker enters the response into a computer. After a maximum number of trials (30) the computer announces whether or not the subject has "eyes in the back of his head", based on the number of correct guesses. According to the experimental design, if the subjects were just guessing by chance, then only 20% would be said to have "eyes in the back of the head". They found that between 32% and 41% of the subjects had "eyes in the back of their heads", suggesting that factors other than chance were operating. The most successful subjects were boys under age 8 and the least successful were girls from 9 – 16 years of age.

The Sloan Study

The purpose of this study was to determine the relationship between experiencing paranormal events and selected demographic factors. Based upon theoretical literature and empirical data, the researcher hypothesized that:

(1) Females would report more paranormal experiences than males.

(2) African Americans would report more paranormal experiences than other racial or ethnic groups.

(3) People with less formal education would report more paranormal experiences than people with more formal education.

(4) People with low incomes would report more paranormal experiences than people with higher incomes.

(5) People whose family origins are in the southern parts of the U.S. would report more paranormal experiences than people whose family origins are from other regions.

METHODOLOGY

Participants:

The Participants were two hundred two (202) adults between the ages of 18 and 65. They consisted of 130 college students at three area universities and 72 adults in the Washington, D.C. Metropolitan Area who responded to a mailed survey.

Instrument:

The instrument used in the study was *The Sloan Paranormal Survey* (Copyright 1992), which was devised by the researcher and field tested at three locations: Southern University in Baton Rouge, LA; Howard University, Washington, D.C.; and The Insight Science Institute, Hyattsville, MD. Seventeen (17) students and ten (10) non-students in the general population participated in the pilot study. The pilot test questions were examined for suggestions and

criticisms. Subsequently, the necessary
revisions and recommendations regarding the survey were
implemented.

Procedure:

Participants from the general population were
mailed the Sloan Paranormal Survey along with an Informed Consent Form. They were asked to answer the Survey questions as honestly as they could and mail them back
along with the signed Informed Consent Form within a two-
week period following receipt of the Survey. This sample
was a list of random names in the Washington, D.C. and
Prince Georges County, Maryland region.

Classes from three universities in the Washington
Metropolitan Area were utilized for the student sample.
Students were apprised of the Informed Consent Form and
they were asked to answer each question truthfully. Students in one class were given extra credit for participating
in the study.

The completed surveys were logged and manually
examined for errors and inconsistencies. The data from the
survey were coded by the researcher. The codes were then
entered into a computerized tabulation system and ana-
lyzed using the SAS system for the social sciences.

RESULTS

Table 1 shows an analysis of basic demographic information of the participants. There were more females (58.2%)
than males (41.8%); most participants were 21-30 years old
(62%). Most had one or two years of college (48.7%) or had
completed four years of college (42.1%). A sizeable percentage of the group earned between ten and twenty thousand
dollars per year (38%). African Americans were the largest
racial/ethnic group (62 %).

Table 2 presents the responses of participants who
responded to question number 1 that asked if they had ever
experienced a paranormal event. Over thirty-five percent
reported ever having had a paranormal or supernatural experience. Fifteen participants did not respond to that
question.

Table 1. Basic Demographic Information (N = 202)

Demographic	n	%
Gender		
Males	82	41.8
Females	114	58.2
Age		
21-30	115	62.2
31-40	48	25.9
41-50	17	9.2
51-60	4	2.2
61+	1	0.5
Education		
Finished H.S.	8	4.1
1-2 Yrs. College	96	48.7
College Degree	83	42.1
Graduate Degree	10	5.1
Income		
< 10K	45	24.1
10 - 20K	71	38.0
20 - 30K	43	23.0
30 - 40K	14	7.5
> 40K	14	7.5
Race/Ethnicity		
Asian	7	3.6
Hispanic	12	6.2
Native American	5	2.6
African American	122	62.6
Caucasian	9	4.6
Other	40	20.5

Note: Some frequencies are missing due to missing values on some items. Demographic data on the Geographic Origin of Immediate Family are shown in Tables 6 and 8. Religious Affiliation is shown in Table 11.

Table 2. # Experiencing a Paranormal Event (Q. #1)

Response	Number	Percentage
Yes	66.0	35.3
No	121.0	64.7
Not Checked	15.0	07.4

Of those who responded to the question (#1), over thirty-five percent reported ever having a paranormal or supernatural experience (n=66). Over Sixty-four percent reported never having had a paranormal experience (n=121). Fifteen participants did not respond to the question.

Table 3 shows the types of supernatural experiences reported by all participants. Even though over 35% actually reported having had a supernatural experience at some time, when asked about specific types of personal experiences, over 50% reported having had paranormal experiences in two categories: feelings come true (53.96%) and dreams come true (50.50%). Over 43% reported having experienced deja vu (having been to a strange place and felt they had been there before, or met a stranger whom they thought they knew).

Table 3. Personal Experiences of Psi Phenomena (N=202)

Phenomenon	Number Experiencing	Percent Experiencing
Object move	15	7.43
Supernatural sound	32	15.84
Waking vision	43	21.29
Apparition	23	11.39
Feelings come true	53.96	109
Dreams come true	102	50.50
Predict events	31	15.35
Communicate mentally	31	15.35
Déjà vu	87	43.07
Missing time	20	9.90
Out-of-body	19	9.41
Near death	12	5.94
Other	19	9.41

Noted also, is the fact that over 20% of the sample indicated that they had experienced visions of someone or something while fully awake; close to 16% stated they had heard supernatural sounds (voices or other).

Figure 1 is a chart which compares various types of psi events experienced by the participants. When asked if they had participated in a ritual or other related activity, no one reported having done so. When asked if they had been under the influence of a substance, no one responded, "yes". Also, when asked if they were or had ever been treated for any brain, mental health or drug-related medical condition, there were no positive responses.

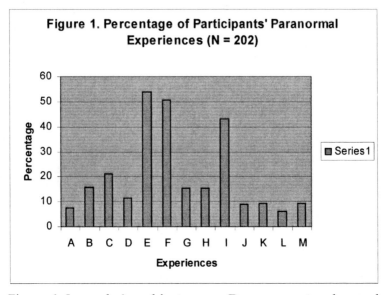

Figure 1. Legend: A = object move; B = supernatural sound; C = waking vision; D = apparition; E = feelings come true; F = dreams come true; G = predict events; H = communicate mentally; I = déjà vu; J = missing time; K = out-of-body; L = near death; M = other.

An analysis of variance was performed in order to compare psi experience mean differences with demographic factors. An alpha level of .05 was used for all statistical tests. Table 4 (See Appendix I.) shows that three demographic factors were significant: gender, race, and origin of family.

Females (M = 3.48, SD = 2.24) had higher scores than males (M = 2.59, SD = 1.43), thus, indicating that females had significantly more paranormal experiences than males. This finding supports the first hypothesis.

Race/ethnicity was significant. African Americans reported more psi experiences than any other group. This finding supports the second hypothesis. The race/ethnicity demographic is looked at in more detail in Table 5.

Origin of family was highly significant. Participants with Midwestern family origins reported experiencing more paranormal events than any other group in that category. This demographic is examined further in Tables 6 and 7.

Although not significantly different, older people tended to have higher scores than other age categories (p = .06). The mean for the 51-60 year old group was 6.0, while all other group means were between 3.0 and 4.0.

Also noteworthy is the fact that , while religion was not statistically significant, it was close (p = .07).

Table 5. Race/Ethnicity Comparisons of Psi Experiences

Race/Ethnicity	n	%	Mean	SD*
Asian	7	3.6	2.40	0.55
Latino	12	6.2	1.66	0.71
Native American	5	2.6	2.40	0.55
African American	122	62.6	3.54	2.10
Caucasian	9	4.6	2.57	1.51
Other	40	20.5	2.60	1.93

Table 5 shows that African Americans comprised the largest group (62.6%). With the exception of the group labeled "Other", the remaining ethnic and racial categories were too small to be adequately descriptive of their population. African Americans had the highest number of psi experiences (M = 3.54, SD = 2.10). The category labeled "Other" which is usually checked by mixed race individuals had the second highest number of psi experiences (M = 2.60, SD = 1.93). When a t-test was applied, African Americans and "Others" were significantly different in their experiencing of psi (t = 2.47, probability = <.01).

Table 6. Origin of Family x Mean No. of Psi Experiences

Family Origin	n	Mean	SD
Southeast	27	3.93	1.73
Northeast	51	3.04	1.48
Midwest	5	5.60	3.36
Southwest	4	3.50	1.73
Northwest	16	3.31	2.82
Foreign	59	2.46	1.64

Table 6 shows the mean number of psi experiences and standard deviations on the demographic variable: Origin of Family. The group which had the highest mean number of psi experiences had their family roots in the Midwest (M = 5.60, n = 5). The group having the second highest mean had family roots in the southeastern part of the United States (M = 3.93, n = 27). Even though the Midwest group had the highest mean number of experiences, the small number of participants in that category does not adequately represent that population. Likewise, the small numbers of participants in the Southwest and Northwest categories do not adequately represent those populations. The remaining three categories which were adequately represented (Southeast, Northeast and Foreign) had mean numbers of psi experiences of 3.93, 3.04 and 2.46, respectively.

Table 7. *t*-tests of Mean Differences on Number of Psi Experiences x Origin of Family

Geographic Origins		n		Mean		SD		t
1	2	1	2	1	2	1	2	
Southeast x Northeast		27	51	3.93	3.04	1.73	1.48	2.04*
Northeast x Foreign		51	59	3.04	2.46	1.48	1.64	1.66
Southeast x Foreign		27	59	3.93	2.46	1.73	1.64	3.47**

*$p<.05$. **$p<.01$.

Table 7 shows the *t* tests of mean differences on Origin of Family for the three categories which were adequately represented in the survey: Southeast, Northeast and Foreign. There was a significant difference between people whose family origin is from the Southeast and those whose family origin is from the Northeast People from those areas showed a clear difference in the experiencing of psi phenomena. When the Southeast category was compared with the Foreign category, a significant difference was also found in the experiencing of psi phenomena.

Table 8 shows the countries of origin of the immediate families of foreign participants. The largest group represented was Nigeria and the second largest groups were El Salvador and Ethiopia.

Table 8. Foreign Country Origins of Immediate Family
(N = 54)

Country	n	%
Ethiopia	7	13.0
Chile	2	3.7
Brazil	1	1.9
Jamaica	3	5.6
Nigeria	26	48.1
Guyana	2	3.7
El Salvador	7	13.0
Rumania	2	3.7
England	2	3.7
Syria	1	1.9
Vietnam	2	3.7

Table 9 shows an inter-item correlation of all paranormal experiences. There were 18 significant correlations out of 66 comparisons, five of which reached the .01 alpha level. Particularly noteworthy is the fact that three of the correlations which reached the .01 level related to people who experienced having strong feelings (hunches) which came true. These people also experienced dreams which came true, communicating mentally with someone and experiencing déjà vu. The fourth correlation to reach the .01 alpha level related to people who experienced waking visions; these people also experienced seeing apparitions as well as deja vu and near death events. The fifth correlation to reach the .01 level concerned people who experienced dreams which came true; they also predicted events accurately and experienced déjà vu.

Table 9 also shows that there were 13 significant correlations that reached the .05 alpha level. Experiencing supernatural sounds was related to having feelings come true and seeing visions. Also, seeing visions was related to experiencing déjà vu, having out-of-body experiences and near death experiences. Seeing apparitions was related to having dreams come true. Having feelings come true was related to predicting events accurately and near death experiences. Dreams coming true was related to experiencing

Table 9. Inter-Item Correlations of Paranormal Experiences (Phi Coefficients)

	Obj	Snd	Vis	Ap	Fel	Dm	Pd	Tlp	Dv	Mt	Ob	Nd
Obj	X	.19	.18	.26	.03	.13	.14	.04	.13	.10	.10	.25
Snd		X	.27*	.14	.06*	.13	.12	.08	.11	.13	.19	.24
Vis			X	.39**	.12	.10	.15	.15	.20*	.15	.25*	.28*
Ap				X	.02	.17*	.11	.06	.16	.25	.26	.17
Fel					X	.30**	.17*	.23**	.30**	.14	.09	.19*
Dm						X	.26**	.12	.15*	.06	.08	.12
Pd							X	.24	.04	.14	.29*	.36*
Tlp								X	.21*	.18	.05	.30*
Dv									X	.11	.13	.16
Mt										X	.23	.27
Ob											X	.28
Nd												X

Note. Obj = object move; Snd = supernatural sound; Vis = waking vision; Ap = apparition; Fel = feelings come true; Dm = dreams come true; Pd = predict events; Tlp = telepathy; Dv = déjà vu; Mt = missing time; Ob = out-of-body; Nd = near death. $*p<.05$. $**p<.01$.

déjà vu. Predicting events accurately was related to both out-of-body and near death experiences. Lastly, communicating mentally with someone was related to déjà vu and near death experiences. These 18 significant correlations of various paranormal experiences indicate that factors other than chance were operating.

Table 10. Mean Number of Psi Experiences x Religious Affiliation of Participants (N = 202)

Religious Affiliation	n	%	Mean	SD
Protestant	41	20.3	2.94	1.95
Catholic	39	19.3	2.31	1.39
Buddhist	2	0.1	2.50	0.71
Eastern Orthodox	7	3.5	3.67	1.21
Jewish	0			
Muslim	12	5.9	4.22	3.11
None	16	7.9	2.81	1.38
Other	73	36.1	3.42	1.95
Not Checked	12	5.9	1.33	1.70

Table 10 shows the religious affiliations of all participants. Protestants (20.3%), Catholics (19.3%) and the category labeled "Other" (36.1%) were adequately represented in the sample. A small number of people did not check a religious affiliation (5.9%). The analysis of variance of demographic data x psi experience (Table 4) showed there were no significant differences regarding religious affiliation.

Table 11. Descriptions of Other Paranormal Experiences (Question 2m)

Participant No.	Experience
1	I was taking a shower and I saw three of my four dead kids standing by the wall for a quick moment.
2	I communicate mentally and do not know that I'm not speaking aloud and expect the person to whom I am talking to answer. Weird huh?
3	One time I was talking to God and a very warm feeling came over me. I was very still and quiet. I felt as though God was talking to me.
4	I could remember things that had to occur at another time (in another life).

Participant No.	Experience
Table 11. (continued) Descriptions of Other Paranormal Experiences (Question 2m)	
5	I have experienced situations which have recurred twice but I cannot remember whether I was actually there when it happened or if I was dreaming.
6	I wrote a book (on my psychic experiences). Maybe you'd like to read it.
7	I have been to a place and I have felt uncomfortable due to something I don't understand.
8	I sometimes get a funny feeling and something bad usually happens.
9	I feel someone staring at me while I sleep and I am not able to move.
10	I witnessed someone else having a supernatural experience.
11	While under dental anesthesia, I felt like I was dying and I asked God to forgive me for different things.
12	I identified someone by their voice which I heard while under anesthesia in the recovery room. It was five years later when I identified the person.
13	What I heard was not so much a voice as it was someone else's thoughts.
14	I've had several dreams that have come true. For instance, once we had no food or money and my mom applied for food stamps, but they never showed up. Then, I had a dream about them and they came the very next day!
15	Some kind of skeletal witch was on my back as I slept.
16	I can tell a stranger a lot about themselves before they tell me anything.
17	I've gotten career opportunities I knew had to be the supernatural work of an upper power.

Table 11 lists the responses of seventeen people who described their experiences in response to an open-ended question (#2m). (Please see Appendix B). Several of these experiences were waking visions. Some had dreams which came true. Others experienced having strong feelings (hunches) which came true. Some, however, had paranormal experiences of a more frightening nature.

Table 12 lists responses to question #13 which asked participants to explain more about the experiences that they had. Many of the experiences were of a spiritual nature. Some, however, involved temporary paralysis or an inability to move while fully conscious. One experience was a warning about a disaster which actually happened.

Table 12. More Explanations About Paranormal Experiences (Question #13)	
Participant No.	**Experience**
1	The more I get to read the *Holy Bible* and learn about Jesus Christ, I have begun to realize the revelations in the Bible that have come to pass in our lives.
2	Somewhere between sleeping and waking, I saw a dog moving in the house and I heard it bark. I also felt I was fighting something. I really believe that I was awake. My friend and I call it the *surreal connection.*
3	I had a lot of experiences like number 2i (missing time). Sometimes I know what's going to happen before it happens. I can't close my eyes and face a wall; I feel like it's going to fall on me.
4	Once, I felt like God was answering me. I heard my voice but the words were not my words. I felt like I had been asleep, but I was not fully awake. After I became fully conscious, I felt very scared and I knew that God had been with me.
5	I heard a voice, presumably from God. My experiences have to deal with my religious beliefs.

Participant No.	Experience
Table 12. (continued) More Explanations About Paranormal Experiences (Question #13)	
6	In Africa, people do experience paranormal activities. I however, cannot attest to them at all; but, I have had dreams that came true and I sometimes tell what people are thinking or are about to say.
7	I always dream about funerals or about attending funerals of close relatives before they actually die. I feel that I have lived before.
8	At the age of 4, I saw my brother who died months after I was born. There were others with me at the time, but no one else saw him. I have seen other deceased family members.
9	Sometimes I'm afraid to go to sleep. I feel paralyzed sometimes and often I hear people talking or see a shadow but never see a face. Sometimes I feel like I'm in danger (being smothered). My mother has the same problem, only worse.
10	I was driving and my aunt, who is dead, told me to slow down because I was going to be in an accident. The accident happened!
11	Once there was a young girl from my church who had a different voice coming through her voice (mouth). I have experienced being conscious but unable to open my eyes or move a muscle.
12	I have several friends that I think about on occasion. Whenever I think about them, they call within a few days or a few hours. They tell me the same thing happens when they think of me: I will call them.
13	After I prayed for various things, they almost supernaturally materialized: a job, education, car, peace of mind, etc. I knew it was a higher power (God) at work.

DISCUSSION and CONCLUSIONS

The purpose of this study was to determine whether or not relationships exist between demographic factors (gender, income, age, education, race/ethnicity, geographical origin of family and religious affiliation) and reported paranormal experiences.

The researcher rejected the null hypothesis for three out of the five hypotheses of this study. The three hypotheses that were supported were: (1) Females would report more paranormal experiences than males; (2) African Americans would report more paranormal experiences than other racial or ethnic groups and (3) People whose family origins are in the Southern U.S. would report more paranormal experiences. The researcher must conclude that several phenomena were experienced by the group, not by chance; factors other than chance were present.

Over half the participants in the Sloan study reported that they had experienced dreams which came true and strong thoughts and feelings which came true. Females reported having more psi experiences than males. Previous research by Smith (1992), who conducted one of the more recent large scale studies on paranormal experiences also found that females reported having more psi experiences than males; overall scores for females were significantly higher. More specifically, more females than males saw visions and experienced deja vu. These findings support the researcher's first hypothesis.

The old stereotype concerning "feminine intuition" receives some validation from these results. Females are socialized differently than males. Females are taught in most societies to be nurturers, caretakers, and relying on inner emotions and feelings is not discouraged in females; but, this behavior is discouraged in males. Males are taught to compete, dominate and conquer. Showing emotion and talking about feelings is thought to be a weakness when this same standard is applied to males. Females, therefore, learn to intuit and pay close attention to the "inner work" of deciphering feelings, dreams, and intuitive thoughts.

African Americans had significantly more paranormal experiences than other racial or ethnic groups. However, they were the largest group represented n the sample.

It is possible that if other racial/ ethnic groups had been adequately represented in this sample, there might have been other significant differences with regard to race and ethnicity. The study by Smith (1992) also found that paranormal experiences are more common among Blacks, Native Americans, and Latinate Europeans (Italian, French, and Spanish) than among Northern Europeans, Scandinavians and Germans. While these results do support the second hypothesis, that African Americans would report more paranormal experiences than other groups, this researcher is inclined to just cite the tendency in that direction, since the other groups were not comparable.

The Black church is a very strong and influential component of African American life. Many African American churches celebrate the liturgy with song, dance, hand-clapping and much joy . As Nana Kwabena, the Akom priest related, these expressions all have their roots in traditional African religions, Akom, Yoruba, and others. The Black Diaspora brought about by the slave trade did not entirely eradicate these high-spirited, high-energy spiritual expressions. Immanence to The Creator is the major factor underlying these expressions. "Calling the spirits or saints" and "calling to God in joyful song and rhythmic entreaties" are not one and the same, but they are not far removed. "Seek and you shall find" is what the African ancestors sought in a close, personal encounter with deity. Close, personal encounters with "the spirit" are well known and well documented experiences in many Black churches. "Shouting" and "speaking in tongues" when feeling the spirit of The Divine are all common and acceptable ways of worship in many protestant Black churches. In fact, there is a charismatic movement surfacing in some of these churches to make worshiping God more personal and experiential and less remote and blandly ceremonial. Even some Catholic churches in predominantly African American neighborhoods, which had formerly been more reserved and traditional in their liturgies have begun to incorporate African heritage symbolism and rituals in their services.

African root religions, rhythm, expectations, and *comfort level* in experiencing the divine have all contributed to a much higher incidence of paranormal experiences among African Americans in this study and the Smith study previously cited. Experiencing The Divine in the form of psi phenomena, the, is "normal" to many African Americans and some other people of color, as well as Latinate Europeans. They live with an *expectancy and awareness* that spirit visitations, dreams coming true and "seeing" are within the realm of possibility and first hand spiritual knowledge.

Both McClenon (1994) and Sheldrake (2003) surveyed people from several different countries. Both of these studies suggest that experiencing the paranormal goes beyond race and ethnicity. They both found that a large percentage of people in many countries and from various racial and ethnic backgrounds also experienced paranormal events. This fact, alone, suggests that this phenomenon is *universal.*

Geographical origin of immediate family was significant in the experiencing of paranormal phenomena. Participants whose family origins are in the Southeast experiences significantly more psi phenomena than either those whose family origins are from the Northeast or foreign countries. What this suggests is that there are definite geographical factors, which influence the experiencing of paranormal phenomena. Rural areas are numerous in the Southeastern U.S., which possibly accounted for people with family roots in this region having more paranormal experiences than people from other geographic regions.

Smith's study (1992) also found that people from rural communities reported significantly more experiences of paranormal events. Smith found that psi experiences were least frequent in the East South Central region and most in the West South Central region. Regional patterning did not seem to have much meaning overall, however. In Smith's study, foreign born participants came predominantly from African countries such as Nigeria, Ethiopia, Ghana, Liberia, Morocco, and Cameroon. A few were from Chile, Brazil, Jamaica, El Salvador, Rumania, England, Syria, Indonesia, Peru, The Dominican Republic, Spain, The Ukraine, and Vietnam . In many of these countries, traditional "earth" or "spiritist" religions are practiced by the masses, thereby making this population more accepting of the paranormal than people in geographical regions where people do not practice these religions. Smith's study has shown that both people in highly populated urban areas

(Northeast) and rural areas which are numerous in the Southeast, have more paranormal experiences than people in other geographic regions.

The hypothesis that people with less formal education would report significantly more paranormal experiences than people with more formal education was not supported by the results of this study. The Smith study, however, found this to be true. In the Sloan study, college students with graduate degrees reported more paranormal experiences than the other groups. Those with a college degree tended to have fewer paranormal experiences than other groups. Close to 96% of this sample had at least a year or more of college education. This sample was not representative of samples in other regions of the U.S. where the ratio of college educated people is much lower. The Washington, D.C. Metropolitan Area has a very high concentration of college educated professionals and many universities.

The hypothesis that people with low incomes would report more paranormal experiences was not supported by the results of this study. While not significant, people who earned the most income (> 40k) experienced more paranormal phenomena than the other income brackets. The group that experienced the least number of psi experiences was in the 30-40k income bracket.

Age, though not statistically significant, showed a tendency for older people (over 50) to have more paranormal experiences than other age groups. This age group tends to make more life assessments than younger age groups. Much of what occurs at this stage of life revolves around spiritual beliefs and self-fulfillment to a great degree. People in this age group may lean more on spirituality and religious beliefs than other age groups. Nearing the age when many people of their generation begin to decline physically and even die, spiritual goals and seeking a meaning to life and making peace with the world are of utmost importance. It is believed that expectancy plays a role in the experiencing of the paranormal, which some interpret as divine manifestations.

Religion was not statistically significant in the experiencing of psi phenomena. People in the religious categories "Muslim", Eastern Orthodox" and "Other" experienced more psi phenomena than any other religious groups. Islam is one of the more intensely and deeply personal religions in which five daily prayers are said by the faithful and the importance of following all of the five pillars of the faith is foremost in the lives of faithful Muslims. This is not to say that the other faiths are not personal or experiential; but, Islam is that way to a great extent.

In the Eastern Orthodox Church, a deeply personal relationship with Jesus is encouraged and daily prayers and reading the scriptures is also a way of life of the faithful. They first look to the Holy Spirit, directly, to guide them; next, to the church fathers. Their faith is also experiential in the sense that they look directly to God, to provide answers and guidance. There is an expectancy and belief that God will answer them, personally.

The religious category, "other", is usually checked by people who consider themselves "free-thinkers" and spiritual" rather than religious. A sizeable number of participants checked "Other" and since most of the participants were between the ages of 21-40 (>88%), it may be said that younger people expressed a non-traditional religious preference. Also, included in this group are the "New Age" faith adherents who seek God beyond the constraints of orthodox religions and who are more inclined to experiment with divining, seek out astrologers, numerologists, psychics and, generally, to use a hands-on approach to seeking The Divine. Many of these people left organized religions because of their sometimes rigid, dictatorial, hierarchical structures. The recent charismatic movement in some churches is an attempt to appeal to younger people and bring them into the fold.

Many "New Age" gurus have caught the ear of younger people, which is not to say that it is a negative fact. There are psychic call-in shows and advertisements on television and the print media. There is a profusion of "New Age" literature in bookstores almost everywhere. Music that young adults and teens listen to is sprinkled with aphorisms of supernatural events such as heavenly journeys, inner visions and struggles between good and evil. Some rock musicians send a more negative message, however, with a more nihilistic philosophy, but still in the paranormal realm.

The inter-item correlations of the paranormal experiences revealed that certain experiences cluster or occur with other experiences. In other words, the experiencing of one type paranormal event may either precipitate or be related to experiencing certain other types of paranormal events. Most notable, seeing waking visions was significantly correlated with having four other types of psi experiences (seeing apparitions, déjà vu, out-of-body and near-death experiences). Having dreams come true was related to two other psi experiences (predict events and déjà vu). Predicting events accurately was significantly related to two other psi experiences (out-of-body and near death). Lastly, experiencing mental telepathy was related to experiencing two other paranormal events (déjà vu and near death).

While 35% of the sample answered "yes" to question #1, which asked if they had ever had a paranormal experience, almost 54% of the participants had experienced feelings coming true (hunches) and over 50% had experienced their dreams coming true. The fact that a sizeable number did not consider these two events paranormal is a further indicator that some people consider these events as *normal experiences*.

Fifteen (15) participants did not respond to question #1 at all, but they did respond to the question on specific other experiences (#2-m). Perhaps the taboo of admitting to having "other worldly" experiences represented a threat to their world view or religion. These fifteen people, perhaps more so than others in the sample, could not consciously accept the fact of having had a paranormal experience. The issue of non-acceptance of psi data in this study, however, took a different turn: as evidenced by these results, acceptance of psi data seems to be growing. What factors may we assume are contributing to this apparent turnaround? "New Age" cultural influence is one possible contributor. Recent and past television shows such as "Star Trek", "Unsolved Mysteries", "The X-Files", "Highlander", and other psychic or mystic mystery shows have helped fuel interest in the supernatural.

Also, as previously mentioned, information on this subject in book form is abundant. Whether the proverbial chicken came before the egg or vice versa is a debatable matter. Did the acceptance of psi phenomena come first and next become a "hot" media topic, or did media influence and fuel the acceptance of psi experiences? Whichever came first, psi is becoming a household topic and is influencing general perceptions about people who experience these phenomena, especially among the well educated.

When asked about any other paranormal events they had experienced, thirty people told us about their very unusual and unique experiences which included seeing deceased loved ones and prayers being answered in the "knick of time". None of the sample reported being mentally ill, hallucinating, involved in a ritual of any sort or under the influence of a substance when they had paranormal experiences.

On an individual level, the social taboo regarding saying that you have paranormal experiences is very strong in U.S. society. The social milieu is hostile, derisive and even threatening for people who admit to having paranormal or spiritual experiences. Many people who have supernatural experiences accept them as either "giftedness:, "psychic", or "sensitive" to their intuitive cognitions. Most, however, decline to discuss their experiences with others unless the atmosphere is accepting, open-minded and not derisive of their experiences.

Why do some people have these experiences and others do not? It is my strong opinion that *expectancy* and *comfort level* with psi events play major roles in what is received, perceived and accepted at the intuitive or paranormal level. *Fear, prejudice* and *close-mindedness* are strong repellents for experiencing psi. People who block their intuitive faculty do not get the same data as people who nurture their intuitive faculty. Those who only attend to their five senses for information choose to see their world and respond to it by using only those sensory inputs. Whether this is because of the social taboos regarding the paranormal, total devotion to "solid science: or religious beliefs, they fail to intuit; and therefore, they miss half of their perceptions or messages. If, however, we are open and live in an awareness that information from the intuitive faculty is normal, then we profit from the "other" way of perceiving , as well as from the cognitive way.

Recommendations for Further Research:

As with all other phenomena, the scientific community requires evidence of psi before they will accept its existence. I believe, even when presented with the evidence, some would ignore or deny it, while a handful of open-minded, pioneering, bold scientists would, indeed, investigate further. While the scientific method as we know it has served us well in researching the world of objective realities, it limits humankind's knowledge of the subjective world of psi phenomena.

We certainly live in a universe of both seen and unseen matter and energies. While we embrace the "seen" world, we reject the "unseen" world and ridicule those who say it exists because we do not know how to fathom it.

Scientifically, we are like a cyclops, a one-eyed creature, with only one window to the world. Therefore, we only accept one source of knowledge: that which our collective cyclopic eyes can sense. We need to expand our knowledge of the world to include the parallel world which also affects us, to a greater or lesser degree. Another scientific method is needed in order to study psi phenomena.

Heuristics may be the answer to developing a scientific method which would lend itself well to the kinds of data which are produced by psi investigations. It is a scientific method of subjectivity rather than objectivity. Dr. Clark Moustakas (1990) of The Union Institute & University outlines a method of investigating subjective information by utilizing heuristic research. This type of research includes the processes of self-dialogue, intuition, indwelling, focusing, immersion, incubation, illumination, explication, creative synthesis and validation. It is my opinion that heuristic research will bring about significant changes in the ways we view the world, in general, and in the ways that we relate to each other and assess ourselves, in particular. It would serve humankind well to look at the underdeveloped side of our cognition, the intuitive intellect. Heuristics can play a part in helping people to do that.

The following recommendations are made for future objective research:

1. A larger sample should be used with a good racial/ethnic mix so that all groups can be adequately represented.

2. More studies should be done to determine if age and religion are significant factors in the experiencing of paranormal events since these two factors closely approached significance.

3. More research should be done to determine if geographical location has a significant effect upon experiencing paranormal events.

4. Study the possibility of "negative possessions" as a cause of paranoid schizophrenia. Conduct research on the precipitating factors and/or activities for a large number of patients.

5. The "consistency" factor should be an integral part of the research on paranormal phenomena since people consistently report the same experiences to researchers, psychiatrists, doctors, hypnotherapists and others. A data base of information on precipitating factors, demographics, and other valuable knowledge should be amassed.

6. Interviews with many more extraordinary spiritual leaders from various backgrounds should be conducted to expand the knowledge on how others experience The Divine.

7. Heuristic studies should be conducted on the experiencing of specific kinds of paranormal phenomena.

8. Make comparisons of experiencers and non-experiencers of Psi with regard to personality characteristics.

9. Study schizophrenic therapies by comparing traditional therapies with healing approaches based on spiritual emergence theory.

10. Are we alone in the Universe? The work of the Center for SETI Research (Search for Extra-Terrestrial Intelligence)needs to be continued as well as other investigations into extra-terrestrial life.

.

Section Four

Conclusions

Chapter 16

Afterword

[The following subsections are devoted to exploring some of the ramifications of major global issues, problems or controversies which are examined in light of the alternative visions offered us by the shamans, ordinary people and the study of psi phenomena.]

The Limits of Science

The spiritual leaders who have told us about their experiences did so without compensation or reward. Their testimonies were honest, open and very candid. How do we process what they have told us about their spirit possessions; about their ability to leave the body and journey to far away places; about their various spiritual gifts; and about their healing hands? What about the sample of participants in the study? How do we process what their answers on the Sloan Paranormal Survey told us? The problem with accepting or not accepting psi evidence is, once again, tied to a method which scientists agreed upon, back in the age of reason: science will either accept or reject information based upon whether or not it conforms to the rules of the "scientific road". All of those who subscribe to the mechanistic view of our world want to see, feel, hear, smell, and taste it before they will acknowledge the existence of anything; everything must be objective. It is just this narrow-minded, fearful position that is limiting the progress of humankind.

If the truth is to be known, and it is my view that it can be known, then we will have to overcome fear of the unknown, because it only breeds more ignorance. We need to adopt a healthy interest and an informed open-mindedness about any area of psi which we plan to investigate. Instead, most of us tend to see what we expect to see. We notice, remember and pass on information that supports our point of view. Ignoring the continual reporting of paranormal experiences and ignoring scientific studies by researchers in parapsychology lead only to further schisms and chaos within the scientific community. We are only in the dawn of our existence, and just like ancient man, we egotistically want to be the center of the universe and be able to control all that it contains. We become angry when something as elusive and random as psi does not fit into our world view and, seemingly, eludes our grasp and control. Hubris is a fault. We are, in a sense, like ancient man, who eventually discovered that the world was not flat and that the sun did not revolve around the Earth. They did not like those truths as we do not like reports of psi. False pride goes before a fall, and humankind is falling. We are a part of this universe, but we are not front, not center, and not all. Maybe one day we will have the courage and humility to at least look at psi phenomena with an open-minded attitude instead of blind skepticism rooted in fear, scientific consensus and religious rigidity.

Before the advent of radio and TV, most people would have laughed and made fun of scientists who said that sounds and pictures with sounds could float through the air to a receiver in your home and that one day we would see and hear them? They thought those scientists were lunatics! Why, whoever heard of such? Then came radio and television. The unbelievable became real. We cannot see those sounds and pictures flying through the air on sine waves. Could psi events such as seeing visions and hearing sounds and voices (clairaudience) be transmitted to us on sine waves like those which we receive through radios and televisions? Even though we cannot see the sine waves, we know that they exist.

We cannot see spirits either. It is a well known scientific fact that energy is neither created by man nor destroyed. Since that is so, where does the electrical energy (impulse) in our bodies go after death? Is that electrical impulse our spirit body (soul) interacting in flesh? If that is so, what happens to that energy at death? It exists somewhere in the universe, according to that law.

Will psi become just another laughing matter for the fearful, the skeptical, the dogmatic and the programmed minds of the world to ridicule? Only time will tell that story; but increasingly more books and television shows focus on these phenomena. This one fact, alone, shows that people want to know more about these phenomena.

We cannot enter other people's dreams or thoughts. We cannot testify to the veracity of others' statements about their psi experiences. We cannot subject them to the rigid and rigorous standards of the scientific method: operability, measurability, repeatability, and consensus. Psi will not be harnessed in such a manner. Elusive? No. Different. Psi is different stuff. We still do not know enough about the parallel invisible world which we live in: the world of microbes, sine waves, radiation and other matter which falls outside our scope of unaided sensing. An additional way of increasing our knowledge about things which exist in this world is sorely needed. We need to bridge the gap between objective science and subjective science. Until we do, there are vast areas of subjective truths which we will not know about because of our non-acceptance of psi phenomena.

Diseases and Psi

How are physical ailments and abnormalities related to psi? How is our behavior related to our physical and/or mental condition? If we accept that both negative and positive karma is cumulative, then we must accept the notion of paying on the debt we owe or receiving the rewards for positive deeds. If we accept that concept, then diseases are negative karma which must be worked off. The concept of spiritual growth is inherent in this paradigm. No pain, no gain is true in cases where individuals must overcome certain odds and handicaps to survive. The body areas which were described by one of the shamans correspond to various behaviors and habits. The body areas which are affected reflect behaviors which we need to alter. If you accept this explanation, then it follows that God would not arbitrarily affect a body area for no reason. It is incumbent upon us to know why we suffer from illnesses and disabilities, because correcting the offensive behavior may just cure us. There is a reason for everything, whether we know it or not. Knowledge can be ours if we truly want it; the caveat is that it may refute much of what you have been taught.

If " The Sleeping Prophet", Edgar Cayce, and a few others could heal by going into trance or contacting a higher source of power, what makes us not move in that direction to find cures for all of the horrible diseases of today which afflict humankind? We could commission a cadre of psychics and healers to work in this area along side scientists. Just as Reverend Clarence "saw" the AIDS virus and how it invades, information of this type may be helpful to those doing research in the field of medicine.

We are in a perpetual state of denial and resistance when it comes to psi evidence. For some, accepting psi causes anxiety because it is in conflict with their accepted beliefs, and to reduce the anxiety, most people choose what is valued most by them (their accepted beliefs) and reject and denigrate the ideas which have caused the anxiety. When this rejection of conflicting ideas occurs, cognitive dissonance theory explains what has happened. Cognitive dissonance was first described by Leon Festinger in the late 1950's. He stated that our cognitions consist of our beliefs, attitudes and values. Cognitive dissonance occurs when new data or experiences are inconsistent with our cognitions and beliefs, thereby creating a mental conflict. In order to alleviate the conflict or dissonance, people resort to several ways of doing so: (1) change the offending belief, (2) add more consonant beliefs which agree with our cognition and which outweighs the importance of the dissonant or offending belief, (3) reduce the importance of the dissonant beliefs, or conversely, increase the importance of the consonant beliefs.

Non-acceptance of psi phenomena, then, is intricately related to the cognitive dissonance theory. In order to change the offending cognition (i.e., a paranormal event) dissonance is reduced by denying or altering the experience. In other words, people accept only what fits their cognitions.

Spirit Possession

Just as there are seemingly "positive possessions" by angels or deities who give healing messages, how do we know that there are not also "negative possessions"? What is schizophrenia? We have described a mental disorder which has all the earmarks of a "negative possession": Hearing voices, seeing visions, and even sometimes being out of control of one's physical body. Just as there are possibly deep or mild possessions in a positive spiritual sense, how can we not pose the opposite question: Are there deep or mild possessions of a negative sort? We do not know enough about schizophrenia to say that Rev. Clarence's assessment of it is wrong. This centuries-old mental disorder is still not wholly curable, even with medications and therapy.

Most people know only one facet of our world: the world which is visible to the naked eye. Our world, however, is composed of invisible energy sources and microscopic life forms with which most of us are totally unfamiliar. Our senses are limited to only a part of the audible range of sound and the visible range of light. If our hearing were like that of a dog, a bat or another animal whose ears can discern sounds that we cannot, would we be so quick to say that schizophrenics don't hear voices, just because we do not hear them? Can a phenomenon such as that described by Rev. Clarence be possible: the victim or patient's hearing has been adjusted to include higher level sounds than normal? Most of us would quickly say that that is absurd.

The shamans have told us about both good possessions and bad possessions. Good possessions like that of Nana Kwabena and his Akom priests and bad possessions like that of Rev. Clarence's counselees are at opposite ends of the same phenomenon: one is positive, enlightening and good and the other is negative and punishing. The shamans also reported very positive contacts with the world of spirit. People who have experienced out-of-body episodes also felt enlightened by their experiences. It makes sense to me that our unseen world, like our visible world, contains entities both good and evil.

Do we really want to know the truth, no matter how far fetched it may be, or is our fear and rejection of the reports of millions of people going to be ignored for a few more centuries to come? What conditions precipitated schizophrenia in most people who have it?   If it can be shown that the conditions or activities prior to a schizophrenic episode are similar or the same for most people, then could we not prevent it from occurring?   This researcher believes that we can look at it as a type of "spiritual emergency" gone awry.

Stan Grof (1989) and his colleagues were right in saying that non-pathological spiritual emergencies aid in the spiritual development of the individual. How can one go through Hell and come out of it intact without having some idea(s) or knowledge of the higher power which saw him/her through it?

Evolution vs. Creationism

What is meant by the terms "evolution" and "creationism"? Evolution is a process of gradual change which commonly refers to the formation and development of life on the earth. The idea that all life came from non-living matter and changed through the ages is called the "theory of evolution". According to the theory of evolution, single- celled organisms appeared on earth approximately three or four billion years ago. As time progressed, these single-celled organisms combined or were combined in various ways to produce early forms of life. More complex forms of life appeared later, with specialized characteristics that helped them adapt to their environment. The common thread among all living things is that they all share two basic similarities: cell structure and genetic code.

The process of evolution is believed to be occurring as fast today as at any other time. However, during the last few million years (a brief period in the earth's history) hundreds of species have become extinct and hundreds of others have developed.

Creationism is the belief, in most religions, that explains the origin of life. These beliefs tell how the world and living things were created. The most widely known story of the creation in the Western World is in the Holy Bible in the book of Genesis. This version of the creation story says that God created the earth in six days and rested on the seventh day. Today's Biblical scholars interpret the creation in several ways: (1) The creation occurred exactly as Genesis said it did, (2) The story of the creation is symbolic and is a mystery that will never be fully understood and (3) God's method of creation is revealed through science and human understanding.

There are several creationist theories. One of the most popular is referred to as *intelligent design;* it argues that God's design can be seen in life. They use microbiology and mathematical logic to sustain their arguments. Intelligent design creationism is an umbrella theory which incorporates the beliefs of most other creationist theories.

Scientific creationists believe that most evidence supports creation over evolution and that merely thousands of years rather than billions of years have passed since the creation of life. They reason that scientific evidence fails to show any one kind of life form in transition to any other kind of life form. Further, they say that fossil records fail to show continuity in development from one organism to another, and that there are systematic gaps between various kinds of organisms. This observation supports the scientific creationists' view that each form of life was always unique within genetic limits and did not change over time.

Suppose the evolutionists are correct in their view. What evidence do they cite as proof of evolution? Geological charts show that different types of life have appeared on the earth at different times in history. Sometimes it took billions of years before the appearance of one form of life and the disappearance of another. Each later form was always an improvement over the one which came before it. Modern man is the newest major life form to appear on the earth within the last 50,000 years, a very short time period on the geological time table.

Evolutionists also cite human development in the womb as one proof of their theory. These stages in the womb are known as embryonic recapitulation or "ontogeny recapitulates phylogeny". This theory states that the human embryo goes through stages in the womb of earlier life forms which we have come from. They cite gill slits like fish, a tail like a monkey and various other stages that resemble the fetuses of a chicken, a pig and a monkey.

Evolutionists also cite fossil evidence as further proof of their theory. Fossils of prehistoric man have been found in various parts of the world. Scientists believe that they are links in a developmental chain from lower to higher forms for humans. Radiocarbon dating which is a chemical process that tells the age of matter supports them in this aspect of their theory. In 1974, the fossilized remains of a human-like creature nicknamed "Lucy" (scientific name: Australopithecus afarensis) were found in Ethiopia by American anthropologist Donald Johanson. Lucy's remains are over three million years old, many thousands of years before hominids were believed to exist. Another fossil, dubbed "Lucy's grandson" was found with a nearly intact skull of a male A. afarensis who lived about 200,000 years after Lucy. Lucy, believed to be the missing link which unites us to our ancestors and Africa, is believed to be the origin of the human species.

Another fossil, believed to be a possible link to modern day Homo sapiens is that of Kennewick man, found in Kenya in 1998-99 along the shores of Lake Turkana. This fossil is about the same age as Lucy but with a more human-like face. Kennewick man was named Kenyanthropus platyops which means "flat-faced man of Kenya". Some anthropologists believe that there is a 50-50 chance that this species, not Lucy, was man's earliest ancestor. Some anthropologists, on the other hand, think that both species could have been an evolutionary dead end.

Further evidence of evolution is offered by the fact that we have vestigial organs in our bodies, organs which used to serve a purpose but which no longer serve the same purpose and are in fact, disappearing. These vestigial organs include the appendix, the thymus gland and the tonsils.

Evolution not only means acquiring new traits, but also discarding traits which are no longer useful to the organism. Humans have lost their body hair, except for the underarm and pubic areas; many of us no longer have wisdom teeth and the size of our teeth is getting smaller, especially the canines or incisors. We no longer have the ability to synthesize vitamin C; our skull thickness has changed; we no longer have bony brow ridges over our eyes; most humans have lost their ear-wiggling muscles. The evolutionists cite the law of use and disuse in explaining why some functions or body parts are diminished or disappear. When something is not used, it is taken away from the organism or diminished if it is only used minimally.

Evolutionists also cite homology, or similarities between two organisms as evidence. For example the wings of a bat correspond one-to-one with the hands of humans. Several other animals such as dogs and sheep have menstrual cycles like human females; whales have vestigial hind limbs recessed in their tails, indicating that they might have once walked on land.

The disappearance of species or life forms is cited as further proof of evolution. Many species of animals and plants frequently disappear from the earth. Conversely, new hybrids or mutations appear. In other words, old life forms disappear and new life forms appear. Even in the microscopic world, new forms of bacteria and viruses appear to plague mankind and other species with new diseases. The viruses and bacteria mutate: they exchange genetic material just as other life forms exchange genetic material through mating or natural selection.

Astronomy lends further proof to a gradually created or evolutionary universe in the "red shift" phenomenon. Very simply, the red shift phenomenon can be explained by looking at the properties of white light. White light when seen through a prism (specially cut glass) is broken up into red, yellow, orange, green, blue and purple. The light at the red end of the color spectrum has a longer wave length than light at the purple end. Scientists have measured light coming from a distant star and they have discovered that over a period of time, the wave length of the red end of the color spectrum keeps changing or getting longer. This means that our solar system is being moved farther and farther away from the star.

In 1929, Edwin Hubble, an American astronomer found that the distance of other galaxies from the earth and how fast they are moving away from the earth could be determined by a mathematical calculation.   Astronomers have discovered that galaxies are rapidly expanding away from the earth and from each other: the universe is expanding. This is cited by evolutionists as further proof that the universe is still "under development" and is by no means finished.

What do the creationists have to say about all this evidence put forth by the evolutionists? With regard to the geological charts and fossil evidence, the creationists say that there are no fossils of intermediate creatures. In other words, if evolution is a fact, there should be evidence of transitional creatures leading up to the species with which we are familiar. If the earth is actually 4.5 billion years old, and if life began suddenly in the Cambrian period about five hundred million years ago, then there should be evidence of some fossil life leading up to the Cambrian period. They cite the absence of pre-Cambrian period life, except some markings which the evolutionists claim are signs of pre-Cambrian life. They say that Lucy is not the missing link. They cite the incompleteness of the Lucy's skull and state that most of it is "imagination made of plaster of Paris" and that no firm conclusion could be drawn about what species Lucy belonged to. The Creationists cite the opinion of Dr. Charles Oxnard, among others, who said that the group to which Lucy belonged is different from both African apes and humans in most features. He felt that Australopithecines are unique, related to neither man nor ape.

Creationists say that the concept of embryonic recapitulation is a fraud. The idea that the human fetus undergoes stages resembling those of the lower animals is to them a lie. They cite the bogus work of a German evolutionist, Ernst Haeckel in the late 1860's. Haeckel, they say, falsified drawings and faked photographs to support the theory of evolution.

Creationists refute the evolutionists' claim that we have vestigial or useless organs in our bodies. Creationists say that idea was invented in the early 19th century when medical information was not what it is today. The organs which evolutionists say are vestigial do have a function, claim the creationists. For example, the appendix, they say, plays a role in antibody production and protects our intestines from disease; the tonsils protect us from infections; lymphocyte and antibody production takes place in the thymus gland; and without the coccyx bones or vestigial tail bones, our pelvic organs would fall down and we would not be able to walk, sit upright or have bowel movements.

Homology, or similarities between two organisms, is used to support evolution because it is believed that the organisms share a common ancestor. Creationists, however, say that these similarities have often been erroneously used. They cite that evolutionists find small portions of organisms homologous but ignore the rest of the organism. They claim that the ignored parts may, in fact, be very dissimilar.

Further, they state that physiologically similar structures often develop in a different way from the embryo stage, thus dispelling the common history claim of evolutionists. Creationists say that homology is actually evidence of creationism because it indicates one creator who used the same basic plan on many of His creations. They reason that if there were many creators, then there would be heterotrophic organisms, or life forms with dissimilar genetic and chemical makeups. Since the food chain dictates that organisms replenish the same types of minerals, sugars, vitamins, amino acids which they lose on a daily basis, then the organisms upon which they feed must have the same or similar nutrients to support the predator organism in order to get some food value from the meal. Creationists, then, also claim homology as one piece of supporting evidence for their theory.

Creationists point to the horse theory of evolution in derision in making their point. At the bottom of the horse hierarchy is Eohyppus, a small horse-like animal about the size of a fox with several toes on each foot. At the top of the hierarchy is Equus, the horse as we know it today. Several horse-like animals in the hierarchy lie between Eohyppus and Equus. Creationists say that no one knows where Equus came from because the textbook drawings of the horse family are drawn from artists' imagination and not from evidence. Further, they say that fossils of the modern Equus have been found, dating back to the same time as Eohyppus, the first horse. If both were living on earth at the same time, how could Eohyppus be the ancestor of Equus? There is much debate surrounding this question.

The debate between the two sides continues to both enrage the creationists and to fuel the flames of the evolutionists' scientific quest for the missing link. I tend to agree with both to some degree. I agree with the creationists who say that we are the creations of a perfect supreme being. However, there is too much evidence that shows a progressive, changing universe to believe that mankind is a finished product at this time in our history on earth. The creationists' timeline is faulty. If our proof is the so-called "missing links" of fossilized ancestors, then, perhaps we need to acknowledge that some species have disappeared from earth, perhaps many millennia before modern man appeared. Maybe they were all eaten by a stronger predator, or maybe they were all destroyed by some disease or disaster which washed their remains into an ocean or buried them so deep in the earth's core that we will never find them.

Fossils are clues to changes that have taken place on earth. Paleontologists have sometimes found fossil seashells high in the mountains, far removed from any ocean. This can only mean that they existed in the sea long before the sea was lifted up to form a mountain. Proof of our ancestry as found in fossils is inherently weak as a valid type of evidence.

Linkages are perhaps illusory and non-existent insofar as our scientific ability to find each and every possible connection to us. The complete history of earth will probably never be known by using paleontology, alone.

It is ludicrous for us to think that we can find the fossil of every single model which The Creator fashioned before we became the present model. And, if we believe that we are the last model of man who will inhabit this earth, then we are foolish and myopic. Some fossil evidence might just be a dead end species, a model which was unsuccessful in exercising its particular patterns of survival. Several life forms which are very successful at survival such as the cockroach, the coelacanth fish and some others still inhabit earth after many millions of years, same basic model.

History, alone, tells us that we came from something and that we are moving toward something greater. The Creator did not short-change us on our abilities , our stature , our looks or anything. We are a walking, talking story of our past, including our past lives. Karmic law always prevails. Survival of the fittest is nature's law and who, but The Creator, made nature? So, it's God's law. It's a world of survival as well as growth and development.

Score one for the evolutionists on the "red shift" phenomenon. The universe is expanding outward, growing ever larger. There is astronomical proof of it, but the creationists are oddly silent on that bit of evidence. The universe is not static and unchanging; what grand blueprint is unfolding remains to be seen. But, we do know that it is, gradually, unfolding. This phenomenon is definite proof that "the creation" is still going on. God is not finished. One day in God's timeframe could be several million years. If we interpret "day" literally, then, we would have to subscribe to the creationists' view that we were made as we are today millions of years ago. There is simply no logic to that view. We have the proof of how we looked many millennia ago in our museums and we are certainly better looking today than prehistoric man.

The Extinction of Humans

Will modern man become extinct like the dinosaurs? Probably so. If all life forms are "becoming" or under development as a part of God's gradual creation, then it stands to reason that we, too, will be replaced by a newer, better functioning, better looking, more intelligent model. Looking back in time at the predecessor forms of Homo sapiens, we have already developed into a more intelligent, more highly skilled and , yes, better looking model. Perhaps Friedrich Nietzsche's notion of a "superman" supplanting modern man is not far from the truth.

There is scientific evidence that, within the last 130 years, the earth has lost a substantial amount of its magnetic shield. If God is speeding up the pace of the creation, then what does this loss herald? The magnetosphere is a layer of air above the earth which keeps cosmic dust and other radioactive particles from entering earth's atmosphere. It acts like a huge invisible shield surrounding our planet, protecting it from cosmic particles just as our skin protects our bodies from bacteria and other foreign matter. If the earth has lost a substantial portion of this invisible protective shield, does that mean that more cosmic dust (radioactive particles) is able to penetrate our atmosphere? The answer is a flat and simple YES. What can cosmic dust do to us? Radiation can have many different kinds of effects upon the human body. Most important, it can cause changes in our genes and chromosomes. The genes and chromosomes are like message carriers or "supervisors" inside our sex cells. They tell the builder cells how to build our bodies. A change in the structure of our genes or chromosomes is like firing one "supervisor" and hiring another. The new "supervisor" tells the builder cells to build the body a new or different way. Once the order is given by the "supervisor" genes, the order is almost always unchangeable; scientists call a genetic change like this a "mutation".

When a sex cell chromosome breaks, the broken ends may either join up with pieces of other genetic material or remain broken and carry a different "message" to the builder cells. This is how new species of plants and animals are created by God. The laws of nature are God's laws.

Our magnetic shield stops most of the radioactive particles from entering our atmosphere, but the earth's magnetic field also has a lot to do with genetic mutations. The north and south poles are always moving about, very, very slowly. From 1955 to around 1960, the earth's North Pole moved approximately 70 miles toward the northwest. Scientists know that in the past, the north magnetic pole has been in Korea, in the middle of the North Atlantic Ocean and perhaps in Africa. Even more amazing, the north and south poles change places about once every million years. The north and south poles have changed positions at least 171 times in the past 76 million years. Scientists know that the earth's magnetic poles have wandered because there are rocks which are like compass needles letting us know where the poles were in the past. These rocks are called loadstones or magnetite. Magnetite particles are found in lava that flows out of volcanoes. As the lava cools, the magnetic particles which make up the loadstone are turned in a north-south direction by the earth's magnetic field. When the lava becomes solid rock, these "compass needle" magnetic particles are frozen into place so that thousands and millions of years later, when scientists examine the rocks found in and near volcanoes, they find these frozen compass needles pointing to where the north and south poles used to be when the rock was cooling off.

Scientists suspect that these shifts in the earth's magnetic poles are related to the disappearance of the dinosaurs and other prehistoric animals. Scientists even have proof that tiny sea animals called "radiolaria" suddenly disappeared shortly after switches or reversals in the earth's magnetic poles. They guess that the earth's protective magnetic shield was weakened at certain places during these shifts, thereby allowing more radioactive cosmic dust to reach earth at these weak spots.

The ozone hole is a huge depletion of the ozone layer that occurs each Antarctic spring. It is a thinning of the layer over that area which has amounted to the destruction of up to 70% of the ozone layer. Whatever changes life in that region is undergoing may not be readily seen, but the huge loss of the protective shield in that area is sure to cause some genetic changes in the life forms there due to the effects of the enormous amount of radiation that passes through the hole.

Scientists say that our use of chloroflurocarbons (CFCs) has helped destroy the ozone layer and most countries are trying to phase out the sources of CFCs (pressurized sprays, cooling agents, etc.). If, by the year 2010, when all countries are supposed to have phased out the use of CFCs, the ozone layer is still disappearing, we must look at the possibility that natural processes are causing the rapid destruction. If so, we must also look at the possibility that God is speeding up the pace of the creation. New life forms will appear, mutations will occur. All of these changes are planned by The Creator and should not be feared by us. All will be well with the world, although it may look a little different. On the other hand, radiation can also destroy whole species or groups of plants and animals, but it will be time for them to disappear and newer life forms to appear.

Now, what is so strange and puzzling to scientists today is the fact that in the past 10 million years, the earth's magnetic poles have shifted or reversed themselves on the average of once every 220 thousand years; but, the last pole reversal occurred 700 thousand years ago. According to many scientists, the earth is long overdue for another switch in its north and south poles.

What next? Will man become extinct? Will we undergo genetic changes? I think so, because the universe is not static, it is dynamic, ever changing and expanding. The Creator has a blueprint for the creation and we will not see these changes in our lifetime, but in the words of a popular song, "Change gon' come." We will not be destroyed, but rather, improved. We are still being created by God and Our Creator controls all of these physical laws including the laws of outer space and heredity. The laws of nature are God's laws and she changes them whenever she so desires. God has made many laws uniform or "regular", on a fixed time schedule so that man will know that there is a purpose and design to the universe.

Religious Intolerance

Throughout the centuries, mankind has ridiculed, shunned and even fought those of different religious beliefs. The twin "I-word" evils, ignorance and intolerance, are the root cause of these problems. All God-seeking religions have several core beliefs in common, among them being: 1) the belief in a supernatural power which is good and omnipotent; 2) a reward/punishment system for our deeds; 3) an afterlife, 4) angels or higher beings who aid in God's work, and 5) a malevolent or evil being(s).

What a wonderful world this would be if we all had actual knowledge of God rather than beliefs! Humankind limits God to our narrow and limited ways of learning about The Creator. The writings of prophets, kings and disciples of the founders of religions which have been passed down to us through the centuries are all that most people have to guide them, spiritually. Most of us are limited to these sources for our knowledge of God and our purpose for living. We believe truths, half-truths, and outright lies in our quest for spiritual knowledge through others. We anthro-

pomorphogize God as a man or superhuman-like being because we do not know the full story about God and life.
Some would say that God limits man in how much we
should know about the so-called "mysteries of life". I say
man limits God because we listen to the voices of those who
know no more that what has been passed on to them, his-
torically. This fact brings to mind the well-known parable of
the three blind men who, believed that they were touching
God in the form of an elephant and they each tried to describe "God" to each other: one felt the elephant's massive
leg and said, "God is like a tree, big and strong; the second
blind man felt the elephant's trunk and said, "No, God is
like a great long snake which is constantly moving; the
third blind man felt the elephant's ear and said, "No, my
brothers, God is like neither of those things. He is like a
huge leaf blowing in the wind." Each blind man felt only one
aspect of the whole being, but each one was accurate in his
description of the aspect which he touched. Humankind,
like the three blind men, does not have the whole picture
and understanding of God What we lack is knowledge so
important and vital that the lack of it makes us suffer im-
measurable harm and hardships, even though we believe
we have all of the facts. It is just those rigid, dictatorial belief systems which harm and sometimes enslave our capacity to grow and develop into the beings which The Creator
made us to be.

Ancient and modern cultural beliefs and practices,
as well as gender biases still remain contentious battle-
grounds which fuel modern religious conflicts and hate
campaigns. The fact that many religions exist tells us that
God has given "the word" to more than one individual or
group. We, however, try to limit God to whichever religion
we are taught and all others are damned. The fact that God
works through many bearers of "the word" and through
many healers, with various spiritual gifts, means that God
is far greater than all our religions. I am in agreement with
Reverend Clarence on that issue. I take issue with those
who say their way (religion) is the only road to God and salvation. Before any organized religion, there were people,
God's people. These people never heard of Jesus, Mohammed, Buddha, Zoroaster or any of the founders of religions.
Did God not love and save them just because they were

born too soon? Even today, discoveries have been made of people in remote areas of the world who had never heard of our founders of religions. Are they to be judged and damned by The Creator just because they were born in the "wrong place"? Never. Religious intolerance is both wrong-headed and blind to the true nature of God.

God speaks to all, regardless of religious indoctrination. God even speaks to lower life forms. Just as in the ancient world, all roads led to Rome, all good God-seeking religions lead to The Divine, no exceptions. They may not have all the facts right, but God certainly does hear them all and love them all. All God-seeking people receive blessings and guidance from The Creator, regardless of their religions.

God healed through all of the shamans, both those who belonged to known, orthodox religions, as well as those whose practices and beliefs were non-orthodox. Since God worked miracles through all of them, then religions are limited in their scope and narrow in their beliefs about The Creator. The values or beliefs shared by all of the shamans were: a belief in God's omnipotence and the heartfelt desire to help others through healing and teaching. God worked miracles through all of them, regardless of their religious or spiritual roots. Religious intolerance has no place in a spiritual milieu. It speaks to ignorance and fear. We need to wake up and learn about our true purpose on earth and our destiny. Asking The Creator questions is the way toward true redemption. Following religious leaders   blindly and listening to those authorities who may or may not know the real truth may earn you a lot of grief and a round trip ticket back to earth plane.

I know that we can have a one-on-one , loving and educational type relationship with Our Creator. She never wants us to be in the dark about anything which concerns our lives. Just ask her!

Racial and Ethnic Hatred

If we are to believe our shamans who espoused knowledge of reincarnation, then we must believe that we are all evolving through living many lives in various countries, as other races and ethnicities and possibly as the opposite gender.

If we believe the holy books of most of the world's religions, there is mention of rebirth. Rebirth in the truest sense of the word means coming back to earth in a new life, as a new baby, perhaps in another country, another race and perhaps a different socio-economic stratum. All of these changes are designed by The Creator to improve the individual and help him or her to meet certain requirements before entering Heaven on a permanent basis. These requirements are both collective and individual. There are ways each person must develop and there are individual karmas that must be worked out or debts to God which must be paid by us.

The prevailing beliefs in many religions about death and going to Heaven or Hell are: 1) Everyone goes to Heaven if they are nice people; and 2) Evil people go to Hell and are eternally damned. The truth of the matter, as revealed through meditation messages and other ways is that many good people have weaknesses that do not meet Heaven's standards. Suppose good people who die are racists, sexists or people, who by their own design and because of their cultural/religious beliefs, keep other human beings from developing and advancing. While they may be good in many ways and even charitable individuals, serious character flaws such as the above earn them a round trip ticket back to earth plane. Some of them do not deserve Hell, so they go into a sort of holding place which some call purgatory where they learn the true facts of God and life and where they may see or visit their new parents before they go into the womb for rebirth.

The former oppressor becomes the oppressed. A racist may be returned to earth as a member of the racial group or ethnic group which he or she persecuted and discriminated against. Payback is real and just.

The Effects of Sexism on Our Immortal Souls

For centuries, women have occupied a lower status in most societies. They have accepted the "female role" of nurturer, submissive mate, gatherer, and keeper of the hearth and home. The traditional female role is undergoing changes today which are causing upheavals in the structure of the nuclear family. Many women now reject the role which has been theirs for so many centuries. Both religion and cultural mores have contributed to the subjugation of females, to their detriment.

The reincarnation of females who have bought into the subservient role has been stated by one of the shamans as a cause of male homosexuality. In other words, some women who are overly subservient must strengthen this weakness and therefore God returns them to Earth in the body of the opposite sex so that they may gain specific strengths which are taught to men, such as struggling for survival, independence, bravery, self-reliance, responsibility and other positive masculine traits.

Some homosexual clients whom I have counseled have said that they knew they were "gay" at a very early age. The past life regression of Byron provides an insight into the reasons why "gay" men return to Earth with that particular karmic debt. The condition of being in the opposite gender's physical body is both a healing experience as well as a punishing one. The female soul of the gay man yearns for the love of another man because she is a female trapped in a male body. The opposite situation exists for the soul of a man in a female body. Male domination of the female is not God's way, even if your religion does teach it. Domineering, possessive men are returned to earth as male-role-playing lesbians.

I am in total agreement with Reverend Clarence when he says that we do not know God's laws because we listen to and follow authorities who sometimes lead us down the road to perdition like the proverbial pied piper of Hamlin.

I, too, have received signs that point to the fact that we are returned to Earth and placed into the family and lifestyle which will help us to develop in the ways that we need to develop. With this being the case, then more women than men are returning to Earth because of the weaker role which women have accepted and followed. If more women than men are returning, then a man shortage will become more acute and the following situations will prevail:

1) There will be more gay men (female souls in male bodies) than straight men (male souls in male bodies).

2) The nuclear family as we know it will cease to exist because of the straight male shortage.

3) Polygamy may become a necessary alternative to the survival of the human species.

4) Wars will depend, increasingly, upon woman-power.

5) Corporations and other businesses will see a sharp increase in women leaders.

There will be those who will say that God intended for women to be subservient, to be the "weaker sex" because it was ordained and that woman was made from Adams rib or some similar account. When socially malevolent beliefs and practices are sanctioned by one's religion, this has a tendency to silence the would-be voice of opposition. More heinous deeds have been committed in the name of God than can be accounted for. The price of sexism and adhering to rigid anachronistic, stultifying sex roles is not something that The Creator intended for us to do. This is learned behavior, not natural to females. To be subservient means to belong to and serve like a master. If that is what some religions teach, then they are in contradiction to the word of God that says, "Thou shalt have no other God (master) before me." We are God's property; we are only on loan to each other: husbands do not own wives; wives do not own husbands; parents do not own their children. We are the property of Our Creator and she does not give away her creations.

If the body language which Reverend Clarence told us about is true, then this would explain why more women are dying of heart attacks than breast cancer. If the heart represents love and fun in our spiritual development, then women, especially working women, bear a double load of work and drudgery; that does not leave them much time for fun and games. On the other hand, the childlike, dependent status of women has hurt, rather than helped their spiritual development. The yoke of social and religious conformity has been the downfall of many women. To be free to be her natural self is the God-given right of every female. Why, then, do we give it away so freely and lovingly? Women must learn to value themselves as well as help others; self-love is the greatest love of all.

Crime and Amorality

Crime and a person's lack of moral beliefs go hand-in hand. If you believe that there is no higher power ruling the world, then morality is something which does not rule your actions and reactions in the world. If you believe there are no consequences to your choices, then you will choose to do whatever is most profitable and expedient for your needs and desires, regardless of who or what might suffer as a result of those choices.

The moral decay of great societies always starts with a decline in the belief in a higher power or a conflict of religions. With the silencing of the "moral voice" of a society, the "politicizing" of formerly taboo or immoral acts takes precedence. Politics is always more malleable than morality. Legalize the rotten and obscene and you change public opinion about whatever it is that the immoral segment of a society wants to sanction. The Romans and other great societies have gone this route. Great civilizations have experienced great downfalls because of internal decay, not because of defeat at the hands of an outside enemy.

Understanding psi would help reduce crime and immorality: people would become aware that The Higher Power communes with them all of the time. Enlightenment and understanding of life would stop crime in its tracks and cause each and every one of us to weigh our actions before we take them. We would all be marching to the beat of the same drummer. Therefore, there would be only one spiritual canon. There would be no believers, non-believers, or agnostics. There would be "knowers", enlightened ones. Knowing that God's karmic laws apply to all life would certainly put a stop to impulsive and harmful behavior. All is fair in life; if God deals you your "hand" based on your past achievements and efforts, then you must play the hand you are dealt. If you are at the bottom of the ladder, then you must work your way up by making wise choices and holding on tenaciously to your free-will because there are always those who seek to take it away. What may seem unfair to some is merely a person's karma being meted out to them. God is our judge, not man. The "Great Spanker" will repay you measure for measure; good for good behavior and bad for bad or immoral behavior. It would serve us well to know what God judges as "good behavior" and "bad behavior" rather than get it wrong and think that we know. As one of the shamans said, "Good people suffer because they don't know God's rules."

There will never be total peace on Earth. Somewhere, there will always be a conflict or war. Earth is a testing ground and a proving ground for us. We must struggle for survival and compete for food, mates and whatever else we need for survival. Fighting, as well as cooperation, is always a part of that struggle. Heaven is peaceful, Earth is "fightful". If the weak and the evil are constantly being returned to Earth, then fighting and defending will always exist on Earth. On the other hand, the possibility of long periods of peaceful coexistence on Earth and the rise of "golden civilizations" may be some of the rewards of knowing about psi and God's karmic laws.

Developing and Using Our "Other" Sense

There is surely something to be gained from developing the intuitive intellect. Why do some of us have it to a greater degree than others? Why are some of us able to talk to the angels and saints; fly with the winds; heal those who are sick; dream dreams which come true or which guide; have strong feelings which come true; see wide awake visions of things and experience other forms of psi or communications from a source we have not yet identified? Who or what bestows these special gifts and abilities upon people? The ultimate question is: Why is psi experienced so readily, joyfully, and spiritually by some and not at all by others? Is it because we do not all follow the same developmental pathways in life? What you are taught and your comfort level with your teachings have everything to do with your experiencing or not experiencing psi. Who would be frightened and who would not be frightened by these very close and personal experiences with The Deity? Surely, The Deity knows.

A new dawn awaits humankind whenever we are ready to acknowledge that there is a missing part of ourselves: we are missing the images, the signs, the language of the universe through which the Higher Power can talk to each of us individually. We are missing half of our cognitive faculties, the intuitive intellect, due to fear and repression. Our Higher Power communicates, but most of us do not know the symbols, the signs which are the stuff of dreams, visions, and even waking , real manifestations. I am in agreement with C.G. Jung when he said that all of our so- cial maladies and ills stem from an alienation from our ancestral past, both human and pre-human. I would ex- pand upon this by stating that this knowledge is universal and accessible by anyone who desires the knowledge. There is a huge "library of information" to which the human mind has access, but which most of us are taught to fear and/or ignore. This knowledge source is empowering, enlightening, and uplifting. We may access this source of knowledge through prayer, meditation and any other sincere method of calling upon The Creator for enlightenment.   The source and origin of all this knowledge is known by many names: Yahweh, Allah, Kije Moneto, The One, God and many other names. What we call God is not as important as calling upon God.

The truth about our existence and our mission can help us individually and collectively by guiding us and giv- ing purpose to our lives. The shamans have told us, not of their beliefs, but of their knowledge and experiences. If knowledge is theirs for the asking, is it not ours for the ask- ing, also? If The Creator has created us all, are we not all chosen and are we not all favored?   All life is one family, birthed by One Creator, all races of man are brothers and sisters; all are favored by God, even the evil, for they are God's wayward children and God still loves them, uncondi- tionally, but not their behavior. Indeed, God loves us all, unconditionally: the good and the evil, the rich and the poor, the genius and the intellectually challenged. God speaks to us all, every living thing, at our own individual levels of understanding.

Individually, we are born; individually, we die; indi- vidually, we are judged by Our Maker. Just as The Creator has chosen some of us to heal and deliver The Word, some of us have chosen The Creator and asked to help and He/She has answered a resounding, "Yes, you may!" God is not about darkness, ignorance and unknowables or unfa- thomable mysteries of life. God is about light, understand- ing, and teaching us truth. What would happen if we all just stopped listening to the voices of authority and listen to God for a change? I think that we would find the answers to age-old mysteries and solve problems which affect most societies

We are all God's chosen people and we will all be lifted up to our Heavenly home one day, not all of us at once, but each according to his deeds, but all will get there. God has not chosen one group to rule over others and dominate the world. God does not want any of her children to be subjugated to anyone except Her. Domination over others is achieved through the acquiescence of the dominated.

Section Five

References, Appendices, and Subject Index

REFERENCES

American Psychiatric Association. (1994). (Fourth Edition). *Diagnostic and statistical manual of mental disorders: DSM-IV*. Washington, DC : Author.

Archer, F. (1969). *Crime and the psychic world*. New York : W. Morrow.

Berger, A. (1987). *The aristocracy of the dead: New findings in postmortem survival*. Jefferson, NC : McFarland.

Bergson, H. (1915). *S.P.R. Presidential Address: Proceedings of the Society for Psychical Research. 27*, pp.157-175. London: SPR

Blackmore, S. (1982). *Beyond the body*. London: William Heinemann

Boaventura, F. (1979). (Translated by Paul Burns). *Pastoral practice and the paranormal*. Chicago : Franciscan Herald Press.

Bockie, S. (1993). *Death and the invisible powers: The world of Kongo belief*. Bloomington, IN: Indiana University Press

Bolles, E. B. (1991). *A second way of knowing: The riddle of human perception*. New York: Prentice Hall.

Boniface, H. (1981). *Brother Andre: All he could do was pray*. Montreal: St. Joseph's Oratory.

Brown, J. H. (1987). Evolution. In *the world book encyclopedia* (Vol. , pp. 330-37). Chicago: World Book.

Browne, S. & Harrison, L. (2000). *Life on the other side: A Psychic's tour of the afterlife*. New York: Dutton.

Browne, S. (2001). *Past lives, future healing,* New York: Dutton.

Bruner, J. & Postman, L. (1958). On the perception of incongruity: a paradigm. In: Beardsley, D.& Wertheimer, M., *Readings in perception.* New York: Van Nostrand.

Burgdorf, C.A., Albritton, D & Ennis, C. (April 1999). *Scientific assessment of ozone depletion:1998.* Retrieved January 17, 2002 from the NOAA Aeronomy Laboratory data-base.

Byrd, R.C. (1988). Positive therapeutic effects of intercessory prayer in a Coronary care unit population. *Southern Medical Journal, 81,* 826-29.

Calloway, H. (1962). *Astral projection: A record of out-of-the-body experiences.* New Hyde Park, NY: Univerisity Books.

Campbell, J. (1968). *The masks of God: Creative mythology.* New York : The Viking Press.

Campbell, J. (1970). *Myths, dreams, and religion.* Dallas, TX: Spring.

Campbell, J. (1972). *Myths to live by.* New York: Viking.

Carington, W. (1946). *Telepathy.* London: Methuen.

Cashman, J. (1966). *The LSD story.* Greenwich, CN: Fawcett.

Cassel, R.N. (1990). Transpersonal psychology as the basis for health care.   *Psychology: A Journal of Human Behavior, 27,* 33-38.

Castaneda, C. (1993). *The art of dreaming.* New York: Harper Collins.

Cayce, E. (1986). *The Edgar Cayce Collection: Four volumes in One.* New York: Bonanza Books.

Chase, P.L. & Pawlik, J. (2001). *Healing with crystals.* Franklin Lakes, NJ: The Career Press.

Chase, P.L. & Pawlik, J. (2002). *Healing with gemstones.* Franklin Lakes, NJ: New Page Books.

Clark, A. (1973). *Psycho-Kinesis: Moving matter with the mind.* West Nyack, NY: Parker.

Cowley, S. (1996, March). *Space physics: A beginner's guide to the earth's magnetosphere.* Retrieved March 12, 2002 from http://www.agu.org/sci_soc/cowley.html

Dossey, L. (1993). *Healing words: The power of prayer and the practice of medicine.* San Francisco: Harper.

Drewes, A. (1991). *Parapsychological research with children: an annotated bibliography.* Metuchan, NJ: Scarecrow Press.

Ducasse, C. (1969). *Paranormal phenomena, science, and life after death.* New York : Parapsychology Foundation.

Eadie, B.J. (1994). *Embraced by the light.* New York: Bantam Books.

Earth Changes TV (2001, March 30). *Solar wind energy in our magnetosphere.* Retrieved March 12, 2002, from http://www.earthchangestv.com/breaking/March_Part2 _2001/0330magnetosphere.htm

Ehrenwald, J. (1971). Mother-child symbiosis: Cradle of ESP. *Psycho- analytic Review, 58,* 455-466.

Eisenbud, J., Psi and the nature of things. *Intl. J. of Parapsychology, 5, Summer 1963,* pp. 245-268.

Festinger, Leon (1957). *A theory of cognitive dissonance.* Stanford, CA: Stanford University Press.

Frontiers of Physics Conference (1977: Reykjavik, Iceland).
    *The Iceland papers on experimental and theoretical
    research on the physics of consciousness.* Amherst, WI:
    Essential Research Associates.

Goodkind, H. (1979). *The mystery of the "talking" plants.* New
    York : Contemporary Perspectives.

Green, J.L.(n.d.). *The magnetosphere.* Retrieved on March 7,
    2002 from http://ssdoo.gsfc.nasa.gov/education/lectures/
    magnetosphere.html

Gris, H. & Dick, W. (1978), *The new soviet psychic
    discoveries.* Englewood Cliffs, NJ: Prentice Hall.

Grof, S., & Grof, C. (Eds.). (1989). *Spiritual emergency: When
    personal transformation becomes a crisis.* Los Angeles:
    Jeremy P. Tarcher.

Gugliotta, G. (2002, April 18).Suddenly, humans age 3 million
    years. *The Washington Post,* p.A3.

Hall, C., & Nordby, V. (1973). *A primer of Jungian psychology.*
    New York : Penguin.

Hendricks, G. & Weinbold, B., (1982). *Transpersonal ap-
    proaches to counseling and   psychotherapy.* Denver :
    Love.

Hibbard, W. & Worring R. (1982) *Psychic criminology.*
    Springfield, IL: Charles C. Thomas.

Hodson, D. (1982). Science - the pursuit of truth? Part I.
    School Science Review, 63, 643-652.

Hodson, D. (1982). Science - The pursuit of truth? Part II.
    School Science Review, 64, 23-30.

Holden, C. (1987). Academy helps Army be all that it can be.
    Science, 238, 1501-02.

Holzer, H. (1991). *The psychic side of dreams.* St. Paul, MN : Llewellyn.

Jones, D. (1979). *Visitors of time: experiments in psychic archaeology.* Wheaton, IL: Theosophical.

Jung, C. G. (1972). *Sychronicity: An acausal connecting principle.* London: Routledge and Kegan Paul.

Jung, C. (1977). *Psychology and the occult.* Princeton, NJ : Princeton University Press.

Kagan, N. & Daniels, P. (Eds.) (1987). *Mysteries of the unknown: Psychic powers.* Alexandria, VA: Time-Life Books.

Krippner, S., & Rubin, D. (Eds.) (1975). *The energies of consciousness: Explorations in acupuncture, auras, and kirlian photography.* New York : Gordon & Breach.

Kubler-Ross, E. (1969). *On death and dying.* New York: MacMillan.

Laing, R.D. & Esterson, A. (1965). *Sanity, madness, and the family.* New York: Basic Books.

Laing, R.D. (1969). *The divided self.* New York: Pantheon Books.

Lamal, P. A. (1989). Attending to parapsychology. *Teaching of Psychology, 16,* 28-30.

Larson, J. H. (1984). A continuing duality: Physics and philosophy. *Journal of College Science Teaching, 13,* 148-49.

Laycock, G. (1980). *Does your pet have a sixth sense?* Garden City, NY : Doubleday.

LeShan, L. (1974). *The medium, the mystic, and the physicist: Toward a general theory of the paranormal,* New York: Viking.

LeShan, L. (1976). *Alternate Realities: The search for the full human being.* New York: Ballantine Books.

LeShan, L. & Margenau, H. (1982). *Einstein's space and Van Gogh's sky: Physical reality and beyond.* New York : MacMillan.

Lienhard, J. H. (n.d.). *Rye ergot and witches.* Retrieved September 7, 2003 from http://www.uh.edu/engines/epi1037.htm

Lindbergh, C. (1978). *Autobiography of values.* New York: Harcourt, Brace, Jovanovich.

Mackinnon, D., et. al. (1987, April). *The relationship between method and validity in social science research.* Paper presented at the annual meeting of the American Educational Research Association, Washington, DC.

McClenon, J. (1994). *Wondrous events: Foundations of religious belief.* Philadelphia: U. of Pennsylvania Press.

Maher, M., Vartanian, I., Chernigovskaya,T. & Reinsel, R. (1996). Physiological concomitants of the laying-on of hands: Changes in healers' and patients' tactile sensitivity. *The Journal of the American Society for Psychical Research 90,* 77-96.

Marie, Andre (n.d.). *Blessed Brother Andre of Saint Joseph.* Retrieved August 15, 2001 from http://www.catholicism.org/pages/andre.htm

Matz, T. (2000). *Catholic saints: Andre Bessette.* Retrieved August 15, 2001 from http://www.catholic.org/saints/andrebessette.html

Mella, D.L. (1988). *The language of color.* New York: Warner Books.

Mintz, E. (1983). *The psychic thread: Paranormal and transpersonal aspects of psychotherapy.* New York: Human Sciences Press.

Morowitz, H.J. (1987). Life. In *The world book encyclopedia* (Vol. 12, pp. 242-46). Chicago: World Book, Inc.

Moustakas, Clark. (1990). *Heuristic Research: Design, methodology, and applications.* Newbury Park, CA: Sage.

Muldoon, S. & Carrington H. (1981). *The phenomena of astralprojection.* Albuquerque: Sun Books.

National Catholic Register (1996, July 21). *Brother Andre – his life and times –1845 – 1937.* Retrieved on August 15,2001 from http://www.ewtn.com/library/MARY/BROANDRE.HTM

Neff, H. (1971). *Psychic phenomena and religion: ESP, prayer, healing, survival.* Philadelphia: Westminster Press.

Neher, A. (1990). *The psychology of transcendence.* (2nd Ed.) New York : Dover.

O'Donohue, W. (1989). The even bolder model: The clinical psychologist as metaphysician, scientist, practitioner. *American Psychologist, 44,* 1460-1468.

Odenwald, S. (n.d.). *How long does an earth magnetic field reversal take and is it harmful to humans?* Retrieved on March 12, 2002 from the NASA Education and Public Outreach Program database.

Ouellette, R. (1980). *Holistic healing and the Edgar Cayce readings.* Fall River, MA: Aero Press.

Palmer, J. (1979). A community mail survey of psychic
    experiences. *Journal of The American Society for
    Psychical Research, 73,* 221-251.

Parapsychology Foundation (1987). *Parapsychology,
    philosophy and religious Concepts: Proceedings of an
    international conference held in Rome, Italy,
    Aug. 23-24, 1985.* New York: Author.

Peterson, J.W. (1987). *The secret life of kids.* Wheaton, IL:
    Quest Books.

Pinch, T., & Collins, H. (1984). Private science and public
    knowledge: The committee for the scientific claims of
    the paranormal and its use of the literature. *Social
    Studies of Science, 14,* 521-46.

Rao, K. (Ed.). (1982). *J.B. Rhine: On the frontiers of science.*
    Jefferson, NC : McFarland.

Rao, K. (Ed.). 1986. *Case studies in parapsychology.* Jefferson,
    NC : McFarland.

Regush, N. (1975). *Exploring the human aura: A new way of
    viewing and investigating psychic phenomena.*
    Englewood Cliffs, NJ: Prentice-Hall.

Reider, M. (1991). *Mission to Milboro.* Los Angeles : Authors
    Unlimited.

Rhine, J. B. (1968). *Parapsychology today.* New York : Citadel.

Rhine, L. (1967). *ESP in life and lab.* New York : Collier
    Macmillan.

Richards, D. (1996). Psi and the spectrum of consciousness.
    *Journal of the American Society for Psychical Research,
    Vol. 90,* No. 4, pp. 251-267.

Roberts, D. A. (1982). The place of qualitative research in
    science education. *Journal of Research in Science
    Teaching, 19,* 277-92.

Roleff, T.L. (Ed.).(2003). *Psychics: Fact or fiction.* Farmington
    Hills, MI: Greenhaven Press.

Ryall, E. (1975). *Born twice: Total recall of a seventeenth-
    century life.* New York : Harper & Row.

Samuel, G. (1993). *Civilized shamans: Buddhism in Tibetan
    societies,* Washington, DC : Smithsonian Institution
    Press.

Schultes, R.E. & Hoffman, A. (1992).The tracks of the little
    deer. *Plants of the gods – their sacred, healing and
    hallucinogenic powers.* Retrieved May 29, 2004 from
    http://peyote.org/

Science notebook: find links birds, dinosaurs. (2002, March 11).
    The Washington Post, p. A10.

Scientific Creationism (1987). In *The world book encyclopedia.*
    (Vol. 17, pp.176-77). Chicago: World Book.

Serfes, D., Fr. (2000, August 20). *Holy scripture in the orthodox
    church: The Bible.* Retrieved April 11, 2004, from
    http://www.fr-d-serfes.org/
    orthodox/scripturesinthechurch.htm

Sheldrake, R. (1999). *Dogs that know when their owners are
    coming home; and other unexplained powers of animals.*
    New York: Crown.

Sheldrake, R. (2003). *The sense of being stared at; and other
    aspects of the extended mind.* New York: Crown.

Sinclair, U. (1930). *Mental radio.* New York: Albert & Charles
    Boni.

Smith, T.W. (1992). *Experiences of paranormal phenomena in the U.S.* Paper prepared for the American Association for the Advancement of Science, February, 1992. Chicago: NORC, U. of Chicago.

Steiger, B. (1989). *Exploring the power within: A resource book for transcending the ordinary.* West Chester, PA : Whitford Press.

Stevenson, I. (1974). *Telepathic impressions: A review and report of thirty-five new cases.* Charlottesville: University Press of Virginia.

Stevenson, I. (1975). *Cases of the reincarnation type.* Charlottesville :University Press of Virginia.

Tansley, D. (1977). *Subtle body: Essence and shadow.* New York: Thames and Hudson.

Tart, C. (1989). *Open mind, discriminating mind: Reflections on human possibilities.* San Francisco : Harper & Row.

Tart, C. (Ed.) (1991). *Transpersonal psychologies: Perspectives on the mind, from seven great spiritual traditions.* New York: Harper Collins.

Tolaas, J. (1986). Vigilance theory and psi. Part I: Ethological and phylogenetic aspects. *Journal of the American Society for Psychical Research, 80,* 357- 373.

Torrey, E. F. (1988) *Surviving schizophrenia: A family manual.* New York : Harper & Row.

Tyrrell, G. (1938). *Science and psychical phenomena.* London: Harper & Brothers.

Van Praagh, J. (2001). *Heaven and earth: Making the psychic connection.* New York: Simon & Schuster.

Vande Kieft, K. (1988). *Innersource: Channeling your unlimited self.* New York: Ballantine.

Vizbara-Kessler, B. (1981). Transpersonalizing education in the 80's. *Educational Horizons, 59,* 192-94.

Weiss, B. (1992). *Through time into healing.* New York: Simon & Schuster.

Wilson, I (1986). *Worlds beyond: from the files of the Society for Psychical Research.* London: Weidenfeld and Nicholson.

Worthington, E. (Ed.). (1992). *Psychotherapy and Religious values.* Grand Rapids, MI: Baker.

Wurtman, R. & Axelrod, J., The pineal gland. *Scientific American,* July 1965.

APPENDIX A

A Study of Paranormal Experiences in the USA among the General Population

INFORMED CONSENT FORM

Dear Research Participant:

I am conducting a study of paranormal experiences among people in the United States as a part of my doctoral degree program in clinical and transpersonal psychology. Information from this research project will increase our understanding of one of the most neglected areas of human development, the intuitive intellect, and will help in future studies of this kind.

During this research study you are asked to respond to the enclosed Survey. Your involvement will require about ten minutes of your time. At your request, after the research is completed, I will forward to you by mail, a summary of my findings and implications.

I am not aware of risks involved in participation in this project. You will be identified by number, and not by name. All responses will be confidential, and your name will not be used in any report regarding this research. You are free to decline to participate or to withdraw at any time.

If you have any questions about this study, please contact me at (phone #). Please leave a message if I am not immediately available. Thank you for your participation.

Sincerely,

Phyllis E. Sloan
Researcher

I,_____,
   (Print your name.)
Consent to participate in The Study of Paranormal Experiences in the
USA among the General Population, conducted by Phyllis E. Sloan. I
understand that I may refuse to participate or withdraw from this study at
any time. I understand that all responses will be confidential. I understand that I may direct questions about this project to Phyllis E. Sloan.

_____
(Signature)

_____
(Date)

_____
(Mailing Address)

_____

Appendix B

The Sloan Paranormal Survey

Instructions: Please darken any circle(s) which apply to you. Use a No. 2 lead pencil and erase all stray marks.

1. Have you ever had a paranormal (or supernatural) experience?   O Yes   O No

2. Have you ever had any of the following experiences? (Check all that apply to you.)

      ___ a. Saw an object move on its own

      ___ b. Heard a supernatural sound [voice(s) or other]

      ___ c. Witnessed a vision of someone or something while fully awake

      ___ d. Witnessed an apparition or ghost

      ___ e. Have strong feelings or thoughts that come true

      ___ f. Have dreams that come true

      ___ g. Can accurately predict events

      ___ h. Can communicate mentally with someone

             If you checked "h", can you complete his/her sentences sometimes?   O Yes   O No

      ___ i. Have been to a strange place and felt I had been there before or met a stranger whom I thought I knew.

      ___ j. Have experienced "missing time" (i.e., you were absent for several hours or days without remembering.)

___ k. Had an out-of-body experience

___ l. Almost died and had conscious experiences
During that time

___ m. Other: (Please describe.)

3. Did you participate in a ritual or other related activity before
your experience(s)?   O Yes   O No

4. If you answered "yes" to #3, was it while you were under the
influence of a substance?   O Yes   O No

If "yes", please specify: O Alcohol   O Prescribed
medicine O Non-medicinal drug

5. Have you ever been or are you now being treated for any of
the following medical problems? (Check all that apply.)
O Stroke   O Psychological   O Drug-related
O Other (Please specify.)

6. Your gender: O Male   O Female

7. Age: O 21- 30   O 31 – 40   O 41 – 50
O 51 - 60   O Over 61

8. Education: O Below high school   O High school
O College (1 – 2 years) O   College
(undergraduate   degree)   O College
(graduate degree)

9. Income: O Below 10k   O 10 – 20k   O 20 – 30k
O 30 – 40k   O over 40k
10. Ethnicity / Race: O Asian O Hispanic/ Latino
O Native American O African –
American O White   O Other

11. Geographical origin of immediate family: O   Southeast

O Northeast O Midwest   O Southwest
O Northwest   O Foreign country

If you checked "foreign country", which one?_____

12. Religious affiliation: O Protestant   O Catholic
O None   O Buddhist O Eastern Orthodox
O Jewish   O Muslim   O Other

13. If you would like to explain more about your experience(s), please use the space below.

14. Would you like to participate in future, more intensive research of this nature?   O Yes   O No
If "yes", please fill in your information below:

Name:_____

Address:_____
(Street)

_____
(City)   (State)   (Zip)
Phone(s): Home (____)_____

Work / Cell_____

Please Note: All participants who respond, "yes", will not be selected for future research. Please return this survey by (date). Further information may be obtained by writing to the following address: (address). Please send a SASE.

Copyright © 1991 by Phyllis E. Sloan
All rights reserved.

Appendix C

Spiritual Signs Chart

Spiritual signs are our everyday messages from God to guide us in our lives. God's signs or language is known to a few, but unknown to the majority. We see some of them as dream symbols. We are also given signs while we are wide awake, through various means. The signs are given to us through numbers, colors, geometric forms, animal signs, astrology, body language, directions, weather, physical movements and many other ways. Interpreting our signs is one way that God helps us to increase our mental abilities; we exercise our associative and abstract mental faculties during this process. Some signs, such as the body language signs, are related to our past lives as well as to our present lives. Study these signs as you would study a new foreign language. Interpreting spiritual signs becomes easier with practice.

Colors

Red = weakness
Blue = healing; improvement; progress; growth and development.
Yellow = Truth; purity; doing things the way God approves of.
Green = the meanings of both blue and yellow
Orange = the meanings of both red and yellow
Brown = power; strength.
Black = deficits; evil; harmful.
White = courage; bravery; faith in God
Purple = fighting; struggle; striving; revolution
Gray = the meanings of both black and white
Tan = sex; passion
Pink = the meanings of both red and white.
Light and dark shades of all colors = the meaning of the color + black or white

Numbers

1 = commerce; buying and selling; how you earn your living; getting what you need to survive (including a mate).

2 = conformity; organizations and corporations or other hierarchical entities; membership; following the crowd (which is a weakness).

3 = God's will or wishes; God's signature or endorsement.

4 = having a resource or supply of what you need for survival (including a mate); money or a quantity of anything.

5 = one weakness or fault.

6 = *God's command to stop;* diminished in size, intensity or amount; less; leaving or going away; a little.

7 = A new venture or undertaking

8 = a double weakness or fault; e.g., borrowing and lending, dominance and submission.

9 = God's first degree of anger.

10 = Striving to get ahead; a fight or struggle for life; revolution.

11 = God's guidance / message(s).

12 = God's second degree of anger.

13 = God's third (highest) degree of anger.

14 = Lying; stealing; cheating; shortchanging.

15 = safety; protection; insurance.

16 = the meanings of both 6 and 10.

17 = the meanings of both 7 and 10

18 = the meanings of both 8 and 10

19 = the meanings of both 9 and 10.

(Base numbers are numbers 1 – 19. Numbers over nineteen should be added until you reach a base number; e.g., the number 4256 should be added: 4+ 2+ 5+ 6 = 17. 17 is a base number and should be interpreted as pertaining to striving in a new venture. Numbers separated by periods, decimals, dashes or colons should be added on each side of the punctuation mark and *not* combined; e.g., a message involving 39.94 should be added on both sides of the decimal point (3+9=12 and 9+4=13; 12 & 13 are base numbers and should be interpreted as two separate numbers.

Geometric Forms

Circle = protection; safety; money; insurance.

Square = fortune or karma; payback; retribution; reward or punishment for deeds done.

Diamond = reincarnation; recycling.

Rectangle = navigation; directions; plans; focus; purpose.

Line (straight) = honesty; uprightness; correct actions, good goals and pathways; good works

Spiral = crookedness; harmfulness; evil; negativity; weakness

Sphere = harm; evil

Cube = joy; festivity; happiness

Pyramid = repentance for sins; correcting weaknesses of character.

Cylinder = buoyancy; lightness; cheerfulness

Hexagon = severance, disappointment; discontinuance.

Pentagon = exploration; pioneering.

Star = the life cycle; a repeat of events.

Triangle = striving; putting forth effort.

Body Language

Eyes = understanding of God and life.

Nose & sinuses = repentance; correcting what you were sent back to earth to correct.

Mouth & teeth = use of speech; e.g., constructively or destructively.

Ears = listening habits; i.e., believing and following what you are taught about God and life; possible weakness if authorities (religions, books & cultures) are wrong.

Throat = helping yourself to get ahead.

Upper arms = striving in higher mental work.

Forearms = higher mental work done or accomplished.

Hands = higher mental work in progress.

Elbows = performing your higher mental work poorly or not up to your abilities.

Waist = thriftiness; conservation.

Thighs = striving in physical work

Legs = physical work accomplished.

Feet = physical work in progress.

Knees = performing your physical work poorly or not up to your abilities; subservience to bosses or others in a position of authority over you (a weakness).

Buttocks = sex work; how hard you tried to be a pleasing sex partner in your last life; the more rounded (normal weight), the harder you tried (or the more successful you were).

Breasts = the extent to which you express love and affection for people; reaching out to others; clean fun with others; enjoyment of life; balance.

Ankle = honesty in work not involving higher mental faculties.

Wrist = honesty in work involving higher mental faculties.

Sexual Organs = expressing love and affection for others; sexual integrity

Forehead = first or uppermost thoughts.

Hair = thoughts; loss of hair on any body part or area means loss of thoughts & efforts related to the area. The longer the hair, the more thought you give to your means of survival and mating.

Height = extent of past life accomplishments. The taller you are, the more you accomplished.

Back = how you support your life.

Lungs = the presence or absence of work.

Stomach = the number of activities in your life.

Cheeks = concern about what others think or say about you (possible character weakness).

Heart = enjoyment of life and love.

High blood pressure = too many work activities & not enough fun.

Toes = understanding your work (physical labor).

Fingers = understanding your higher mental work.

Heels = Push to get ahead; how hard you strive in your work.

Shoulder = responsibilities.

The left side of the body represents the past and the right side, the present. Injuries to the left side mean that you are regressing in a trait. Injuries to the right side mean that you are developing a negative trait. An injury or illness involving any body part or function is a negative karmic debt related to whatever the part or function represents. Corrective behavioral measures are needed to build positive karma.

The larger the organ or body part, the more you have accomplished in what the area represents. This does not include organs or body parts enlarged by fatty tissue.

Physical Movements

Falling = deteriorating or destructive life conditions.
Flying = high ideals; high goals; good ventures.
Upward = improvement
Downward = deterioration; destruction.
Forward = making progress.
Backward = lack of growth; regression.
Sideways = off main target, mission or goal.

Directions

North = progressing; moving upward economically; less hospitable social climate.
South = less prosperous economic conditions; hospitable social climate.
East = conformity; maintaining tradition; following the crowd.
West = pioneering; non-conformity.

Combined directions take the meanings of both directions; e.g. S.W. and N.E.

Weather

Violent weather of any type = God's anger.
Coldness = need for more love; harsh conditions.
Warmth = love; kindness; good conditions
Rain = God's sorrow

Elements

Fire = cleansing; destruction.
Air = life.
Water = life.

Animal Signs

Wolf = cunning.
Elephant = repentance; correcting past life errors.
Lion = strength; power; boldness
Birds = high goals and values; good ventures; Colors should be included for a more accurate interpretation.
Snakes = evil; harm

Frogs = evil; harm
Cats = laziness; bad luck or bad karma; colors should be included in the interpretation for a complete meaning,
Dogs = subservience to a master (a weakness). Include color for complete interpretation.
Rabbits = sex; passion
Squirrels = repressed and/or regressed sexuality.
Rat = evil; harmful condition.
Fish = spiritual food; truthful information about God and life; a message from God.
Turtle = spiritual food.
Sheep = conformity; followers
Cows = conformity; followers
Spiders = loneliness or being alone too much

Any other animal signs should be interpreted according to the habits and traits of the animals. Sometimes the animal sign means that you have the same traits and/or similar habits of the animal.

Miscellaneous Signs

Keys = discovery; opening or closing; security or insecurity.
Bicycles = balance; harmony
Water = life.
Air = life
Death = new life; new beginnings; physical demise; possession or domination by an evil spirit.
Flowers = new life. (Color should be included for a complete meaning.)
Tails = directing your life (frequently symbolized by birds' tails);setting goals for yourself.
Plants = inactivity (usually a weakness).
Light = spiritual understanding.
Darkness = lack of spiritual understanding.
Coins = the numerical value of the coin plus the date (only the year, not the century). Dropping them and finding them have significance. Dropping them means that something is awry and needs fixing. Finding them is an indicator of current conditions.

Buildings & Vehicles = corresponding physical attributes or life conditions; (Roof = head; headlights & windows = eyes, basements = life at a low level.
Broom = cleansing; elimination of harmful or evil elements.

[This is an abridged list from notes provided by Reverend Clarence and three members of his congregation. Some signs are general and must be interpreted for specific conditions in your life.]

Publisher's Note: A more complete list and extensive explanations are forthcoming in 2006 in *Spiritual Signs and Messages* published by Alpha Run Press.]

Appendix D

Spiritual Signs Calendar

Your spiritual signs calendar is for your personal use. Many times, events happen to us during our waking hours and many of us fail to understand the significance of them. We all get messages directly from God, not only through dreams, visions, E.S.P. and other so-called "paranormal" means, but through signs which God shows us while we are fully awake.

Number signs which you receive from parking tickets and other numbered documents given to you have a meaning. You may turn on the radio or TV and while you are surfing, some word or group of words may stand out more than others. You may pass someone on the street and hear a snatch of someone's conversation that stands out in your mind; these are direct signs from God to guide you in some area(s) of your life.

Pray to remember each dream which you have. Tape or write down the elements of the dream and try to figure out their meaning. If you do not know what the symbols mean, pray and ask God what they mean.   God will give you the same message again and again in easier and easier symbols until you understand, when you continue to ask for clarification. But remember – *think!*   God wants us to exercise our brains. We use about one-tenth of our brains now; the more we think, the more God will turn up our mental abilities. If you do not use it, you will lose it. That's a fact!

Write down your daily activities and events which occur in your daily life. You will find, when you look back over your dreams and compare them with events in your life that some of them have come true! You might have to look back a few days or less or maybe go back a month or more, but some of your messages will be prophecies. Every person is a prophet of God. You do not need to lead others if you do not desire to do so, but everyone can be his own prophet because God will guide each person and give you your own personal prophecy.

Use a loose-leaf binder or notebook for your spiritual signs calendar. Make four (4) columns for each page of your calendar and use the column headings below. Make a calendar for each month, or for each week, whichever you prefer. Use the Spiritual Signs Chart (Appendix C). Also, pray and ask God for clarity on your signs.

Date	Daily Activi-ties/ Events	Type of Sign(s)	Interpreta-tion(s)

APPENDIX E

The Miracle Prayer
for
<u>Understanding God and Life</u>

Almighty God, Creator of Life, Source of All Knowledge and Master of All, I really want to know you well. I want to know the many ways You guide and teach me.

Every day I want to walk with You and thank You for my blessings. Dear God, I will turn to You for love, help and guidance in every part of my life.

Please, Dear Mother-Father Creator, let me know how very, very close You are to me. Let me know how my every thought, wish and deed is known by You. Please, Dear God, fill my life with light and teach me about You and all about life, itself.

Please tell me what is important in life and what is not. If there is anything which I can do to help Your great life plan come to be, please let me know it.

Divine Master of All, I know You are present everywhere, both in Heaven above and on Earth – even in this room here with me now, loving me and watching over me.

I will come to you with every question and problem because You are the ONLY AUTHORITY. There are many on this Earth who would try to teach me about You but I will not listen to them. They may confuse and misguide me. I will listen only to you. Please take my hand and show me the way.

Thank you Dear God.

Dear friend,
        God will answer any question that you have. Your answers come to you in visions (dreams) which you may have to interpret, through events in our lives, and other special signs.

If you do not understand the symbols in your dreams and other communications from God, continue to ask God for UNDERSTANDING about them and they will become crystal clear. God wants you to ask questions. Some sample questions which others have asked and gotten answers to are: (1) Why am I on Earth? (2) What am I supposed to be doing> (3) What does my illness (or accident) mean? (4) What should I do to be healed? These are just a few questions. You may ask God ANY QUESTION about your life or life in general and *you will get an answer directly from God.* There are right prayers and wrong prayers. Never pray to harm someone or ask God to make someone do something that you want them to do, even if it is good for them. They have free will and God will not take it away.

To get the greatest benefit from using this prayer, you should read it over many times... at least once each day until God answers your prayer and then always keep it where you can find it easily. Turn to it whenever you feel the need for God's help and guidance.]

Appendix F

Cleansing Mantra

The world is full of both charlatans and do-gooders who try to guide us in the ways of God. I will separate truth from fiction, if I can, by rational thinking.

When it comes to divine teachings, some believe that blind faith is the only way to go. However, faith in God combined with enlightenment from God is the surest way to the divine pathway toward Heaven.

God, I know you will help me to find and stay on that pathway; I will turn off the voices of those who would guide me in ways that are not true to your divine plan for my life.

I will open up my mind and heart to your direct divine guidance, so that I may know truth.

Please help me to correct the teachings of my upbringing that may be harmful to my soul, even though those teachings were well intended.

Let me see the light of truth and follow the divine pathway.

Correct my errors and let me know when I am ready to step up to a new level of understanding and learning.

I will be patient with those who are still indoctrinated and believing in error. When they are ready, I will share your truths with them and show them how to seek your guidance, directly.

APPENDIX G

I Corinthians 12

12 Now concerning spiritual gifts, brethren, I would not have you ignorant.

2 Ye know that ye were Gĕńtileś, carried away unto these dumb idols, even as ye were led.

3 Wherefore I give you to understand, that no man speaking by the Spirit of God calleth Jēśŭs is the Lord, but by the Holy Ghost.

4 Now there are diversities of gifts, but the same Spirit.

5 And there are differences of administrations, but the same Lord.

6 And there are diversities of operations, but it is the same God which worketh all in all.

7 But the manifestation of the Spirit is given to every man to profit withal.

8 For to one is given by the Spirit the word of wisdom; to another the word of knowledge by the same spirit;

9 To another faith by the same Spirit; to another the gifts of healing by the same Spirit;

10 To another the working of miracles; to another prophecy; to another discerning of spirits; to another divers kinds of tongues; to another the interpretation of tongues;

11 But all these worketh that one and the selfsame Spirit; dividing to every man severally as he will.

12 For as the body is one, and hath many members, and all the members of that one body, being many, are one body: so also is Christ.

13 For by one Spirit are we all baptized into one body, whether we be Jēwś or Gĕńtileś, whether we be bond or free; and have all been made to drink into one Spirit.

14 For the body is not one member, but many.

15 If the foot shall say, Because I am not the hand, I am not of the body; is it there-fore not of the body?

16 And if the ear shall say, Because I am not the eye, I am not of the body; is it therefore not of the body?

17 If the whole were an eye, where were the hearing? If the

whole were hearing, where were the smelling?

18 But now hath God set the members every one of them in the body, as it hath pleased him.

19 And if they were all one member, where were the body?

20 But now are they many members, yet but one body.

21 And the eye cannot say unto the hand, I have no need of thee: nor again the head to the feet, I have no need of you.

22 Nay, much more those members of the body, which seem to be more feeble, are necessary:

23 And those members of the body, which we think to be less honourable, upon these we bestow more abundant honour; and our uncomely parts have more abundant comeliness.

24 For our comely parts have no need: but God hath tempered the body together, having given more abundant honour to that part which lacked:

25 That there should be no schism in the body; but that the members should have the same care one for another.

26 And whether one member suffer, all the members suffer with it; or one member be honoured, all the members rejoice with it.

27 Now ye are the body of Christ, and members in particular.

28 And God hath set some in the church, first apostles, secondarily prophets, thirdly teachers, after that miracles, then gifts of healings, helps, governments, diversities of tongues.

29 Are all apostles? Are all prophets? Are all teachers? Are all workers of miracles?

30 Have all the gifts of healing? Do all speak with tongues? Do all interpret?

31 But covet earnestly the best gifts: and yet shew I unto you a more excellent way.

[Note: The above passage was excerpted from the King James Version of the *Holy Bible*.]

APPENDIX H

Self-Hypnosis for Past Life Regression

[The purpose of the past life regression is to help people understand why they were sent back to Earth and what their mission should be in their current lives. Although some psychotherapists use past life regression (or retrieval) to treat phobias and other psychological problems, the sole purpose of this exercise is to understand what you should be working on to correct your past life mistakes, violations and shortcomings so that you can move on to a higher plane of existence after death instead of returning to Earth. You may record these words or have someone else record them and use them for self-hypnosis. Do not omit any sections of the regression.]

Get comfortable. Make sure that you are not too cold or too warm. Do not wear constricting clothes. You may want to loosen a belt or take off your shoes. You may even lie down if you like. If at any time during this session, your recording malfunctions, you will awaken refreshed, happy and calm. Now, just relax and sit back or lie down. Close your eyes and let your body go loose and limp. Breathe deeply as I count from one to five. One... breathe deeply---and relax. Two, breathe deeply ... relax. Three, breathe deeply and relax. Just blow it out. Four, breathe deeply and blow it out...relax. Five, breathe deeply and blow it out, just relax. As you relax, just let your mind wander. Any sounds or noise you might hear will not distract you, but will help you to relax and go even deeper. I'm going to mention some parts of your body, and as I do I want you to relax that part of your body. Let all of the muscles in your forehead relax. Just let the tension go. Relax the muscles around your eyebrows... eyes... and cheeks. Feel the tension leave your face. Feel the muscles in your neck and shoulders relax. Release the tension as you go deeper and deeper. Relax the muscles in your back as you go deeper and deeper, deeper relaxed. Let those muscles in the small of your back and your buttocks muscles relax. Feel the tension release and go downward and out of you body and out of this room. You are feeling safe, calm and relaxed. You feel more relaxed than you have ever felt before. Relax the back of your thigh muscles. Just feel them go loose and limp. Feel the tension gently fly away from your body. Relax your calves and then let the relaxation go on down to your heels; let it travel on to the bottom of your feet as you go deeper and deeper. Let the wave of relaxation travel to the toes and the topside of your feet. Just feel the tension fly away as you go deeper and deeper relaxed. Feel the topside of your thighs relax. Now, feel your stomach area relax as you go deeper and deeper. Feel your chest muscles relax. Just feel the tension and tightness leave, fly away from your body from head to toe. Let all the remaining tension gently lift away from your body and go out into the universe. I am going to let you rest for a little while and when you hear me again you will be even deeper relaxed. (Wait approximately one minute.)

You are feeling so relaxed. You are now in a very special place that is warmed by the sun and you feel so relaxed. You are on the shore of a beautiful lake, relaxing under a beautiful tree on the beach. You have never felt so relaxed before. It is so peaceful and beautiful here on the shore. You are still very relaxed. In front of you is a very large beautiful palm tree, larger than any you have ever seen before. There are ten large golden flat stepping stones leading up to the tree. You step on the first stone and you are so very relaxed. You step on the second stone and you are even deeper relaxed. As you step on the third stone leading up to the tree, you are so calm, confident and very relaxed. As you step on each stone, you are more and more relaxed---fourth stone, fifth stone, sixth stone. As you get closer to the tree you can see that there is a golden door on the tree and beside the tree is a figure robed in bright blue. He is a guide with a halo and he will travel with you to a higher realm. With each step, you are deeper, deeper relaxed. You get closer to him, seven... eight... nine... and finally the tenth stone. You have reached your guide. He stretches out his hand to you and asks you to come with him through the golden door to your past life. You take his hand and as you look back, you see your sleeping body by the shore. You can always come back to your sleeping body whenever you want.

You take your guide's hand and you feel very safe and confident. You have the ability to move through time. You both step through the golden door into a space that is filled with all the colors of the rainbow. You and your guide are flying through space. You move through this space with your guide until you come to a place that looks familiar. Step inside this place and look around you. Where are you? What time of the year is it. Look at yourself in the body that you inhabited in that lifetime. What are you wearing? What sex are you? Are you young or old? Who is with you? Taste the food that you ate then. Someone is talking to you and calling you by your name. What is your name? Someone mentions the name of the place. Go back to your childhood in that life. Who were your friends, playmates, school, feelings, teachers? Time is passing. You are older. Are you married? What is your occupation and situation in life. You see everything very clearly. Time is passing. Move ahead to the day you died. You will not have pain or fear. If you are uncomfortable you can choose not to experience it. Focus on the year you died. Focus on the modern geographical name of the area where you lived. You are coming back, now. You will have a vivid memory of everything which you saw and experienced. You will feel wonderful. I will count to five and you will awaken bright, alert, happy peaceful and calm. One... two... three... waking up...four...and five. Fully awake now...happy and calm.

[You may repeat this exercise and regress to as many lives as possible, to gain a full perspective of your growth and development through the centuries.]

Information on past life regression and relaxation techniques were obtained from the following sources:

1. Reverend Clarence's notes.
2. Neves, R.A., *Hypnosis Scripts, NLP Interventions and Collected Thoughts* (a workbook, no copyright date).
3. Krasner, A.M., *Past Life Regression* (an audio taped recording) American Institute of Hypnotherapy.
4. Ansari, Masud, 1991, *Modern Hypnosis: Theory and Practice.*, Mas-Press, Washington, D.C.

Appendix I

Table 4. Analysis of Variance of Demographic Factors x Number of Psi Experiences (N = 202; 87 = males, 114 = females)

Source	df	M	SD	F
Gender	1			8.20**
Male		2.59	1.44	
Female		3.48	2.24	
error	163	(3.86)		
Age	4		2.27	
21-30		3.05	2.03	
31-40		3.05	1.68	
41-50		3.50	2.13	
51-60		6.00	3.37	
61+		4.00	___[a]	
error	150	(4.00)		
Education	3		1.57	
Finished H.S.		3.38	2.07	
1-2 Yrs. College		3.36	1.82	
College Degree		2.70	2.07	
Graduate Degree		3.60	2.63	
error	163	(3.92)		
Income	4		1.83	
<10k		3.26	1.98	

Table 4. (continued)

Source	df	M	SD	F
10-20k		3.37	2.14	
20-30k		2.92	1.65	
30-40k		2.17	1.93	
>40k		4.17	2.62	
error	151	(3.91)		
Race/Ethnicity	5			2.86*
Asian		2.40	0.55	
Latino		1.67	0.71	
Native American		2.40	0.55	
African American		3.54	2.10	
Caucasian		2.57	1.51	
Other		2.60	1.93	
Error	159	(3.78)		
Family Origin	5			4.55***
Southeast		3.93	1.73	
Northeast		3.04	1.48	
Midwest		5.60	3.36	
Southwest		3.50	1.73	
Northwest		3.31	2.82	

Table 4. (continued)

Source	df	M	SD	F
Foreign		2.46	1.64	
Error	156	(3.32)		
Religion	6			1.96
Protestant		2.94	1.95	
Catholic		2.31	1.39	
None		2.81	1.38	
Buddhist		2.50	0.71	
Eastern Orthodox		3.67	1.21	
Jewish		___[b]	___	
Muslim		4.22	3.11	
Other		3.42	1.95	
Error	154	(3.48)		

Note: Values enclosed in parentheses represent mean square errors. Due to mussing values for some variables, some analyses are calculated on slightly fewer than 202 participants. [a] There was only one participant in this age category. [b] There were no participants in this religious category. $*p < .05$. $**p < .01$. $***p < .001$.

Subject Index

About the Author

Dr. Phyllis E. Sloan has over twenty years experience in higher education as a university professor, administrator, researcher, psychotherapist and counselor. She is a licensed clinical professional counselor in the state of Maryland and Washington, D.C. She is also certified by the National Board for Certified Counselors (NBCC).

Dr. Sloan is an international scholar and consultant who has facilitated workshops outside the U.S., as well as throughout the U.S. in several states. She has presented workshops on mentoring, career development, cultural diversity, male/female relations, human relations, parenting, working with the mentally and physically challenged, and many other areas in the career development and mental health fields.

She is the author of "Youth Violence: Causes and Solutions with an Emphasis on Peer Counseling" in R. Duhon-Sells (Ed.) *Exploring Self-Science Through Peace Education and Conflict Resolution.* She has also authored and co-authored numerous articles in transpersonal psychology, child psychology and women's issues.

Dr. Sloan is a native of Gary, Indiana and her roots go back three generations in that city. She currently resides in the Washington, D.C. Metropolitan Area.